WILL IT COOKBOOK?

Yes! Well, hopefully. Unless you've bought one of the cookbooks th[at] out and filled with baked beans. It was supposed to be a super-funny joke, but we couldn't come up with a punch line, so now there are roughly 1,500 bean-books floating out there.

Sorry. Ah, the cookbook, yes (clears throat).

When it comes to food—the good, the gooder, and the shockingly not ungood—Mythical Chef Josh, Rhett & Link, and the Mythical Kitcheneers have just about done it all. Through the internet's most-watched daily show, *Good Mythical Morning*, and culinary spinoff, *Mythical Kitchen*, they've taste-tested, mythbusted, and dreamed up the most inventive, delicious, and ridiculous foods imaginable, all for your eyeballs to eat on-screen. But they've also realized that the mouth does a much better job of eating than the eyeballs, which is why this flavor-packed cookbook (that's hopefully not just beans) is coming to your kitchen.

Inside these pages you'll find fan favorites and new inspirations, including:

- next-level spins like Animal Style Mac 'n' Cheese, Skittle-Milk French Toast, and Grilled Cheese Ramen;
- secret family recipes like Rhett's Top Secret Baked Beans, Link's Mom's Country Fried Steak, and Josh's Carne Asada Burrito of Death;
- and unexpected mashups such as Garlic Bread McMuffins, Chicken and Waffles Potpie, Ramen Nachos, Everything Bagel Fondue, and Pop-Tart Lava Cakes.

Filled with one-of-a-kind recipes, profound life advice, candid photos, and at least one weird story about an angry toaster that's come to life, *The Mythical Cookbook* will help you cook deliciously, eat happily, and live Mythically. And have no fear—while *Mythical Kitchen*'s on-screen creations push food to the limits, the recipes in this book are delicious and doable for real life, in real kitchens. Bring extra napkins to the table—you'll need them.

RHETT & LINK PRESENT

THE MYTHICAL COOKBOOK

RHETT & LINK PRESENT

THE MYTHICAL COOKBOOK

10 SIMPLE RULES FOR COOKING DELICIOUSLY, EATING HAPPILY, AND LIVING MYTHICALLY

Josh Scherer

with Noah Galuten

H

HARVEST

An Imprint of WILLIAM MORROW

TO ALL THE MYTHICAL BEASTS
WHO HAVE EVER PUT RANCH ON LASAGNA, AND TO ALL
THE MYTHICAL BEASTS WHO HAVE NOT

CONTENTS

FOREWORD

In 2012, when we sat down at a card table to record our first episode of *Good Mythical Morning*, we wondered how long we'd be able to keep the show going before we ran out of stuff to talk about. After a few months, we were safely at the bottom of the conversational barrel, turning to topics such as "How to Catch a Fly in Your Hand," "15 Prison Slang Words You Must Know," and "Are Eyebrows Facial Hair?" Thankfully, we discovered another hidden talent besides talking: eating.

Who knew that more than a few people would have an insatiable appetite for watching two guys from Buies Creek, North Carolina, compare bacon-flavored sodas, ingest an entire scorpion, or swallow a Carolina Reaper (we're still trying to forget that last one, as we thoroughly embarrassed ourselves by crying, hiccuping uncontrollably, and questioning the meaning of life itself). Whether or not it makes sense, it's true: people like to watch us eat. Of course, this has never stopped them from complaining about our (or, let's be honest, Link's) mouth noises, but they seem to keep watching nonetheless.

As the years passed and we kept eating an increasing variety of foods, we began to sense a need for recipes that were more complex than simply having our intern, Chase, boil things for safety. Don't get us wrong. Chase was great at boiling. So good, in fact, that he's now a full-fledged producer. But we needed more than boiling. We needed sautéing, baking, and poaching. Maybe even blanching. And deep-frying. LOTS of deep-frying.

We hired Josh Scherer for precisely these reasons. Not only could he blanch with the best of them, but he didn't bat an eye when we asked him to make a Slim Jim–stuffed churro (yes, it's great) or Taco Bell juice (which is exactly what it sounds like: the juice of Taco Bell and not as great). Before long, he was suggesting ideas for what we should try next, including In-N-Out Animal-Style Mac 'n' Cheese. At that point, we realized he was just as weird as we were, and we've never looked back.

Mythical Chef Josh and the Kitcheneers are constantly perfecting the art of having fun with food. They boldly explore the landscape of culinary possibility, often waltzing right through the barriers of what's expected (or even accepted) in cooking. Most importantly, they have the time of their lives with each and every step. There is so much pure joy in the way they bring food to life. You cannot enter the Mythical Kitchen without smiling, unless they happen to be cooking up something that is intentionally designed to freak us out, like a chocolate-covered lamb eyeball to celebrate Valentine's Day. Did somebody say Eye Love You?

You may get the impression that Josh is some mad food scientist, sitting silently in a corner, dreaming up egregious culinary concepts designed to feed the YouTube Algorithm. And you'd be partially right. But while Josh can and does create extreme foods for your viewing pleasure, he never loses sight of the primary goal of any good chef: making sure the final product tastes good. He knows what kind of food real people with real palates actually like, and he whips up so many delicious concoctions while bringing absolutely no pretentiousness to the process. At the same time, he's got a dizzying level of professional skill that would impress the toughest food critic (he can also bench press food critics, though none have accepted his offer).

Josh's willingness to experiment, encyclopedic knowledge of what tastes incredible, and ridiculous culinary skills make him the perfect person to write this book. We're so excited that you're finally holding it in your hands. For years, we've been the lucky recipients of the fruits of his labor, selfishly enjoying one delectable dish after another as millions of people watch with mouths watering and stomachs growling. But now we get to share with you that joy that he and the Mythical Kitchen have given us. Our hope is that, by bringing to life the recipes that follow, you'll get a taste of the wonderful, Mythical world we've created together.

—RHETT & LINK

INTRODUCTION

It all started with a taco shell and a coagulated brick of pork blood. Well, technically it all started with a single explosion of infinite energy and matter that hurled burning-hot gas outward into space-time at the speed of light, but that's not particularly noteworthy. Back to the pork blood taco. Two brave internet explorers (no relation to the browser) put their lives on the line when they asked the age-old question: Will it taco?

GROCERY STORE SUSHI
Will it taco? *No.*

BROCCOLI AND CHEESE
Will it taco? *Yes.*

BABY SHAMPOO
Will it taco? *Hey, this isn't even close to food!*

BURGER
Will it taco? *Well, duh!*

PORK BLOOD
Will it taco? *OH GOD GET US OUT OF HERE IT TASTES LIKE SOMEONE FARTED ON A PILE OF MOLDY COPPER WIRING.*

Aside from leaving the desk with quite possibly the weirdest-smelling breath anyone has ever breathed, Rhett and Link also left that day with another pungent discovery: a whole lot of people want to watch them do strange experiments with food. And also that eating gross things is funny. But mostly the first one. After more than one hundred episodes of "Will It?," countless other series devoted to off-the-wall delicious food, and an entire spin-off channel helmed by a ragtag group of (incredibly smart and handsome) Mythical chefs, we have shotgun-blasted our way through the scientific foodie frontier in ways that no others before have.

Because, when it comes down to it, cooking truly is just thousands of little science experiments that stack up against each other over time to create something delicious. What happens if I cook the eggs at this temperature? Or that temperature? Or with butter? Or without butter? Or if I sauté something first, before boiling it and after roasting it, and hey, maybe those ants on the ground taste good and OH MY GOD it turns out you can't eat that mushroom over there but the eggs inside of fish are DELICIOUS on potato chips! Let's try deep-frying it!

Legendary chef Auguste Escoffier experimented with food until he had more than six hundred methods to cook an egg; we've experimented with food until we found out the exact best potato chip to use to coat a chicken tender (it's Lay's Salt & Vinegar, by the way). We're basically the same. But, of course, experimentation means nothing if you don't come to the right conclusions, which is why we have distilled everything we've learned from creating thousands of bizarrely delicious foods into ten simple rules for cooking deliciously, eating happily, and living Mythically.

Rule 1: Fill your Happiness Pit as early as possible

Rule 2: Share food with people to trick them into liking you

Rule 3: If a hot dog is a sandwich, you can be a chef

Rule 4: When life hands you bacon, don't question it and just eat the dang bacon

Rule 5: Eat together as a family, even if that family is just you, a cat, and an aggressive, sentient toaster

Rule 6: The person who first ate cheese was a weirdo; be like the first person who ate cheese

Rule 7: Set fire to your mouth, not your kitchen

Rule 8: If you can dream it, you can deep-fry it

Rule 9: Eat dessert first, or last, or whenever the heck you want to

Rule 10: Eat something that scares you

"But, *Mythical Cookbook* narrator who is Josh except he's strangely using the royal plural pronoun (except when he's not), what does all that MEAN?!" you ask quite appropriately. That's a great question, little Johnny (at least one of you reading this right now has to be named Johnny), and we're glad you asked. Let's explore together. After reading this book cover to cover you will learn to:

COOK DELICIOUSLY

That's the point of a cookbook, innit? If you've watched *Good Mythical Morning* and *Mythical Kitchen* over the years, you will likely recognize many of these recipes, although some are brand-new food experiments that we just thought of off the top of our collective heads because we figured they would taste good (and we were right—high five!). Every recipe that previously existed from the show has been adapted and tested for the average home chef to be able to successfully cook at home while still maintaining the integrity of the dish (and often making it better!). Sometimes in the Mythical Kitchen we get a little carried away, and it takes us two weeks to make a cheeseburger that dirties every single dish in the kitchen. We don't want you to go through that pain.

In many of the recipes, we've also highlighted

some crucial cooking techniques for you to master! As much as we love our silly little cooking experiments in the Mythical Kitchen, the only reason we're able to come out the other side with delicious food is because we've mastered many of the fundamentals. So, while you're out there making donut fried chicken, you're also going to get a quick lesson about how to avoid air pockets in your fried chicken batter and how to harness the Maillard reaction to make your chicken extra flavorful. You'll also be using one consistent salt—Diamond Crystal Kosher all day!—that's measured out in each recipe. Because knowledge is power!

EAT HAPPILY

Now that you know how to cook delicious food, the next step is eating it. You see, what most people choose to do is put the food in their mouth, and then use their teeth—the molars are our personal favorite—to grind the food into a fine paste before letting it slide down their throat hole. Actually, let's just assume you've got the physical part covered. Instead, we intend to teach you how to do the whole dang thing with a smile on your face. It's not exactly groundbreaking to tell you that food is meant to be enjoyed, but we actually mean it here. Too often, chefs get hung up on how to eat correctly as opposed to happily, and that obsession with being correct can get in the way of happiness. *Don't eat processed foods! Don't cook with seed oils! You didn't season your cast-iron pan with artisanal hand-expressed pine resin from the Cloud Forest of Alderaan? You monster!*

Life is hard enough as it is without stressing over every single detail about what you eat, so this cookbook is a celebration of the foods that bring us joy. And hey, maybe those foods will bring you joy too. No matter what skill level, knowledge base, personal preferences, or monetary constraints you're bringing to this cooking journey, there's a recipe in here that will allow you to eat happily, and,

if not, we always invite you to make substitutions. No one should ever be made to feel less than because they don't know what sherry vinegar is and don't want to spend the money on a sous vide machine. We're in this together.

LIVE MYTHICALLY

Well, if you're already cooking deliciously and eating happily, there's a 63 percent increased chance that you're going to be living Mythically (results may vary). "Be your Mythical best" has been the motto since day one, and that saying permeates everything, even down to your food choices. Hopefully this cookbook teaches you how to have an open mind when it comes to trying foods that you may have previously been unfamiliar with! Hopefully it inspires you to bring a casserole to your new neighbor who just moved in across the street! Hopefully it inspires you to share a spoonful of your tuna salad in the gym sauna with the person next to you! Wait, you're not allowed to eat tuna salad in the gym sauna anymore? Okay, share your pool yogurt with someone, then.

This book won't teach you how to become a health guru, it won't teach you the hard-core science behind the thirty-two steps to roasting the perfect chicken, and it won't teach you how to make your family the perfect dinner in fifteen minutes every single night until the day you die. But this book will teach you how to see food as something that's silly, and fun, and meant to be played with. It'll teach you how to make your life just a little bit more Mythical, one meal at a time.

FILL YOUR HAPPINESS PIT AS EARLY AS POSSIBLE
(BREAKFAST)

According to the most recent research, the brain is the only organ that is capable of producing happiness. A Swiss scientist at the University of Bern in 1863 thought he recognized trace levels of happiness in the gallbladder of a twenty-three-year-old brick layer, but it just turned out to be more bile. The scientist was stripped of his license and lived out his days in disgrace, selling magical gallbladder elixirs door-to-door. But the failings of Professor Hedosz Noddexist are beside the point.

The point is, when you eat food, you aren't just feeding your stomach, you're feeding your brain, which spurs out a little happiness chemical that courses throughout your entire body and manifests in physiological responses such as smiling, laughing, light-to-moderate frolicking, and being just a little bit nicer to strangers, which allows them to do the same for others. No matter what some bodybuilding guru on Instagram told you: food is not just fuel for the body.

Many of us grew up knowing that breakfast is the most important meal of the day, even though no one exactly told us WHY that was true. Something about metabolism? Or maybe it was a hormone thing. Who the heck knows! But we'll tell you right here: breakfast is the most important meal of the day because it gives you an opportunity to crank the happiness chemical up to 11 before you even leave the house.

Studies have shown that drivers who eat plain oatmeal for breakfast are 41 percent more likely to go into a feral rage after getting cut off on their morning commute than drivers who ate a big ol' sloppy, greasy breakfast burrito. And that study came from Professor Hedosz's lab, so you know it's legit.

In all sincerity, happiness is the glue that's always held the food together at Mythical. Well, happiness, and sometimes cheese, because happiness doesn't work well to seal a quesadilla. And that sense of happiness is INFECTIOUS! It all starts with Rhett and Link putting mac and cheese in between the layers of a Big Mac with utter delight, and then someone like me watches that, smiles, and thinks, "What other silly food experiments like that would make ME happy?" And that's how I end up in a YouTube video, deep-frying lamb's brains and dusting them in Nashville hot spice. It's also how you get Nicole, Vee, Trevor, Lily, and all the future Kitcheneers you haven't met yet creating all the wacky stuff that you see on-screen.

There are only two questions we ask ourselves before we make a dish: (1) Does this idea make us happy? And (2) is it a seven-tier wedding cake that's going to ruin our lives for two whole days

and result in a bunch of shattered glass? We had to add that second question after the "Elvis Meals of History" episode; if you know, you know. And that's a distinctly different set of questions than: Is this going to be delicious? Did we really think a Fruity Pebbles pizza would taste as good as a classic pepperoni slice? Absolutely not! But in a pitch meeting, when someone described a rainbow-colored pizza with milk sauce and a cereal crust, we all laughed, shook our heads, and knew we had to do it. Because food is just a tool we use to create happiness. Full stop.

And there's historical precedent to this, folks! For all those who complain about silly internet food "ruining" certain dishes—people have always played and tinkered and changed and corrupted and perverted in the kitchen! And for no reason other than making the edges of someone's mouth curl toward the sky.

In the Middle Ages, cooks used to make a dish called "live frog pie" for dinner parties and large banquets. It did, as you probably guessed, contain a live frog. After a meal full of roast suckling pig, stuffed pheasant, perch cooked in almond milk, and vegetables dressed with all kinds of herbs from the garden, cooks would bring out their various puddings and pastries. As a practical joke, one of the pies would simply be a plain crust sitting on top of a dish. When a guest cut into that special pie, a live frog jumped out and scared the hell out of them.

I repeat: JUST FOR LAUGHS, MEDIEVAL COOKS PUT A LIVE FROG IN A PIE CRUST! This was seven hundred years ago, and it sounds like it could have come straight from a *GMM* episode! Food has never, in the history of the world, been solely about fueling the body. Food is culture, it is tradition, it is comfort, and, above all, it is pure freakin' happiness on a plate.

So, next time you're making breakfast, even if it isn't the Waffle Eggs Benedict, or an Enchilomelet,

or Skittle-Milk French Toast, just riffle through your pantry and see what you can add to your oatmeal that might inject a little spark of joy into the first part of your day. Maybe you crush up some Cinnamon Toast Crunch in there. Maybe you throw some marshmallow fluff and peanut butter on top. Maybe it's just some rainbow sprinkles, because those remind you of going to the ice cream truck with your dad when you were a kid, and you used to love going to the ice cream truck.

So many things can go wrong throughout the course of a single sun cycle. Start every day with an easy win. Start every day with happiness. Feed your Happiness Pit as early as possible. You have our permission.

FRUITY PEBBLE PANCAKES

To quote Jeff Goldblum—er, Dr. Ian Malcolm—in the Oscar-winning nature documentary *Jurassic Park*, "Your scientists were so preoccupied with whether something *could* pancake, they didn't stop to think if it should." We took the lessons learned from Dr. Malcolm to heart and discovered that maybe guinea pig balls should not be pancaked (speaking of which, can we say no to pancaking anyone's balls?). But one thing that absolutely should be pancaked? Fruity Pebbles—after all, they're just colorful, sugary Rice Krispies, so why the heck wouldn't it be great?

(Spoiler alert: *Jurassic Park* is a very good movie. Also spoiler alert: waking dinosaurs from their seventy-five-million-year extinction proves to be a bad idea. Also spoiler alert: they kept on trying, like, seven more times for some reason.)

....

Drop the flour, ½ cup of the Fruity Pebbles, the sugar, baking powder, baking soda, and salt into a food processor or blender and buzz it until you've made what should only be described as Fruity Pebble Pancake Mix.

Combine the buttermilk, melted butter, and egg yolks in a large bowl and beat them up with a whisk. Add the flour mixture to the butter mixture and mix it really well. For better texture and flavor, try to do the right thing here and let that batter rest for 45 minutes in the refrigerator.

Once your batter has rested, work on your shoulder strength and put those egg whites in a bowl and whisk them as much as your rotator cuff will allow, ideally until you have stiff peaks and can do that thing where you hold the bowl upside down and don't end up with egg whites all over the counter. (Or . . . just use a handheld electric mixer.)

Meanwhile, heat up a griddle to 350°F or your preferred pancake cooking vessel (cast iron or nonstick both work) over medium heat.

Recipe continues

Makes about 17 pancakes

2 cups all-purpose flour
1 cup Fruity Pebbles, plus more for serving
2 tablespoons sugar
½ teaspoon baking powder
½ teaspoon baking soda
½ teaspoon salt
2 cups buttermilk
½ cup (1 stick) unsalted butter, melted and cooled
2 large eggs, yolks and whites separated
Cooking spray or some kind of fat (like more butter), for greasing
About 1¼ cups sweetened condensed milk, for serving

Fold those stiff egg whites and the remaining ½ cup of Fruity Pebbles into the batter, getting everything as mixed as you can without overworking it and beating out all that air you just spent so much time making.

Spray the griddle with cooking spray (or grease with fat) and, working in batches, ladle ¼ cup of batter for each pancake onto the griddle or pan. Once the bottom is golden brown and you see bubbles forming on the raw side (2 to 3 minutes), flip them over and cook the other side. Use your brain and eyes and nose to make sure the pancakes are cooking and browning without burning, and adjust the heat up or down as needed. Move them to a plate and continue adding more cooking spray or grease to the griddle or pan as needed to cook the rest of the pancakes.

Warm the condensed milk in a glass measuring cup or pitcher in the microwave to make it easier to pour. To serve, drizzle those things with sweetened condensed milk, sprinkle on more Fruity Pebbles, and have a fruitful, pebbly good time.

Beating Egg Whites Separately for Pancakes?

This is a way to add more air and fluffiness to your pancakes. All you have to do is beat egg whites separately and fold them in at the end. Egg whites are primarily made of protein, and this aeration technique, also used in meringues and soufflés, will give your pancake batter extra structure. The next day, you may say things like, "Wait, why is my arm so sore? Oh yeah, it's because I made pancakes all good." And you did.

WAFFLE EGGS BENEDICT (OR . . . EGGO EGGY BENNY?)

Welcome to Every Brunch Menu in American History, featuring some version of eggs Benedict. But instead of waiting forty-five minutes for a table on a Sunday afternoon to spend eighteen dollars on "eggs with egg sauce," you can make it at home for way less money. Also, when you eat brunch at home, the mimosas aren't the only thing that get to be bottomless. On a serious note, we must recommend that you wear pants while cooking. We have not yet emotionally recovered from the Bottomless Bacon Grease Incident of 2017.

This recipe is all about the value of an Eggo grilled cheese base, and hacking the usually difficult hollandaise sauce by using the blender method . . . while also teaching you that frying a sunny-side up egg is a lot easier than poaching an egg (and you still get the runny yolk!).

....

First up, set a nonstick pan over medium heat. Then take those soggy, floppy, thawed waffles and make two sandwiches by putting a slice of cheese between each pair of waffles. Melt 1 tablespoon of the butter in the pan, then add the Eggo sandwiches and let them cook until they are golden brown on the first side.

Meanwhile, start up your hollandaise. Plop the egg yolks, hot sauce, 1 tablespoon water, the lemon juice, and 1 teaspoon of salt in the blender and let it rip until the eggs are fully combined. Drop the speed to low and slowly drizzle in the melted butter while blending until your hollandaise is emulsified and creamy but still pourable. It should be the consistency of a Sour Patch Kids Go-GURT. If you've never had a Sour Patch Kids Go-GURT, that's just your loss; what an amazing product. If the sauce gets too thick, stir in a few drops of water until the texture is to your liking. If it's too thin, keep those blades spinning. It's an intricate dance of death.

By now the waffle sandwiches should be ready to flip, if they weren't already. Flick another tablespoon of butter in the pan and flip the

Recipe continues

4 Eggo Homestyle Waffles, thawed to room temperature

2 slices cheddar

4 tablespoons (½ stick) unsalted butter, for cooking the waffles and eggs

3 large egg yolks (save the egg whites for the health nut who refuses to eat your Benedict, but tell them to cook for themselves because you're busy MAKING A FUN BRUNCH, JEFF!)

1 tablespoon hot sauce of your choice

1½ teaspoons lemon juice

Salt and ground black pepper

10 tablespoons unsalted butter, melted

2 slices Canadian bacon, at room temperature

2 large eggs

2 tablespoons unsalted butter, for frying

Hefty pinch of minced chives, for garnish

Sprinkle of paprika, to get fancy

waffles over and cook until the other side of the waffles is crispy and the cheese is melted. (A little bit of charring on the edges is A-OK.) Once they are done, transfer the sandwiches to their own plates. Keeping the pan at medium heat, flash the Canadian bacon slices in the pan for about 10 seconds on each side to just warm them up a touch, then place one right on top of each waffle grilled cheese.

Start frying those eggs in the same pan. (You could use another pan to get this done faster . . . but who wants to dirty another pan when you're about to eat brunch with no pants on? This is YOUR day, buddy, and you've EARNED it!)

Add the 2 remaining tablespoons of butter to that same skillet and fry up those eggs until the whites are just set and the yolks are runny, about 4 minutes. Season them with salt and pepper and place one on top of each ham slice.

Finally, drizzle the hollandaise over everything, then get classy as heck and sprinkle those chives from as high up as you can so they bounce around all fine dining–like. Sprinkle some paprika over the top, then stuff your face and go back to bed.

GATORADE MUFFINS

Like a caterpillar in the chrysalis stage, waiting to emerge as a beautiful butterfly, there is a brief period of time when all cupcakes simply exist as muffins. Until the frosting is mounded atop those beautiful dough lumps, they are not the kid's birthday party treat you know and love, but rather a breakfast option, perfect for eating before your daily 5K run. Now that we've established that muffins are a totally healthy food, we might as well make them with Gatorade, because . . . electrolytes? Anyway, electrolytes are basically just minerals, like salt, so when someone tells you they like salted caramel because salt accentuates the flavor of sugar, you can say, "Oh, me too, except Gatorade muffins, because they include potassium and magnesium and not just salt—why are you so basic?" and then you can just brag about your Gatorade reduction while they slowly walk away.

....

Note: This recipe calls for two standard 12-cup nonstick muffin tins, and the frilly little muffin papers to put inside them.

Step 1: Make the Gatorade Reduction. Place the Gatorade in a pot and bring it to a steady boil. Boil until it is reduced to 1 cup of thick syrup, about 40 minutes. Okay, now definitely DO NOT place it in a food dehydrator overnight and grind it up and snort it. We lost a lot of good people that way. Instead, set it aside to cool to room temperature.

Step 2: Make the Muffin Base. Preheat the oven to 375°F. Spray two 12-cup muffin tins with cooking spray, then add the frilly muffin papers and spray those too.

Whisk the flour, baking soda, and baking powder in a large bowl. In another large bowl, beat the butter and sugar until they are fluffy and fully combined, with no chunks of dry sugar hiding around the edges. Add one of the eggs (without the shell, you monster) and beat it for 30 seconds, then add the other one and beat that too. Whisk in the sour cream, and once it's all super incorporated (the sour cream might look a little curdled, but that is totally okay; it will be fine!), add the Gatorade reduction and get it all mixed up.

Makes 24 muffins

Gatorade Reduction
Two 28-ounce bottles Cool Blue Gatorade (or pick your not-poison for a different color and I guess flavor, even though "blue" isn't really a flavor)

Muffin Base
Cooking spray
2 cups all-purpose flour, plus another pinch to coat the blueberries
1 teaspoon baking soda
1 teaspoon baking powder
¾ cup (1½ sticks) unsalted butter, at room temperature
½ cup sugar
2 large eggs
½ cup sour cream
½ cup Gatorade Reduction
2 cups frozen blueberries

Streusel
2 tablespoons unsalted butter, at room temperature
¼ cup Gatorade Reduction
¾ cup all-purpose flour, plus more if needed

Pour the wet mixture into the flour mixture, using a silicone spatula to make sure you're not wasting any of that blue nectar, then whisk the batter vigorously until it's all stodgy and mixed up with no lumps.

Place the frozen berries in a bowl with a pinch of flour and toss until the berries are all lightly coated. Add them to the muffin mixture and fold until combined.

Scoop the batter into the prepared pans, using about ¼ cup batter per muffin cup.

Step 3: Make the Streusel. Combine the butter and Gatorade reduction in a large bowl and beat until it is all mixed up (it will not look totally homogenous, but that is okay). Add the flour and mix it with a fork until you have a thick, crumbly mixture. If it's too thin, add more flour. Crumble the streusel evenly over the muffins.

Bake until a toothpick stuck into the center of the muffins comes out clean, about 15 minutes.

Allow the muffins to cool in the pan for at least 15 minutes before eating. Once cooled, eat them and go play basketball because you are now fully electrolyte loaded.

What Is Creaming?

Creaming is the process of beating sugar and softened butter together until they get aerated and unified, resulting in a lighter, fluffier mixture that doesn't just make your food taste better—it also expands the volume. That means more muffins, more cookies, and more cake to go around! See? Sometimes you CAN get more with less.

GARLIC BREAD McMUFFINS

This recipe was called "The Immaculate Encapsulation" on *GMM* for a reason . . . and the reason is that while butter makes everything better, *garlic* butter makes everything *garlic* better. For this recipe, we get to make Olive Garden breadstick–inspired, garlic butter–infused English muffins and turn them into McDonald's-inspired Egg McMuffins. *Mythical Kitchen*: when you're here, you're loving it.

....

Preheat the oven to 450°F.

Slice each English muffin in half with a hand-whittled English muffin knife. If you don't have a hand-whittled English muffin knife, a bread knife will do just fine. Soften the butter in the microwave until soft and spreadable but not melted, working in 10-second bursts, then add the garlic, black pepper, and parsley and stir it up. Slather each English muffin half with garlic butter, then bake for about 8 minutes, until toasty. Remove the muffins but KEEP THE OVEN ON!

While the muffs are in the oven (it's unclear why we've started abbreviating words, but roll with it), chop your bacon into small bits and add it to a cold saucepan. Turn the heat to medium and use a wooden spoon to move the bacon around until the fat renders and the pig meats are crispy. Drain some of the fat (don't get TOO crazy here and lose all the good stuff), then add the crushed red pepper and marinara. Cook until all the ingredients get to know each other, about 2 minutes.

Okay, okay, okay. You got the gar butt muffs (the abbreviations have gotten out of hand, sorry) and the bacony sauce hanging out—now it's time to fry up some eggs and sausage patties. Lube up your hands with either vegetable oil or cooking spray, and form the Italian sausage into 4 equal patties, about as wide as the English muffins are. Fry up those sausage patties in a skillet over medium heat until they are no longer raw and likely to cause disease. Remove the sausage, wipe down the pan, then melt the butter in the skillet. Fry the eggs however you like them—

4 English muffins
½ cup (1 stick) unsalted butter
4 garlic cloves, palm heel struck and minced
¼ teaspoon ground black pepper
1 tablespoon minced curly parsley
4 slices bacon
Pinch of crushed red pepper
1 cup marinara sauce
Vegetable oil or cooking spray
8 ounces raw Italian sausage (we go spicy over sweet)
1 tablespoon unsalted butter
4 large eggs
4 slices provolone

over easy, over medium, over hard, overexpert mode. All eggs are valid.

YOU MAY NOW CONSTRUCT YOUR SANDWICHES! Geez, finally, right? Add a dollop of bacon sauce to the bottom of an English muffin, then top with a sausage patty, a slice of provolone, a fried egg, and more bacon sauce. Crown this delicious Italian American and American mashup with the top English muffin. Repeat for the remaining three sandwiches. For best results, wrap each sandwich in aluminum foil and throw it back in the oven for 5 minutes to melt the cheese.

Eat it right away, because when you're here, you're loving it . . . and it's also where America and Italian America meet . . . and where garlic butter makes everything garlic better.

POPEYES BREAKFAST BURRITO

We're big believers in the idea that if you have leftovers, you shouldn't just microwave them and turn them into a worse version of something you ate fresh yesterday. We're also big believers in the emotional healing power of a child's laughter, but that has nothing to do with leftovers. No, you should harness the power of creativity, rugged individualism, and American [international readers, please insert the name of your country] ingenuity to transform leftovers into something great. If you're like us and sometimes order way too much Popeyes, possibly because your date stood you up—or you saw a Popeyes and you stood your date up—we have got the ultimate recipe for when you're like . . . "Hey, I want a breakfast burrito but I turned all my bacon into bacon roses to give to my date who I stood up because I got distracted by the seductive orange glow of a Popeyes."

....

Preheat the oven to whatever is called for in the instructions on the back of the Tater Tots bag. One may think that, with all our chef training, we would know better than a shiny bag of frozen tater nuggets. Unfortunately, we do not. Place the tots in a baking dish and bake for . . . as long as the bag says you should bake them. If the bag tells you to do anything—ANYTHING—do it. In bag we trust.

While the tots are baking, add the mayo and hot sauce to a tiny little bowl and gently whisk together. GENTLY, we say! After that, crack all 8 eggs into a large bowl, add the salt and pepper, and whisk harder than you've ever whisked before. HARDER, we say! Heat the butter over medium heat in a large nonstick sauté pan until melted, then add your whisked eggs and cook, continuously moving them around the pan until just set, about 4 minutes. Remove from the heat and reserve all that for later.

When the tots are about 10 minutes from being finished, throw the chicken tendies right on top of the Tater Tots and bake to heat through. (If you're using frozen chicken tendies, just cook those

Recipe continues

One 32-ounce bag
  frozen Tater Tots
½ cup mayo
2 tablespoons hot sauce
  of your choice
8 large eggs
½ teaspoon salt
¼ teaspoon ground black pepper
2 tablespoons unsalted butter
8 leftover chicken tendies
  from Popeyes (or you can use
  your favorite brand of frozen
  chicken tendies, but they won't
  be as good because Popeyes
  chicken is the shiznit)
1 cup shredded cheddar
  (about 4 ounces)
4 large flour tortillas
  (12 inches is preferred)

according to the instructions on the almighty bag. BAG WILL PREVAIL!) Make an assembly line with all your ingredients to be put into the tortillas: shredded cheese, scrambled eggs, chicken tendies, Tater Tots, and hotsaucennaise (copyright pending).

THIS STEP MUST NOT BE SKIPPED, WE ARE SUPER SERIOUS, Y'ALL, WE WILL KNOW IF YOU SKIP THIS STEP AND SHOW UP AT YOUR HOUSE AND BE VERY DISAPPOINTED. Heat a large sauté pan over high heat and griddle each tortilla for 15 seconds on each side. This will make it pliable enough to fold around your ingredients without breaking. Working with one tortilla at a time, add shredded cheese, eggs, chicken tenders, Tater Tots, and hotsaucennaise, then tuck in the sides of your burrito and roll it, forming a tight handheld food bundle.

Give yourself a high five and probably call that date you stood up last night to apologize; that's pretty messed up what you did.

FROZEN FRENCH FRY AND LEFTOVERS HASH

We called this the official breakfast of divorced dads and also *Mythical Kitchen* because holy cow is this easy and delicious. Why eat soggy, dried-out leftovers when you can make them into a hot and crispy breakfast that is, frankly, better than your Chipotle bowl ever was in the first place? This takes frozen French fries, chops them up, fries them up, and hashes them up with a leftover Chipotle bowl or, to be totally honest, ANY LEFTOVERS THAT YOU HAVE THAT WILL TASTE GOOD WITH CRISPY POTATOES AND A SUNNY-SIDE UP EGG ON TOP! Leftover Costco rotisserie chicken? Hash it! Leftover meat sauce? Hash it! A leftover DVD of the HBO series *The Leftovers*? Hash it! Wait. No. Why do you still own DVDs? Just make this Frozen French Fry and Leftovers Hash and stream it instead, but maybe skip season one, because we hear it was kind of boring at first but gets way better in the later seasons.

....

Put 1 big glug of oil in a wide nonstick skillet and set over medium-high heat. While it's heating up, chop up those frozen fries into little bitty pieces because big pieces of potato in hash are lazy and not really hash. Put those right in the oil, stir them around for a second, and then press them down with a spatula into the pan and let those things get sizzly. Don't disturb them. Just leave them alone.

After about 90 seconds, take your leftovers and just dump those right on top, give them all a nice stir, then press them all down and leave them alone again. They need more space.

Meanwhile, heat a small nonstick skillet over low heat and add that last little glug of oil. Crack the egg in there and let it go slow and low until the white is set and the yolk is still runny, about 6 minutes.

Once you think the hash is crispy and golden on the bottom, give it another 10 seconds. Unless it's burning. If it's burning, reduce the heat. Once it's ready, after 10 to 12 minutes, you can start flipping it

Recipe continues

Serves you and only you, no sharing

About 3 tablespoons (or 1 big glug and 1 little glug) neutral oil

One 32-ounce bag frozen crinkle-cut French fries

4 cups your favorite leftovers

1 large egg

Ground black pepper, for serving

Hot sauce, for serving

in little segments. If it's not crispy and brown, keep on going until it is. Once it's all hot and crispy and mixed up, slide it onto your plate or into a giant cereal bowl and then put the egg right on top. Hit it with some pepper and a little hot sauce and then eat it, marveling at how you made a hash with a bunch of junk that was just lying around in your fridge and freezer, and shout to everyone within earshot that you scaled Mount Breakfast and they should all be in awe of you. Or, you know, just eat it. But that sounds less fun.

Leftovers?

Leftovers for this recipe could include anything, such as lasagna, creamy chicken casserole, pot roast, beef and broccoli, or our platonic ideal: leftover Chipotle burrito filling.

SKITTLE-MILK FRENCH TOAST

Or as they say in France, "*Pain perdu avec lait du Skittles et notre belle culture a été bâtardée par les Américains.*" Such a beautiful language! The truth is, on a "Will It Cereal?" episode of *GMM*, we tried to find out if you could just eat a bowl of Skittles in milk. And while you certainly can . . . it's a little weird and chewy. But we discovered that SKITTLE MILK IS AMAZING! And what's better than drinking a tall glass of Skittle milk? Using it to make French toast. This is honestly way easier and more delicious than it has any right to be. But if you want to double down on the flavor, you can totally make a separate glass of Skittle milk to drink with your French toast, just to get totally jacked up on sugar before noon.

....

Step 1: Make the Skittle Syrup. Pour those Skittles into a medium pot with 1 cup water and bring it to a boil. Keep that heat at medium-high and watch those Skittles get en-syruped! Stir occasionally to keep the Skittles from sticking to the bottom, until the syrup reduces to ¼ cup, about 11 minutes. Set aside and warm it back up to serve.

Step 2: Make the Skittle-Milk French Toast. Put the Skittles in a medium bowl with the milk. Let them steep for about 20 minutes, stirring them around every few minutes, until the milk tastes like rainbow.

Pour the milk through a strainer into a large bowl and either eat those weird white ghost Skittles or throw them away. Crack the eggs into the bowl, add the salt, and whisk until everything is all mixed up.

Place a cast-iron or nonstick skillet over medium heat and add 1 tablespoon of the butter. Once it is melty and foamy, add 2 slices of the bread to the milk mixture and flip them around until the bread is super saturated. Lift up each piece, letting the excess liquid drain off, then put it in the skillet and cook until brown and crispy on one side, about 3 minutes. Flip them over and get the other side, about another 3 minutes.

Recipe continues

Makes 8 pieces of French toast

Skittle Syrup
One 2.17-ounce bag Skittles

Skittle-Milk French Toast
One 2.17-ounce bag Skittles
2 cups whole milk
6 large eggs
¼ teaspoon salt
4 tablespoons (½ stick) unsalted butter, plus more for serving
8 slices white bread

Put them on a plate and repeat with the remaining bread and butter until you've got 8 slices of Skittle-Milk French Toast! Serve right away with butter and Skittle syrup. Or if you're a dad, realize that everyone else already ate the French toast while you were making it and now there are just two slices left and everyone else went to go play with their friends and you finally get ONE MINUTE TO SIT ALONE IN PEACE and enjoy your two hot slices of French toast. You deserve it, Dad. Thanks for being you.

Stale Bread?

As we found out in an episode of MythMunchers, using stale, dehydrated bread really does drastically improve your French toast. The problem is, science and technology have advanced to the point where your store-bought bread likely doesn't go stale before you eat it all. Here's what you do: if you're the responsible type with the gift of foresight, lay your bread slices out on the counter the night before. If you're . . . more like us and prefer to fly by the seat of your pants, put your bread in a 350°F oven for 10 minutes while you make your Skittle milk.

ENCHILOMELET

We here at Mythical like to follow the Egg Theory of Before Noon Food (ETOBNF), which famously states: If you put an egg on something, you're ethically allowed to eat it before noon. Every brunch restaurant in America follows this rule. Want to serve a burger? Put an egg on it and call it a breakfast burger. What about a plate of pasta? Put some eggs and bacon in there. Boom: pasta carbonara. Chocolate cake? Slap a sunny-side up on there and saddle up for a balanced breakfast, cowboy! I know what you're thinking . . . they're gonna put eggs inside an enchilada and call it breakfast, aren't they? Wow, that actually sounds really good. We should have thought of that. But NO! We're going the other way and taking that Trader Joe's enchilada that has been sitting in your freezer that you kind of want to eat for breakfast and instead, we're going to make a classic diner-style omelet and put that enchilada right inside. Enchilomelet!

Makes but 1 enchilomelet

2 frozen enchiladas (get creative here—the flavor is up to you, but beef or cheese feels like the best, and chicken feels like a weird way for mother and daughter to be reunited)

One 10-ounce can enchilada sauce

2 tablespoons unsalted butter

3 large eggs

Salt and ground black pepper

2 tablespoons finely crumbled queso fresco

1 extremely optional cilantro leaf (you know . . . for plating)

Step 1: FOLLOW THE PACKAGE INSTRUCTIONS. That's right, folks—cook those enchiladas according to the package instructions. Meanwhile, crack open that can of enchilada sauce and warm it up on the stove over medium heat. In a pot! Not in the can. Actually, in the can might work, but that feels like something a hobo in the 1920s would do, except with a can of beans and not enchilada sauce. We take NO legal responsibility if you try to heat up a can of enchilada sauce directly on the stove.

Step 2: Make an Omelet. Place a nonstick skillet over medium heat and slap that butter in there. Crack your eggs into a bowl with a splash of water and whip them up with everything you've got—you want a nice, smooth, fluffy boy with no white floaters.

Once the butter is melted, pour the eggs into the pan. For the first 20 seconds, you're going to use a spatula (ideally high-heat silicone) to keep sliding the egg edges toward the middle, tilting the pan to let the wet eggs fill into the gaps as you do it. After those 20 seconds, you're going to sprinkle it with salt and pepper and let it sit. Then you wait, and watch, until it looks like that egg is starting to firm up a little. You want it a little wet in the center, and on the border of custardy.

After that, turn down the heat a touch and take your spatula and run it around the outer lip of the omelet, releasing it from the edge. Your eggs should be nice and custardy. Give the pan a gentle shake to make sure the omelet is able to slide around comfortably and doesn't have any sticky spots.

Lift those 2 enchiladas from their cardboard home and slide them right on top of half of the omelet.

Tilt the pan toward the enchiladas slightly and use your spatula to lift up the non-enchilada side and fold it over the enchiladas. Slide that sucker onto a plate, spoon some enchilada sauce over it, sprinkle it with queso fresco, put that *dangerously optional* leaf of cilantro on top, and go ahead: crush that breakfast. Throw away the enchilada packaging and pretend you made everything from scratch.

Omelet Triage?

If your omelet is totally a sticky mess and you are starting to get mad . . . don't worry! Chop up the enchilada on a cutting board, scoop it right into your eggs, and mash it all together—and huzzah! You made an enchilada scramble! Crumble in the queso fresco and top everything with some enchilada sauce and you've got a delicious breakfast that you 100 percent meant to do.

BISCUIT AND GRAVY SKILLET PEETZA

What is a pizza? Is it a pie? Is it an open-faced sandwich? Is pizza merely the friends we made along the way? According to the Associazione Verace Pizza Napoletana (AVPN), the governing body of all pizza rules and regulations, a pizza must have a diameter not exceeding thirty-five centimeters and a raised crust between one and two centimeters tall. We reached out to the AVPN asking for a special dispensation that would allow our monstrously large biscuit raft topped with sausage gravy, eggs, and cheese to be considered a pizza, and they did not seem pleased. They were speaking Italian, so we're not exactly sure what they were saying, but we did manage to catch the words *stupidi* and *americani*. We think those are types of pastas. Anyway, we found a legal loophole by spelling it *peetza*. Take that, Italy!

....

Step 1: Make the Sausage Gravy. If you've never made a sausage gravy, hooooo boy, buckle up because you're about to go to Flavorville (it's about 75 miles east of Flavortown and has a supercool water park). Melt the butter in a medium saucepan over medium heat, then add the sausage and break it up with a wooden spoon. Cook until the sausage is browned and cooked through, about 6 minutes.

Add the flour and cook, stirring, for 3 minutes. Add the milk, ½ cup at a time, stirring until the lumps are gone with each addition. Add the salt and pepper, then cook for about 2 minutes. The gravy should be thick enough to coat the back of a spoon. Hot dang, the Flavorville Water Park lazy river is going to feel great after all this work. But you're not done yet.

Step 2: Make the Biscuit Peetza. Place a rack near the bottom of the oven. Preheat the oven to 450°F.

Grab a large bowl and hold it tightly. Whisper to it. Sing it the songs of old, and the songs of new. Then add the flour, baking powder, and salt and give everything a good stir. There are several different ways to add tiny chunks of butter to your biscuit dough, but we've found the

Recipe continues

Makes 1 peetza big enough for 8 small people, or 6 medium people, or 4 large people, or 1 Magnús Ver Magnússon, four-time World's Strongest Man champion

For the Sausage Gravy

2 tablespoons unsalted butter

4 ounces pork breakfast sausage

3 tablespoons all-purpose flour

1½ cups whole milk

½ teaspoon salt

½ teaspoon ground black pepper

For the Biscuit Peetza

2 cups all-purpose flour

1 tablespoon baking powder

1½ teaspoons salt

½ cup (1 stick) unsalted butter, ice cold

¾ cup whole milk

1 tablespoon vegetable oil

1 cup shredded mozzarella (about 4 ounces)

3 large eggs

Scallions, for garnish (or nothing, for not-garnish)

easiest is to make sure your butter is VERY cold and grate it using the largest holes on a standard cheese grater. (The hardest way involves the Large Hadron Collider, which gets dangerous.) Grate your cold butter into the flour mixture and toss with a fork until evenly dispersed.

Add the milk and stir together with the same fork you've been using. If you've lost that fork, grab another fork. And then another. Where are all your forks? Mix until the dough holds together and no more flour is visible. The goal is to work gently and not fully mash the butter into the dough, but cut yourself some slack and just try your best.

Grease up a big ol' honkin' 12-inch oven-safe skillet with the oil, then add the biscuit dough and press it into an even layer across the bottom and about 1½ inches up the side. Pour your gravy across the crust, then spread it out into an even layer before adding your cheese.

Use a spoon (or your fingers, assuming you are a real one, and we know you are) to create three egg-size holes in the shredded cheese layer. After that—guess what comes next?—crack the eggs into those egg holes and chuck the pan in the oven for about 15 minutes, until the egg whites are set and the biscuit crust is crispy. Let the pizza cool for at least 5 minutes, then top with either scallions or nothing and enjoy.

Should You Have a Large Skillet?

Yes, you should have a large skillet. If you don't have yourself a large skillet, definitely get yourself a large skillet. The ideal large skillet diameter is 12 inches, but we're open to any large skillet you have. Oh, and make sure it is oven-safe. So, no rubber or plastic parts on the handle.

THE TALE OF HORRIBLE, NO-GOOD,
Grumpy Old Smoothie Man

Every morning, the villagers rejoice over breakfast. Burritos with grease-stained tortillas that barely—just barely—hide the cheesy treasures inside. Omelets so fluffy they look as if they should float among the clouds. Coffees and teas and juices and donuts and cakes and, oh, how you wouldn't believe the array of schmears and dollops and drizzles.

The Maple Syrup River is flowing, the bagels roll freely down the lush green hills, and everyone sings merrily, for they are eating breakfast. Well, not everyone. Off in the distance, past Hamsteak Hill and over the tippy top of Bacon Forest, you'll see the scowl of a lonely man who ceased his morning merrymaking long ago. He growls and frowns and winces as he lifts a cup of thick, gray-green sludge to his lips. "Breakfast shouldn't be fun," the angry Glasses Man says. "Breakfast is about routine. Breakfast is about practicality. Breakfast is about nutrition." He takes another long, self-assured slurp. "A spinach smoothie is the only proper breakfast."

He feels a gentle tug on his dusty brown sweatshirt. "But, mister, my mom said that if every villager doesn't eat a delicious breakfast, then Robo Vulture will snatch us up in his talons of steel and drag us to the Gray Place." It is little Stevie Swoopie, the tiniest villager of them all, who climbed all the way up Mount Marmalade to spread the message of breakfast cheer. "Stupid children's stories," Glasses Man says, as he swats Stevie Swoopie's tiny hand away. "Almost as stupid as eating a bowl of sugary cereal for breakf—"

Glasses Man is interrupted by the horrible shriek of a million nails scratching a million chalkboards. The ground shakes and the Granola Grass stirs beneath his feet as a terrifying shadow descends. A voice booms from beneath the beating, metal wings, "HORRIBLE NO-GOOD GLASSES MAN, YOUR SINS CANNOT GO UNPUNISHED!" Glasses Man drops his smoothie and stares up at the monstrous robotic bird. "No. No, no, no, it's simply not possible!" But his protests are drowned out by the sound of the villagers as they ascend the ridge. "Gray Place, Gray Place, Gray Place," they chant. Panicking, Glasses Man looks down and sees Stevie Swoopie's eyes glowing red. "GRAY PLACE! GRAY PLACE! GRAY PLA—"

LINK'S SMOOTHIE

This is the most boring recipe in the cookbook, and we are sorry Link is the way that he is.

....

Put the ingredients in a blender.

Blend.

Keep blending.

Think about creating a new series on YouTube where two best friends with incredible hair—one tall, one with glasses—travel the globe in search of history's most important smoothies. Not necessarily the best smoothies, but the most historically important smoothies. First, of course, we need to decide what makes a smoothie historically important, and we're so glad you asked: it's all about context—Oh great, smoothie's done!

Pour into a glass.

Drink with a straw.

Get a breakfast burrito from a drive-thru on your way to work because you're still hungry.

Makes 1 smoothie

1 cup almond milk
½ cup frozen blueberries
½ cup fresh spinach
1 tablespoon peanut butter

Optional Ingredients
1 scoop your preferred vanilla protein powder (Josh's favorite brand is Optimum Nutrition Gold Standard, and Josh has bigger biceps than Link, so you should probably listen to him.)
¼ cup walnuts
1 tablespoon hemp seeds
1 tablespoon chia seeds

SHARE FOOD WITH PEOPLE TO TRICK THEM INTO LIKING YOU

(APPETIZERS)

Hey there, buddy! Heard you had some trouble making friends, connecting with peers, and sustaining meaningful platonic relationships! Well, don't you fret, because after taking our foolproof, ten-step course on the Law of Apptraction,* you'll never again spend another Friday night alone on the couch staring at your phone.

You see, the law is really quite simple, and rooted in the theory of Quantum Social Perception.† Here's how it works: When you walk into a room full of new people, everyone immediately takes stock of everything about you. Your body language, your hairstyle, your clothing, the tone of your voice, and even your smell all cause synapses to fire in the brains of others, ultimately deciding whether you are friend or foe. A favorable reaction, and you might be asked to join a recreational kickball team! But an unfavorable reaction, and you run the risk of finding out that everyone won free hot wings at a trivia night that you were never invited to.

---

* The Law of Apptraction is not binding and results may vary. Also you will definitely spend more Friday nights on your couch alone, because, let's face it, sometimes that's the best place to be.

†Quantum Social Perception is in no way related to *Quantum of Solace*, which is in no way related to *Ghost Protocol*. Those are two different movie franchises.

Old, outdated advice might tell you to simply change certain aspects about yourself. Perhaps you should take fashion tips from social media influencers. Maybe you should get a trendy haircut. It could even be a good idea to avoid going on half-hour rants about how World War II influenced American dairy subsidies when the original question was "Hey, what's up?" Although this method has worked for some, most people are incapable of changing their personalities, and the salespeople at the cool clothing stores make them uncomfortable.

So, what to do? Enter: the Law of Apptraction. It states that, so long as you are holding a tray of appetizers, you can get away with being as unkempt, disagreeable, and downright weird as you want to be. The Law of Apptraction works by interrupting the usual neuron transmissions that fire in someone's brain when they're meeting a stranger for the first time. As they are passing judgment on your appearance and trying to discern if that is, indeed, a giant salsa stain on your white T-shirt, the olfactory senses kick in, and instead, they find themselves thinking of the giant tray of jalapeño poppers in your hands. What was once a potential threat is now a new friend, thanks to the Law of Apptraction.

And that's not where it stops. Instead of being forced to listen to that person talk about their job in insurance policy risk management or whatever, you'll find they are so enamored with how crispy the poppers are, it's all they'll want to talk about for the next ten to fifteen minutes, drawing others into your pungent orbit. Suddenly, the Law of Apptraction has biohacked the nervous systems of everyone at the party, and they're all marveling at how much of a genius you were to use crispy rice as a coating for a nostalgic appetizer classic. You leave the party as a member of two new meme-centric group texts, and you have started a book club with the party host. You will never read the books, but that's okay, because you'll show up to the meetings with shrimp cocktail in hand.

We must warn you, though, because the Law of Apptraction is an incredibly powerful tool and should not be treated lightly. You must learn to wield it responsibly, and also understand that you will draw in a different type of friend with each different appetizer in your arsenal. If you master all ten recipes in this chapter, here is who you can expect to apptract.

Spam Jalapeño Poppers: Use this recipe to lure adventurous friends with a penchant for understanding nuance and subtlety. Sure, they'll be attracted to the universal combination of creamy cheese with spicy jalapeños, but it's the crispy sushi rice coating that will truly draw them in. These are the friends to go cave spelunking with and then see an arthouse documentary about the history of cave spelunking afterward.

Goldfish Pizza Rolls: These will attract the hardcore nostalgia nerds who are perfect for activities such as bowling, watching *Family Guy* reruns for hours, playing '90s arcade games, and seeing new Marvel movies. The real bonus is: these friends will not insist that Marvel movies are actually powerful social commentaries on current events; they just want to see Spider-Man go *pew pew* with the web shooter.

Ramen Nachos: These will be for your ultimate sharing-is-caring friends who don't care about money or status. The ramen nacho enjoyers will frequently invite you to partake in free activities with them, such as loitering in a park, loitering in a parking lot, or loitering at a public pool. They will never ask you when you are planning to buy a house, and they will always share their fries with you.

KFC Drumstick Burrito Bombs: If you really want to attract the most hedonistic friends, you will enter the room with a plate of chicken legs wrapped in deep-fried burritos. These are the friends who live for the now. These are the friends who seize the Tuesday afternoon with bottomless mimosas. These are the friends you want to see after a bad day, while you drown your sorrows in an entire large pizza dipped in a gallon of ranch dressing.

Steakhouse Taquitos: Ahhhh yes, the steakhouse taquito friend—dark and mysterious, a shadowy figure who does not reveal the hidden depths under the surface. They often wear sunglasses inside and carry a motorcycle helmet, despite never having driven a motorcycle. They will invite you to underground post-punk concerts, but when you show up to the venue, you'll find it's just an empty parking lot. Beware the steakhouse taquito friend.

Baconator Soft Pretzels: The type of friend whose brain gets hijacked by promises of soft pretzels and melty cheese is the same friend who will not leave their home for weeks at a time, but it's cool, because they have subscribed to every streaming service, have multiple throw pillows, and are always drinking hot chocolate. The cozy soft pretzel friend tends to be more enjoyable from October to February, so plan your apptractions accordingly.

Pulled Pork Twinkies: Much like the cakes themselves, these tender and emotionally fluffy friends are always there for you on your worst days. They will cry with you after your cat dies, they will listen to your pettiest work complaints, and they will lend you their weighted blanket when you just need to cry it out. The Twinkie friend is perfect for seeing the new Tom Hanks movie about an old man with regrets. You will enjoy the movie. Because it is Tom Hanks.

Bean Pizza: This friend is equal parts wholesome and adventurous. They love hiking, but more than the actual hiking, they love looking at the view from the top of the hike and saying, "Man, isn't nature beautiful?" This friend will unironically plan a paddleboat date at a local man-made lake on a random Sunday afternoon, where you two just talk about your hopes and dreams for the future. You will get a single beer afterward, and it will be lovely.

Cheeseburger Nuggets: The cheeseburger nugget friend is a human hummingbird. They will pop into view, partake from the feeder, then zoom out as quickly as they came. They will pop a nugget, then vanish, but every six months, when another friend cancels on a Korean BBQ reservation and the restaurant refuses to seat you, the hummingbird friend will be there in five minutes, no questions asked, only to disappear for another year. This is a useful friend to have.

Shrimp Cocktail of Death: You had never ordered bottle service in a club before the shrimp cocktail friend came into your life. You had never eaten a twelve-course abstract art–themed tasting menu either, but goshdangit if you didn't enjoy it. You don't know where the shrimp cocktail friend gets their money because they never talk about a job, but you were the one who showed up to a house party full of strangers with fifty dollars' worth of poached shrimp after all. So, who's the REAL fancy pants here?

SPAM JALAPEÑO POPPERS

Makes 20 poppers, serving 4 to 6 people as long as there is other food and 2 of the people aren't that into food

Spam musubi—griddled Spam with rice and toasted seaweed—is one of the great Hawaiian snack foods. And jalapeño poppers—spicy boy cheesy nug nugs—are one of the great corporate chain restaurant bar snacks. So what happens when you mix them together? We tried putting them in a blender and slurping it down with a boba straw, but that was objectively disgusting. So then we figured, "Hey, let's put a little more thought into this. The Smoothie Fusion Method (SFM) has a 100 percent failure rate, and we should probably stop making that our first attempt every time." Anyway, it turns out that Spam already makes a jalapeño Spam, so we put away the blender and came up with this recipe, which is WAY better than that smoothie, and honestly also way better than most jalapeño poppers.

....

Step 1: Let's Make Sushi Rice. Put the washed, drained rice in a medium pot with 2 cups water and bring it to a simmer. Once it's simmering, drop the heat to low, give it a stir, put a lid on it, and cook for 15 minutes. Remove from the heat and let the rice rest for about 10 minutes. Put the vinegar, sugar, and salt in a small bowl and microwave it for 15 seconds—just to dissolve the salt and sugar. Then add it to the pot of rice, give it a stir, and cover it again. Let the rice sit there until you need it.

Step 2: Make the Spam Filling. Dice the Spam, then heat the oil in a medium skillet over medium-high heat. Once it's hot, fling in those Spam cubes and fry them up, stirring them around, until they're brown and crispy and you have to stop yourself from eating all of them right out of the pan and burning your fingers, about 4 minutes. Once they're done, lift them with a slotted spoon and dump them into a large bowl with the cream cheese and cheddar. Roughly chop the pickled jalapeño slices, add them to the bowl along with the salt, and then stir it all up until you have a delicious, porky jalapeño cheese blob. Set the blob in the fridge to solidify for at least 30 minutes while you get ready to . . .

Step 3: Fry 'Em Up! Fill a heavy-bottomed pot with about ½ inch of oil and set it over medium heat to get it going while you ball up your

Sushi Rice

2 cups short-grain sushi rice, washed and drained

3 tablespoons rice wine vinegar

1 tablespoon sugar

1 teaspoon salt

Spam Filling

Half of a 12-ounce can Spam Jalapeño (You can use any flavor of Spam, but please, for the love of Starbucks, do not use the pumpkin spice Spam. Yes, it exists. Yes, even we have our limits.)

2 tablespoons vegetable oil

One 8-ounce brick cream cheese, at room temperature

1 cup shredded cheddar (about 4 ounces)

¼ cup drained pickled jalapeño slices

1 teaspoon salt

To Finish

Neutral oil, for frying

Ranch dressing, for dipping

poppers. Add some warm water to a small bowl. Wet your hands with a little of the water, then grab a hunk of rice and press it into a thin, flat disk about the size of your palm—yes, that's right, the bigger your hands, the bigger your mouth probably is, and the bigger your Spam jalapeño poppers deserve to be.

Take a heaping tablespoon or so of the filling—or more, if you have giant hands—and put it in the middle of the rice, then close up the rice into a ball and set it aside. Then make more. Keep making more until they are all ready to be fried, or until you are tired of making rice balls.

Now increase the heat to high and look for the oil to start shimmering. While you're waiting, set up some paper towels on a plate so you have somewhere to put the poppers after they've been fried.

Fry up them balls, in batches, turning them occasionally until they are golden brown and crispy on all sides, about 4 minutes total. Here's the deal. You could use an oil thermometer and try to keep your oil at exactly 350°F. But you could also fry Spam jalapeño poppers like your grandmother did and just use your eyes and nose to figure it out. Think of it this way: if they are burning and smell scorched, your oil is too hot. If they don't bubble and sizzle and release steam when you put them in, the oil is too cold.

Also, as you're frying multiple batches, you might start getting low on oil. So what do you do? Come on, guys, you know this one: you add more oil, and then you make sure the oil is hot before you add more balls in.

Once they're fried, lift out the poppers with a slotted spoon and put them on the paper towels to rest and cool off for a few minutes. When you have waited long enough to NOT BURN YOUR FACE OFF WITH MOLTEN JALAPEÑO SPAM CHEESE, dip them in ranch dressing and think about how much better this is than if you just put it all in a blender and drank it.

How Do I Wash My Rice?

Short-grain Japanese rice has a *lot* of starch so as to create that perfect texture for sushi. It's important to rinse the rice a couple of times in cold water to get rid of the excess, though. Too much starch will make your rice gummy, which is bad. If you wouldn't want your gum rice-y, you shouldn't want your rice gummy. Write that down. So if you go to a sushi place and the rice is gummy, you should definitely stop eating there. If that's how they treat the rice, they are probably doing really disgusting things to the fish.

Put the rice in a fine-mesh strainer and lower it into a large bowl of cold water. Use your fingers to swirl it around for about 15 seconds, lift the strainer from the rice, dump the water, and repeat that process one more time. (Okay, fine, you can probably just do it once, since we're making Spam jalapeño poppers and not sushi, but we think you should do it at least twice because WINNERS DO MORE! WINNERS OPEN SUSHI RESTAURANTS! START AN LLC AND GET AN SBA LOAN FOR YOUR SMALL BUSINESS! Okay, wow, that went off the rails. Anyway, how's the rice washing coming along?)

GOLDFISH PIZZA ROLLS

In the mountains of Alto Adige, you will find the small village of Totino, where they are famed for having invented the technique of toasting ravioli. Yet just like how the fast-food chain Wienerschnitzel called themselves Wienerschnitzel even though they sell hot dogs instead of actual Wiener schnitzel (it's pounded and fried veal!), the Totino's corporation of America took that ancient northern Italian recipe for toasted ravioli and decided to call it a "pizza roll," and thus, an empire was born.

Just kidding. Pizza rolls were invented in America in 1968 when a guy named Jeno Paulucci wanted to create an egg roll filled with pizza ingredients. (Jeno's Pizza Rolls were quickly sold to Pillsbury and renamed Totino's Pizza Rolls.) Anyway, the point is that pizza rolls are already a ridiculous idea, so you should absolutely be able to do whatever the heck you want with them, including making the crust out of Goldfish. And you know what? Goldfish Pizza Rolls are delicious, and as soon as you finish making them, stoned gamers will start knocking on your kitchen window asking to be friends.

....

Note: Oh, and you don't *need* a 3-inch-wide goldfish-shaped cookie cutter to make these . . . but boy will they not be goldfish-shaped without it.

Step 1: Make the Goldfish Dough. Chuck the Goldfish crackers, flour, salt, and baking powder into a food processor and pulse it five times to incorporate. Next, crack in the eggs, add ⅔ cup water and the oil, and pulverize until the mixture balls up and comes together like dough. For any dough problems, the solutions are alarmingly simple. Too wet? Sprinkle in some more flour and keep pulsing. Too dry? Add a spoonful of water and keep pulsing.

Once you have a nice dough, form it into a disk, wrap it in plastic, and leave it in the fridge for 2 hours to hydrate and to allow the fish glutens to relax. Now you can . . .

Step 2: Make the Filling. Mix the tomato paste and ¼ cup water together in a small bowl. Give them a good stir so it's not all clumpy

Recipe continues

Serves 4 to 6 as an appetizer at a cocktail party or, who are we kidding, this serves 2 people: you, and you at 1:00 a.m., clawing the leftovers out of the fridge like a starved Gremlin

Goldfish Dough

2 cups Goldfish crackers

2 cups all-purpose flour

2 teaspoons salt

1½ teaspoons baking powder

3 large eggs

¼ cup neutral oil, such as vegetable or canola

Filling

One 4.5-ounce tube tomato paste

¼ cup small-diced pepperoni

¼ cup small-diced orange cheddar

Finish Him!

2 large eggs

Pinch of dried parsley flakes

¼ cup grated Parmesan (about 1 ounce)

Ranch dressing, for serving (optional)

and wet, then add the pepperoni and cheddar and mix everything together. You're done. That's it. That's the filling.

Step 3: Fill Them and Cook Them! Preheat the oven to 350°F. Line a baking sheet with parchment paper.

Now that your dough has rested, divide it in half, and cover one-half in plastic while you work with the other half. Use a floured rolling pin to roll out the dough into a sheet that's about ⅛ inch thick, or at least as thin as you're willing to make it before you say, "That has to be thin enough, right?" But then go a little bit thinner. Repeat this with the other dough half. The most important thing is that both pieces are the same thickness and the same shape.

Beat the eggs with a splash of water to make an egg wash. Brush one of the sheets of Goldfish dough with egg wash, saving any remaining egg wash for later.

Dollop the filling onto the other sheet of dough, about 1 tablespoon or so at a time (or just eyeball it like us and hope for the best because measuring is for architects), spacing it out with an inch or so of space in between dollops (or just eyeball it like us and hope for the best because measuring is for architects). Lay the other sheet, egg wash side *down*, over the filled sheet. Use your fingers to pat out the space in between the filling and press the dough together. Take your goldfish cookie cutter and cut around each dollop, then pull away the excess dough around them. Crimp the edges closed with your fingers if they seem like they have a lot of cheese seepage.

Place the goldfish on the prepared baking sheet, brush the tops with more of the egg wash so they get extra-golden goldfish-y, then sprinkle them with as much parsley and Parmesan as you think looks abundant but not desperate.

Bake until the crust is fully cooked through and golden yellow, about 20 minutes.

Serve these on their own, all classy-like, or in a cereal bowl filled with ranch dressing if you want to live out our shame fantasy.

How Do You Wash an Egg?

An egg wash is a great trick for adding refined, glossy sheen to your baked goods. It is just beaten egg (usually mixed with a little water or milk to thin it out), brushed onto your dough to transform it from "rustic" to "classy." It also doubles as a great way to help any toppings, like sesame seeds, grated cheese, or dried herbs stick to the dough while it bakes, and it helps seal the dough sheets so they adhere to each other.

RAMEN NACHOS

TIRED: Ramen Burgers.

WIRED: Ramen Nachos.

INSPIRED: A car that runs on leftover ramen broth from restaurants. Expect our Mythical prototype to enter markets in 2074.

That's right, we put a five-year-old meme in a cookbook headnote. Take that, ramen burger! We are making Ramen Nachos, the crispy, finger-food version of ramen that nobody asked for but is unquestionably delicious. We take instant ramen and make it way less instant, by cooking it, freezing it, frying it, searing and braising chashu, making Miso Nacho Cheese, and putting it all together to make drunk food you don't even need to be drunk to eat. We'll be honest, this is one of the longer and more complex recipes in this book, but THIS IS WHY WE'RE HERE! Let's make Ramen Nachos.

....

Note: You can fry these for best results, or bake them for still pretty good results!

Step 1: Make Your Ramen Masa! Boil the ramen noodles according to the package instructions, then rinse them under cold water, drain them, and put them in a large bowl. Add the flour, eggs, and ramen flavor packets. Give them all a nice mix, making sure there are no, like, whole egg yolks, because that would be a weird, lazy choice.

Put a silicone baking mat or sheet of parchment paper on a baking sheet, then lay the ramen noodles on top. Try to spread them out into one thin, even layer, enjoying the squishy noodle feeling between your fingers but not licking them unless you're into raw egg and raw flour. Put another silicone mat or sheet of parchment on top and then freeze until frozen, like, 2 hours.

Step 2: Make Pork Belly Chashu! Fill a large pot halfway with water and bring it to a boil. Next, roll that pork belly up into a tight log with the fat side up and tie it tightly with butcher's twine so it holds its shape—nobody wants a floppy belly, let alone a floppy pork belly. Once the water is boiling, gently lay the belly roll into the water and keep it at a gentle simmer for 10 minutes to poach it up. Transfer the pork

Recipe continues

Ramen Chips

4 packages instant ramen (choose your flavor wisely!)

½ cup all-purpose flour

2 large eggs

Neutral oil, for frying (optional)

Pork Belly Chashu

2 pounds pork belly

2 tablespoons vegetable oil

½ cup sake

½ cup soy sauce

⅓ cup sugar

2 tablespoons mirin

1 large knob fresh ginger, peeled

4 scallions, roughly chopped

6 garlic cloves, peeled

Neutral oil, for frying

Ramen Eggs

4 large eggs

½ cup chashu liquid

Miso Nacho Cheese

4 tablespoons (½ stick) unsalted butter

2 tablespoons all-purpose flour

¾ cup whole milk

2 tablespoons miso (any kind will do)

1 tablespoon mirin

1 tablespoon soy sauce

12 slices American cheese

Nachos, Assemble!

Pickled ginger

1 fish cake (narutomaki), sliced

Sliced toasted nori

Thinly sliced scallions

belly to a plate or cutting board and pat it dry with paper towels.

Okay, now drain and wipe down that chashu pot, then place it over high heat and add the oil. Once it is shimmering, sear the crap out of that belly on all sides, using tongs to turn it—you want it to be golden brown all over. Don't be lazy about this or you will be making a super-weird choice to start being lazy this far into a pretty complicated recipe. Don't give up. We believe in you. You can take a break while it's braising if you need a break so badly!

Once the pork is seared all over, add ¾ cup water, the sake, soy sauce, sugar, mirin, ginger, scallions, and garlic and bring the liquid to a simmer. Let it simmer, covered, flipping the pork every 30 minutes or so, until it is nice and tender, about 2½ hours. Transfer the pork to a plate or baking sheet and let it cool. Now would be a good time to measure out ½ cup of strained chashu liquid and put it in the fridge to cool down for later.

Step 3: Make the Ramen Chips. Once the ramen dough is frozen, you're going to want to either preheat the oven to 375°F for an easier but less good version OR heat your fry oil (using a deep fryer or a large, heavy-bottomed pot filled with at least 3 inches of oil, making sure that the pot is no more than two-thirds full) to 350°F for a tastier but messier version.

Remove the silicone mat or parchment and set the slab of frozen ramen dough on a cutting board.

Use a knife to square off the edges of your ramen sheet and get straight lines. Cut the sheet, the short way, into 5 even rows. Now you should have 5 ramen rectangles that are all about the same width. The goal is to cut these into triangles (remember,

a square is just two triangles waiting to be cut diagonally). Cut the rectangles into triangles that are about the size of Doritos. Keep them in the freezer until you are ready to fry them.

Either fry the ramen chips in batches until they are mahogany brown (about 3 minutes) or put them back on that lined baking sheet and bake until golden brown and crispy (about 20 minutes). The goal here is to get them super dry and crispy (you know, like tortilla chips). Once encrispened, whether by oven or fryer, set them aside while you . . .

Step 4: Make Ramen Eggs and Miso Nacho Cheese. Bring a medium pot of water (with enough water for 4 eggs) to a boil. While that's going down, fill a large plastic baggie with the ½ cup of chilled chashu liquid. Use a spoon to carefully lower the eggs into the boiling water, then keep the water at a simmer for EGGSACTLY 6 minutes. While the eggs are cooking, set up a bowl of ice water.

When the eggs are ready, carefully lift them out of the pan and immediately plunge them into the ice bath; let them sit for about 5 minutes to chill through. Once they're chilled, peel them and put them in the baggie to marinate until it's time to eat.

Meanwhile, discard that egg water, add the butter to the same pan, and place it over medium heat. Once the butter is melted, add the flour and stir it constantly, until it is toasted and has lost its raw flavor, about 2 minutes. Slowly add the milk, ¼ cup at a time, stirring constantly to make sure no lumps are forming. Add the miso, continuing to mix until everything has joined into a unified miso sauce. Whisk in the mirin and soy sauce, then remove from the heat and dump in the cheese, stirring until it's all melted.

Recipe continues

Step 5: Assemble the Nachos! You did it! Well, not quite. You almost did it! Preheat your broiler to high, then cut your cooled pork into slices of ½ inch or so. Lay them on a baking sheet in a single layer and blast them right under the broiler until they're all nice and sizzly and the fat is bubbling away, about 90 seconds. Okay! Here we go! It's go time! Red alert!

Take your eggs out of the marinade and slice them in half, keeping all the custardy yolk sitting in their little egg cups. Warm up the miso nacho cheese again on the stove until it's . . . warm. Arrange your ramen chips on a platter. Lightly glaze the pork slices in nacho cheese and lay them on top of the chips. Pour that beautiful brown cheese sauce all over the nachos. Top it with ramen eggs, pickled ginger, and fish cakes and sprinkle the whole dang thing with toasted nori and scallions and, holy pig belly, you have ramen nachos! Honestly, even if you didn't make them and just read all the way to the end of the recipe, we are very, very impressed.

Want to Hear Something Shocking?

Shocking your eggs in ice water does two important things: (1) It stops them from cooking, so you can be a lot more precise about your egg cook. See, when an egg is removed from boiling water, the internal temperature is still hot enough to cook the yolk further than desired. Once it hits the icy depths, boom! All cooking ceases. And (2) it makes them WAY easier to peel.

KFC DRUMSTICK BURRITO BOMBS

If you're a fan of the show, you know that we love to do fast-food Menu Mashups. If you're *not* a fan of the show . . . wow. Okay. I guess first of all, thank you for picking up this cookbook and flipping to this page. What are the odds of that happening? That's pretty wild. Also, you should check out our shows, *Good Mythical Morning* and *Mythical Kitchen*. They're super popular and people seem to like them a lot. Oh, wait a second, are you in the future? Did you find this book in a postapocalyptic time capsule? What's the future like? IS THERE STILL YOUTUBE?

Anyway, if you *are* a fan of the show, you know about our mashups, and this is one of our absolute favorites. All you need to do is pick up some KFC drumsticks, some taco-size tortillas from Chipotle, and a rice-free burrito bowl of all your favorite fillings. Then . . . you just deep-fry them all together to make these amazing deep-fried flavor bombs. Also, if you don't feel like going to KFC or Chipotle, feel free to just use the ingenious idea of wrapping a tortilla around a chicken drumstick and deep-frying it because, holy smokes, what an incredible idea.

....

Ready? Here we go. Heat your fry oil (using a deep fryer or a large, heavy-bottomed pot filled with at least 4 inches of oil, making sure that the pot is no more than two-thirds full) to 350°F. Line a plate with paper towels for draining.

Then heat a nonstick skillet over medium-high heat and use it to warm up your first tortilla until it feels warm and pliable, 5 to 8 seconds per side. (Remove the skillet in between tortilla warmings to prevent burning.)

Next up, lay a drumstick on the tortilla, with the bone sticking out of the end like a handle. Top that chicken meat with responsible dollops of Chipotle filling—for example, about 2 tablespoons of meat, a tablespoon of beans, and a teaspoon of each of the other ingredients.

Recipe continues

Makes 4 drumstick bombs

Neutral oil, for frying
Four 6-inch taco-size
tortillas from Chipotle
4 KFC drumsticks
A Chipotle burrito bowl with
all your favorite ingredients
(we really recommend
barbacoa, black beans, queso,
corn salsa, hot salsa, and
guacamole, but no rice)

Now you're going to want to fold it and roll it into a tight little coin purse–looking satchel of goodness. Fold over one side of the tortilla at the meaty end of the drumstick, then roll the rest of it up, holding it into a secure package, with the bone sticking out at the top. Now tie it tightly with kitchen twine (but not so tight that you rip the tortilla!), not worrying too much if you have a little seepage. Use tongs to lift up the burrito bomb by the middle, with

the tongs helping to hold it together, and lower it into the fryer, drumstick handle facing up, fully submerging the tortilla until it is golden brown and crispy, about 2 minutes.

Take it out and let it cool on the paper towel–lined plate and then do it all over again three more times until you have delicious satchels of double-fried chicken burrito mouth-flavor exploders.

A Hot Tip About Tortillas

Honestly, warming up tortillas before you make things with them might be the most important lesson in this entire book. Have you ever noticed that your tortilla rips when you take it right out of the fridge and try to make a burrito with it? That's because it's cold. Warm it up! It will make your life exponentially better.

STEAKHOUSE TAQUITOS

Here's the thing: rolling something up into a tight tortilla coil and then frying it (or crisping it in a pan) is really, really hard. So hard, in fact, that we wanted to make things a little easier on all of us and make *another* form of the taquito—a tortilla folded in half with stuff inside, crisped in the pan. FUN FACT: *taquito* literally just means "little taco," and in many parts of Mexico, the rolled kind found in freezer sections across America are called flautas, which means "flutes." This recipe is SO MUCH easier and 100 percent as delicious (with a 50 percent margin of error, based on personal taste preferences).

Anyway, the version of these we made on "Will It Taquito?" took roughly 450 Josh-hours and involved a crab cake tortilla and homemade creamed spinach. But do you know what we learned? Crab cake tortillas are a ton of work, and frozen creamed spinach is just as good as homemade. So we simplified everything, got rid of the overpriced filet mignon, and are instead searing up some sirloin steak with onions, mushrooms, and a little thing called STEAK BUTTER, which is objectively the best-sounding phrase in the English language. Okay, let's taquito.

....

Step 1: Make the Steak Butter. Ready to find out how easy it is to make Steak Butter? Okay, here we go: put the butter, garlic, parsley, salt, and pepper in a bowl and mix them together. You just made steak butter. Now set it aside until it's time to use it.

Step 2: Make the Kansas City Sirloin. Place a heavy-duty skillet (ideally cast iron) over medium-high heat and let it get nice and hot. Add 1 tablespoon of the oil. Once it is smoking, season the steak aggressively with salt and pepper and lay it right down in the pan. Cook until you get a nice golden brown sear on one side, about 3 minutes, then flip it over and sear the other side, about 90 seconds. To test the steak's doneness, you can poke it with a finger to see if it has a little bit of firmness but still a decent amount of give left—or you can use an instant-read thermometer. For steak taquitos, you're probably looking for closer to a medium-rare to medium cook, which is an internal temperature of anywhere from 125° to 130°F. But this is gonna get cut up and finished in STEAK BUTTER, so don't worry about it too much—

Makes 11 crispy tacos, one for every member of Danny Ocean's crew. Bernie Mac will eat 2. Scott Caan will go hungry.

Steak Butter

4 tablespoons (½ stick) unsalted butter, at room temperature

2 garlic cloves, palm heel struck and damn finely chopped

2 tablespoons damn finely chopped parsley

½ teaspoon salt

¼ teaspoon ground black pepper

Kansas City Sirloin

2 tablespoons neutral oil (don't let your oil take sides!), such as canola or vegetable

One 8-ounce or so sirloin steak that's around 1 inch thick, patted dry with a paper towel

Salt and ground black pepper

6 white button mushrooms, thinly sliced

½ medium yellow or white onion, thinly sliced

To Finish

One 9-ounce package frozen creamed spinach (ideally Stouffer's)

6 tablespoons neutral oil (1 tablespoon for every two taquitos)

Eleven 8-inch corn tortillas

2 cups shredded Monterey Jack (about 8 ounces)

you can always cook it more later. Or you can overcook it and it won't matter too much because it will be tossed in STEAK BUTTER. The most important thing is getting a nice sear on the steak.

Once the steak is done, take it out and set it on a cutting board to rest. Reduce the heat to medium, add the remaining 1 tablespoon oil, and then the mushrooms and onion. Season them with ½ teaspoon salt and ¼ teaspoon ground black pepper. Fry those up, stirring frequently, until the onion is soft and tender, about 5 more minutes, and reduce the heat to low.

Now that your steak has rested, cut it up into cubes of ½ inch or so. Add your steak butter to the pan, and add that steak back in as well. Remove from the heat and toss everything all around until the butter is melted and has glazed the steak and mushrooms. Transfer the mixture to a bowl and set it aside.

Step 3: Make Your Taquitos! Cook the frozen spinach according to the almighty package instructions, then set it aside. Now wipe down the pan you just used for the steak with a paper towel, add 2 tablespoons of the oil, and set it over medium-high heat.

Place your first tortilla in the pan, and lay a sprinkling of Jack cheese on top, covering the whole tortilla. Then, on just half of the tortilla (remember your training—you are going to be folding these over), add a layer of steak mixture, making sure it's got some mushrooms and onion in there, and top it with a dollop of creamed spinach. Fold the tortilla over and cook until the bottom is crispy, about 90 seconds, then flip it over and crisp up the other side.

Repeat this with the remaining taquitos, doubling them up in the pan if you have the room, and adding more oil each time. Now just eat and enjoy. You did a great job (unless you didn't, but that's okay too).

Build Back Butter

Compound butter is a delicious trick to spruce up your everyday cooking. Take any flavors you like and mix them up into some softened butter. After that it can just live in your fridge and you can toss it into anything to make it delicious. Got some chili-lemon-garlic-herb butter? Toss it into a pan and cook some shrimp with it and you've got shrimp scampi. Grilling a steak? Throw some Steak Butter on top after it's cooked and you've got a heck of a steak. The possibilities are endless. Also the pastabilities. It's really good for finishing pasta too.

BACONATOR SOFT PRETZELS

"The Baconator is tough to take, in that texture," said Rhett.
"As a mousse, yeah," Link agreed.
". . . Which I did not like, for the record."

—GMM, *"WILL IT PRETZEL?"*

Due to this sad review of our work—a creamy, soft, aerated meat fluff stuffed inside a pretzel—we found ourselves needing to somehow *improve* this recipe before it made its way into this very book. But that is for the best, because it turns out it is a *terrifying* amount of work to convert a Wendy's Baconator into a mousse, regardless of whether one should stuff it inside a pretzel.

So, not to undercomplicate things, but what if—hear us out—we just made a soft pretzel, covered it in slices of bacon and cheddar, and baked it until it formed a cheddar-bacon pretzel?

The answer to that question is: yeah . . . it's a lot better.

....

Step 1: Cook the Bacon. Slap the bacon into a skillet over medium heat and cook it until most of the fat is rendered but the bacon isn't super-duper crispy (don't worry, it'll get crispy when it's baked on the pretzels), about 6 minutes. Using a slotted spoon, remove the bacon and set it aside, saving that smoky, wonderful bacon grease for later.

Step 2: Make the Baconator Pretzels! Pour the warm water into a big bowl, add the sugar and salt, and mix to dissolve. Pour in the yeast and let it sit for 5 minutes to get all nice and foamy. If it *doesn't* foam up, cancel all your plans and throw a funeral for your yeast, because it is dead. Then wait the customary five days of mourning before buying new yeast and trying all over again. (Or you can just skip the funeral, you monster!)

Add the oil, then the flour, and knead the mixture in the bowl until it comes together. Then slide it onto a clean work surface dusted with

Recipe continues

Makes 6 pretzels

The Bacon
8 slices bacon, diced

Soft Pretzel
1 cup plus 2 tablespoons warm water
¾ teaspoon sugar
¾ teaspoon salt
2¼ teaspoons (¼-ounce packet) active dry yeast
1½ tablespoons neutral oil, plus more to brush the dough
3⅓ cups all-purpose flour, plus more for dusting
½ cup baking soda
2 large eggs
Coarse salt
1 cup shredded medium cheddar (about 4 ounces)

Baconator Sauce
Bacon drippings
½ cup mayo
¼ cup ketchup
¼ cup yellow mustard

flour and knead it until it feels like a cohesive dough—about 5 minutes, depending on how jacked you are.

Form that dough into a ball and put it back in the bowl, drizzle a little more oil over the top—just enough to barely coat it—and brush it over the surface. Cover the bowl with plastic wrap, set it somewhere kind of warm, like on top of your stove, and let those yeast monsters eat the sugar and burp it out into gas bubbles (that's actually pretty much how yeast works; isn't that freaking cool?). Once the dough roughly doubles in size—after about an hour—you are ready to roll.

Preheat the oven to 450°F. Set a big pot of water (6 quarts) on a stove over high heat.

Divide the dough into 6 roughly even pieces. (Cut it in half, then cut each half into thirds—oh no, we're back in school again, but also why didn't they just teach us how to make pretzels in school? It would have been way more informative and delicious.)

Roll those dough pieces into long, thin ropes, then twist them up like a pretzel. No, literally, twist them up like a pretzel. Once the water is boiling, add the baking soda, a little at a time to prevent it from foaming up like a volcano. Boil each pretzel for about 20 seconds, then flip it over and boil the other side for another 20 seconds. Transfer them to a baking sheet (ideally lined with parchment paper), leaving some space between them.

Beat the eggs with a splash of water, then brush the tops of all the pretzels with the egg wash. Sprinkle them with salt, cover them with bacon bits, and blanket them with cheddar.

Bake until the pretzels are golden and the bacon and cheese are crispy, about 15 minutes.

Step 3: Make the Baconator Sauce and Get to Dipping! Whisk together the reserved bacon fat, mayo, ketchup, and mustard and pour it into your most adorable ramekins. Dip those delicious Baconator pretzels and be glad that there isn't beef mousse piped through the center.

What Is Baking Soda For?

Boiling pretzels in a solution of water and baking soda is what gives them their color, crunch, and soft, chewy interior. Not to get too science-y, but baking soda is *alkaline* and alkalinity is the opposite of acidity. You may not realize this, but white flour actually has acidity—something that Big Flour doesn't want you to know. By using the alkaline baking soda solution, you are affecting the pH balance (remember that from school, where you thought you never had to think about it again?) and changing the chemical makeup of the pretzel. Or to put it more simply: baking soda make pretzel tasty.

PULLED PORK TWINKIES

These were inspired by the *GMM* episode about regional fair food across America (Hams Across America?), in which we took oven-roasted BBQ pork and baked it inside a Twinkie-shaped corn muffin. It is an awesome, cakey corn muffin that *looks* like a Twinkie but, instead of never going bad, will 100 percent go bad if you leave it on the counter all week. But it also tastes like corn bread with delicious, tender chopped BBQ pork inside it, all in an ergonomic-mouth-convenience-shaped treat.

....

One Small Note: If for some reason you *don't* want to spend seventeen dollars on a Twinkie pan, well, first of all, you need to reassess your priorities—those student loan payments can wait. But second, you can absolutely just make these in regular muffin tins and they will still be very good.

One Other Note: It's really hard (and kind of pointless) to make a really small amount of BBQ pork. So while you could quadruple the full recipe for Corn Twinkies and make a whole mess of these, you can also just enjoy some bonus pulled pork and throw it onto some buns, or save it in the fridge for future meals. (It also freezes really well.)

Step 1: Make the BBQ Pork. Preheat the oven to 325°F.

Whisk together 1 cup water, the salt, brown sugar, pepper, paprika, granulated onion, and mustard powder in a medium bowl to make your pork rub. Place your pork shoulder in a large Dutch oven or deep roasting pan. Rub the pork all over with the pork rub (oh, *that's* why they call it *pork rub*), patting it in with your hands. Turn the pork fat side up and cover the pot with the lid or the roasting pan tightly with aluminum foil.

Roast the pork for 4 hours. Remove the lid or foil, crank the heat to 400°F, and continue to cook until the pork is super brown, caramelized, and has a nice bark to it, about another hour. Let the pork rest for at least 15 minutes. Transfer it to a cutting board and use the biggest knife you have to chop that thing up. You could also use forks to pull it, but truthfully, you want a smaller chop on this thing because

Recipe continues

BBQ Pork

3 tablespoons salt

3 tablespoons light brown sugar

1 tablespoon coarse-ground black pepper

1 tablespoon smoked paprika

1 tablespoon granulated onion

1 teaspoon mustard powder

One 4-pound boneless pork shoulder

1 bottle your favorite store-bought BBQ sauce (we're big fans of Stubb's and Sweet Baby Ray's)

Corn Twinkies

Cooking spray

1¾ cups all-purpose flour

1 cup fine yellow cornmeal

⅓ cup sugar

¾ teaspoon baking powder

½ teaspoon baking soda

¾ teaspoon salt

3 large eggs

1 cup whole milk

6 tablespoons unsalted butter, melted

3 tablespoons honey

you are *checks notes* putting it inside a corn Twinkie. Transfer it back into the baking vessel from whence it came and toss it all up with that rendered fat and seasoning in there. Place 2¼ cups of pork into a bowl and toss it with some of the BBQ sauce. You'll know when you've added enough BBQ sauce. There you go. One more squirt. Okay, good, looks perfect.

Step 2: Make the Corn Twinkies. Preheat the oven to 375°F. Use your cooking spray to grease up your preferred corn-baking vessel—be it Twinkie or muffin pan.

Whisk up the flour, cornmeal, sugar, baking powder, baking soda, and salt in a large bowl. In a smaller (but no less important) bowl, whisk the eggs, milk, melted butter, and honey. Pour the wet ingredients into the dry ingredients (okay, fine, the big bowl was more important, but you still totally needed both) and mix everything together with a spoon or spatula until fully combined.

Fill up each prepared well about one-third of the way with the batter. Layer in 2 tablespoons of BBQ pork, trying to keep it as centered as possible and away from the sides of the pan. Pour over more of the Twinkie batter, making sure to fill each well only two-thirds of the way up, so you don't have a Twinkie slop monster growing out of your pans, delicious as that might sound.

Bake until a toothpick inserted into the middle of a Twinkie comes out clean (well . . . not clean, but it should only have BBQ sauce on it, not Twinkie dough), about 20 minutes.

Let cool in the pan for 10 minutes, then gently remove the cakes and eat them up, dipping them into more BBQ sauce to let your Fair Food Flag fly.

BEAN PIZZA

(7-LAYER SHEET PAN PIZZA)

We made a bean pizza on a "Will It Pizza?" episode of *GMM* that was topped with everything with the word *bean* in it except for maybe jelly beans. But even though we are a massively fiber-deficient country (seriously, you should be eating way more fiber), we decided that . . . maybe that was too many beans.

But do you know what's *not* too many beans? 7-Layer Dip. And do you know what sucks about 7-Layer Dip? Having to lift up your hands *twice* to eat it. You have to pick up a chip, then move it over to the dip, and then lift it up again?! Heresy. So instead we are making a super-home-cooking-friendly grandma-style pizza, which requires WAY less pizza-shaping skill than a traditional round pie and doesn't need a pizza peel or a pizza stone or any of that junk. And you can eat it while only having to lift your hand *once*. See? Life *can* be better.

....

Note: You CAN mix this dough by hand instead of using a stand mixer, but it will make your life a lot harder. Just assume you will need to double the kneading time if you are doing it without the help of a robot.

Step 1: Make the Pizza Dough. In the bowl of a stand mixer fitted with the dough hook attachment, combine the water, olive oil, and sugar, stir to combine, and pour in the yeast. Give the yeast about 5 minutes to foam up and prove that it is as active as it says it is. If it is not . . . you're gonna have to let that little guy go. Get some new yeast and start over. Then get mad at your store for selling you old yeast. Or get mad at yourself for keeping yeast in your pantry that long.

Add the flour and salt and knead on medium-low speed for about 7 minutes. The dough should start to lose its shagginess and get a little more cohesive. If it feels super dry and like it's not coming together? Add a splash of water and keep going. See how intuitive that is? It should be a little bit tacky and sticky. Transfer it to a CLEAN surface. Lightly oil your hands and give it a few kneads by hand.

Recipe continues

Serves 4 to 6, if you're, like, watching a football game and sharing, or let's be honest, it serves 2 people, unless you're alone, then just eat the pizza and indulge—being alone isn't so bad

Pizza Dough
1¼ cups warm water
2 teaspoons olive oil, plus more for shaping
Heaping ½ teaspoon sugar
2¼ teaspoons (¼-ounce packet) active dry yeast
2¾ cups bread flour
2 teaspoons salt

Guacamole
2 medium avocados
1 serrano, seeded and minced (optional)
¼ cup diced yellow or white onion
Juice of 1 good lime or 3 bad ones (about 2 tablespoons), plus more if needed
½ cup chopped cilantro leaves
1 teaspoon salt
Ground black pepper

Toppings for Baking
Two 16-ounce cans refried beans
2 tablespoons olive oil
2 cups shredded Monterey Jack (about 8 ounces)
1 cup shredded cheddar (about 4 ounces)
½ cup sliced black olives

Toppings to Finish
½ cup sliced scallions
1 medium tomato, diced
½ cup sour cream

APPETIZERS   59

Now you can form it into a ball by picking it up and stretching it inside itself, like you're stuffing a sock. The top of the dough will get smooth as it stretches and forms into what kind of looks like a doughy balloon. Set that dough into a lightly oiled large bowl, cover with plastic wrap, and let it sit on the counter until it has doubled in size, 1 to 3 hours, depending on how warm your kitchen is. Wash your stand mixer bowl and hook before the residual dough gets hard and sets and you're like, "Wow, this is really hard to clean. I really should have cleaned this before it all dried out."

Once your dough is rested and ready, take your olive oil and drizzle some directly into the bottom of an 18 × 13-inch baking sheet and spread it around. Put the dough ball right on the baking sheet. Stretch the dough, using your fingertips to press into that dough and spreading your fingers wide as you move. Continue shaping it and pressing with your fingers, trying to get it all the way to the edges of your baking sheet, keeping it as evenly stretched as possible. As it starts to get bigger, you can even lift up the edges with your fingers and gently pull it, being careful not to make any thin spots or rips. In fact, find any thick spots and push on those (like Whac-A-Mole, except instead of being inside of a pizza parlor, you are inside of a pizza).

If the dough doesn't fill the baking sheet all the way, that's okay. It will relax even further while it rests.

Cover the pan with plastic wrap and let the dough proof for another 20 minutes, allowing that dough to settle into the pan (don't tell it that you are about to cook it alive!). Preheat the oven as high as it will go (ideally about 500°F, but 450°F will work too).

Meanwhile . . .

Step 2: Make the Guacamole. Dump the avocado flesh right into a bowl. Add the serrano (if using), onion, lime juice, cilantro, salt, and pepper to taste and mash it all up with a fork. Taste and adjust the seasoning, adding more lime juice if you want it extra bright. Press some plastic wrap directly on the surface of the guacamole and set it aside.

Step 3: Bake the Pizza. Put the refried beans in a medium saucepan and warm them up over medium heat, covered, until just bubbling. If they are crazy-thick canned beans, add a splash of water to thin them out a little. They should be thin enough to spread on pizza dough with a spoon. Set them aside.

Now that your dough is nice and relaxed, lift up the edges of the dough again and stretch it out toward the corners, like you're putting a bed sheet over a mattress (even if you've never made your bed, just pretend you know what you're doing here), and then press the edges up against the corners of the pan.

Drizzle the olive oil over the top of the pizza, then use your fingers to spread it across the surface. Poke a few holes in the dough with a fork. Parbake it for about 15 minutes, until the pizza is just set and firmed up and has some browning on the bottom. This will make your job *way* easier, since spreading refried beans on raw pizza dough is incredibly hard to do.

Once the pizza is just set, take it out and use a spoon to spread a thin, even layer of beans across the whole pizza.

Next, sprinkle those cheeses on top of the beans, making sure to get cheese up to the edges and into the corners of the pizza (a crispy cheese edge is a VERY good thing). Sprinkle the olives on top of the cheese and put the pizza back in the oven.

Recipe continues

Bake for another 10 to 15 minutes, until the crust has browned. When the top looks all brown and perfect, use a spatula to lift up an edge of the pizza and look at the bottom. If it is not all golden and brown and perfect (a little bit of blackening is A-OK), take that whole pan and drop it down to the literal floor of the oven to get that super-direct heat. Finish baking it there, checking it every minute or so until the bottom looks perfect.

Once it is perfect, or you have realized that perfection is a myth and you are satisfied enough with how it looks, take it out of the oven and use a spatula to transfer it to a cutting board.

Step 4: Top That Pie! While the pizza is still piping hot, sprinkle those scallions over the top. Let the pizza rest for a minute, or until it won't immediately melt sour cream upon contact. Use a pizza cutter (or a knife if you don't have a pizza cutter, even though pizza cutters are amazing) to cut the pizza into 8 slices . . . or do whatever you want. You can cut a weird circle out of the middle if you're dying to. Who are we to tell you how to cut a pizza?

Finally, sprinkle the tomato over the whole thing, then use a spoon to dollop on the guacamole and sour cream, making sure to get some on every single slice.

Eat your 7-layer dip in pizza form, just as nature intended.

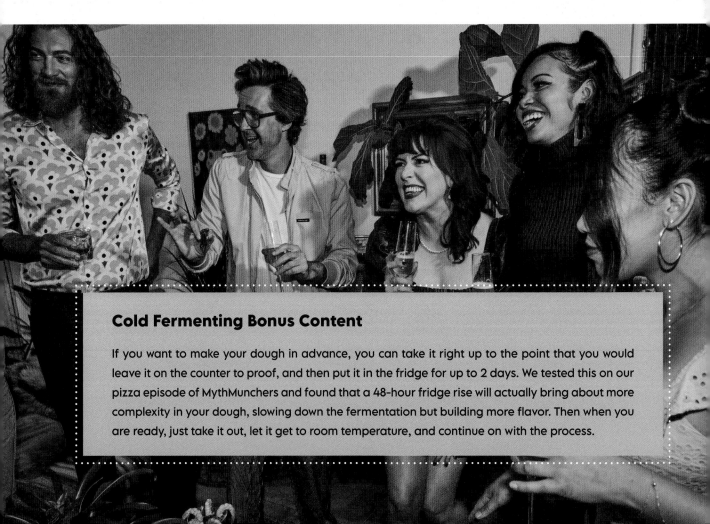

Cold Fermenting Bonus Content

If you want to make your dough in advance, you can take it right up to the point that you would leave it on the counter to proof, and then put it in the fridge for up to 2 days. We tested this on our pizza episode of MythMunchers and found that a 48-hour fridge rise will actually bring about more complexity in your dough, slowing down the fermentation but building more flavor. Then when you are ready, just take it out, let it get to room temperature, and continue on with the process.

CHEESEBURGER NUGGETS

Human beings are born with certain inalienable rights. There's life, there's liberty, there's the pursuit of happiness, and then there's the right to not be forced to choose between chicken nuggets and a cheeseburger when you go to a fast-food restaurant. The tyranny has lasted too long, Burger King! End your monarchical reign of terror, give up the power to the people, and let us have the cheeseburger nuggets! We know they have the technology, though they refuse to deploy it. Until then, we suppose, you'll either have to form a populist shadow government that operates rogue Burger King franchises across the world until it gains enough popular support to overthrow . . . or you can just make them at home. The former is more fun, but the latter is way easier.

....

Combine the beef, cheddar, ¼ cup of the panko, the onion, pickles, ketchup, mustard, Worcestershire, salt, and pepper in a large bowl. Now, you just gonna stare at it, or are you gonna get your hands dirty and mix it all up? (To be clear, you can use a fork to mix it up, but it's so much more fun to squish your hands through raw beef!)

Once the beef mixture is thoroughly hand mashed, form it into about 20 small disks, 2 inches in diameter and ½ inch thick. Do you need to break out a ruler for this? Absolutely not. You can use a laser-guided global positioning gauge to assure your measurements are accurate. (PSYCH, just eyeball it.) You may want to lube up your hands with vegetable oil or a nice spritz of cooking spray. Arrange your raw nuggets on a baking sheet and freeze for 15 minutes while you set up a dredging station.

Preheat the oven to 450°F. Line a baking sheet with a wire rack, or just grease a baking sheet if that's all you have. (If you got suckered by the infomercials and have an air fryer, definitely use that!)

Put the flour in one bowl. Crack the eggs into another bowl and whisk those up. Put the remaining 2 cups panko in another bowl. Ah

Makes 20 nuggies for you and your friends. Or your kids. Or just you. Or your cat (wait, no, don't feed these to a cat).

1 pound 90/10 ground beef
½ cup shredded sharp cheddar (about 2 ounces)
2¼ cups panko bread crumbs
¼ cup minced yellow or white onion
2 tablespoons minced pickles
2 tablespoons ketchup
1 tablespoon mustard
2 teaspoons Worcestershire sauce
½ teaspoon salt
¼ teaspoon ground black pepper
1 cup all-purpose flour
2 large eggs
Any sauce you want to dip them in, which could include but are not limited to: Buffalo, BBQ, ketchup, ranch, sriracha mayo, mustard, hot mustard, honey mustard, soy sauce, fish sauce, cheese sauce, condensed cream of mushroom soup, chocolate sauce, butterscotch, and the little bit of bean liquid that's left at the bottom of a Chipotle burrito bowl

crap, that took less than 15 minutes. To pass the time while the nuggets set up, scroll through your Instagram for 7 minutes and get mad about the people from high school who are more successful than you. We know that's what you were going to do anyway.

Great, now that you're all riled up, bread those nuggies! Dip each nugget in flour, then into the egg, then in the panko, and place them on the prepared baking sheet. When all the nuggets are loaded, bake for 15 minutes, or until golden brown. Let cool for 5 minutes, then serve with one to fifteen of your favorite sauces.

SHRIMP COCKTAIL OF DEATH

Statistically speaking, you're going to die before you cook every recipe in this book. Sure, if you really want to pull a *Julie & Julia*, you COULD easily cook everything, but, based strictly on the numbers, you won't. And not only is that okay, that's beautiful. Life without death is like French fries without ketchup—meaningless, dry, and oh my god, please stop taking my fries; if you wanted fries, you should have ordered fries. We've been cooking peoples' "last meals" on *Mythical Kitchen* for quite some time, and there are some things we've noticed. Despite the fact that people could have any food in the world—A5 Wagyu, foie gras, complex pastries, rare truffles, caviar—they mostly want something simple that reminds them of their childhood. For Josh (hi, it's me speaking in the third person!), the ideal start to his final meal on Earth is a perfect, ice-cold shrimp cocktail. When Josh was growing up, shrimp cocktail was the fanciest food he had ever heard of, and despite the fact that it is served at his favorite $12.99 all-you-can-eat lunch buffet, it is still incredibly fancy. If we're gonna go out, let's go out with a little class, eh?

....

Step 1: Make the Cocktail Sauce. Combine the ketchup, hot sauce, lemon juice, Worcestershire, horseradish, and pepper in a little bowl and use a whisk, or your finger if it's just you eating this and you feel like being gross, to mix it together.

Step 2: Make the Shrimp. Cut the lemon in half, then squeeze the juice into a medium saucepan and chuck the lemon carcass in. Add 1 quart of water, the salt, Old Bay, bay leaves, peppercorns, and mustard seeds to the pot and bring to a boil over high heat.

Prepare an ice bath by filling a medium bowl with AT LEAST 8 ice cubes and 2 cups of cold sink water. Reduce the heat under your pot to medium, drop in your shrimp, and cook until the outside is a bright pink, about 2 minutes. If you're using smaller shrimp, the cook time will be shorter. A good rule to follow is: your shrimp should be in the shape of a J; if they curl into the shape of a C, you've gone too far. Remove

Makes 12 shrimp, so, like, divide that number by however many shrimp you feel like you could eat, and that's how many servings this is. For us, this is half a serving.

For the Cocktail Sauce
⅓ cup ketchup

1 teaspoon hot sauce (Tabasco can't be beat for cocktail sauce)

1 teaspoon lemon juice

1 teaspoon Worcestershire sauce

1 teaspoon prepared horseradish

¼ teaspoon coarse-ground black pepper

For the Shrimp
1 lemon

¼ cup salt

2 tablespoons Old Bay seasoning

2 bay leaves

1 tablespoon black peppercorns

1 tablespoon mustard seeds

12 jumbo shrimp, peeled and deveined (the bigger the better, so 8/12 count is best, but those are expensive, so use whatever shrimp you can get your hands on)

To Serve
Shredded iceberg lettuce (this is EXTREMELY optional!)

the shrimp and send them into the icy bath, colder than death itself.

If you want to be EXTRA proper on the serving, here's what to do. Take either a martini glass or a coupe glass, fill the bottom with shredded iceberg lettuce, then top that with cocktail sauce. Dry your shrimp on paper towels, and hang them off the rim of the glass. Enjoy, and also consider writing a last will and testament. It's never too early to be prepared!

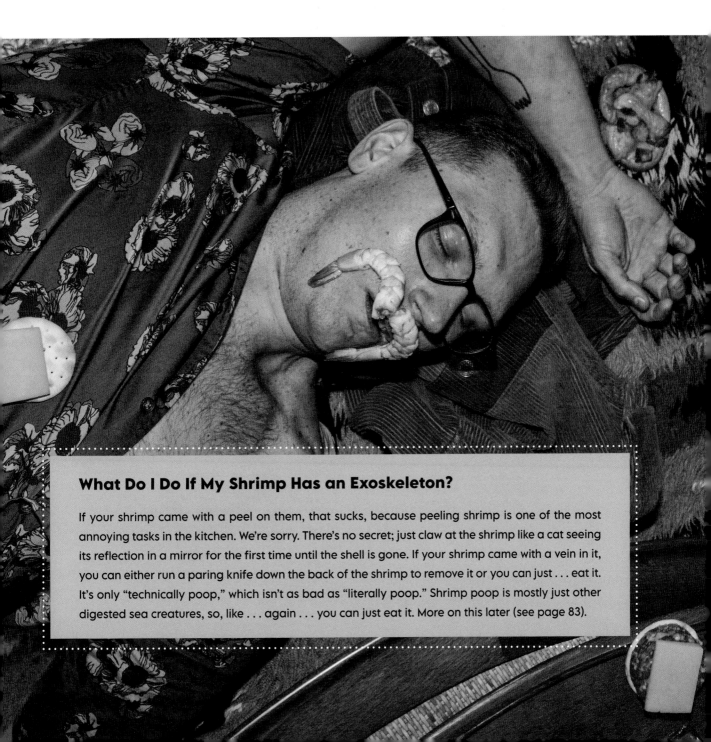

What Do I Do If My Shrimp Has an Exoskeleton?

If your shrimp came with a peel on them, that sucks, because peeling shrimp is one of the most annoying tasks in the kitchen. We're sorry. There's no secret; just claw at the shrimp like a cat seeing its reflection in a mirror for the first time until the shell is gone. If your shrimp came with a vein in it, you can either run a paring knife down the back of the shrimp to remove it or you can just . . . eat it. It's only "technically poop," which isn't as bad as "literally poop." Shrimp poop is mostly just other digested sea creatures, so, like . . . again . . . you can just eat it. More on this later (see page 83).

IF A HOT DOG IS A SANDWICH, YOU CAN BE A CHEF

(SANDWICHES)

The word *chef* gets thrown around a lot. People put it on backyard-grill dad aprons. They say, "What's cooking, Chef?" when they walk into the kitchen and someone is making literally anything. They throw it onto Instagram bios as a personality trait. Heck, a ragtag group of YouTube cooks who all have wildly different professional backgrounds might even call themselves "Mythical Chefs," despite none of them currently working in a restaurant.

But the word *chef* also gets used as a tool for elitist gatekeeping, to make "civilians" feel like this hallowed word is meant to be used only for the *precious few* artistic geniuses who are qualified to grill four hundred steaks in a night, or tweeze micro cilantro onto a GIANT plate with a *tiny* amount of food in the middle. Or hey, maybe they even get their own episode of *Chef's Table* in which they say that they're so talented that they should be allowed to cheat on their wife (this is a real thing that happened!).

Here's the dirty truth about being a chef: it kind of just means "manager." Technically, it came from the word *chief*, from the old French for "head." So, for every tortured genius trying to earn three Michelin stars for their nine-seat restaurant in Napa

Valley (don't get us started on Michelin stars . . .), there's an executive chef of a Hard Rock Cafe in a casino in Florida who's just trying to make sure that the staff schedule is up to date and the order guide is being adequately managed so that they can hit their numbers, get their annual bonus, and feed people one of the TEN burgers on their menu in a timely and consistent manner. *Chef* can mean a lot of things, even in the most literal definition.

Here's something else that the rock star chef industrial complex doesn't want you to know: a lot of chefs don't actually cook at home. Quite frequently, they came up cooking in restaurants and never ever had to learn how to make dinner for fewer than 120 people at a time. When they're off work, the *last* thing they want to do is go to a grocery store, buy raw ingredients, take them home, and then turn them into a meal. It is very likely you would rather eat a homemade meal made by a passionate stay-at-home-mom than a meal made by a professional chef who's been jaded by a decade of slinging eggs Benedict every Sunday morning when all they wanted to do was sit on the couch, eat a bowl of Frosted Flakes, and watch the game.

This is all to say that if you want to call yourself a chef, you absolutely can, and any chefs who get

mad about it because "you aren't a real chef" are probably overcompensating for some much larger issues that you don't have to bother yourself with. If you're the Taco Tuesday chef for your family or friends, more power to you. Claim the word and let it be anything that makes you feel positive, happy, and empowered to cook food.

But more important, there is absolutely NOTHING wrong with being a home cook. Sure, chefs have a demanding and important job, and we all love eating at restaurants, but home cooks are the real heroes, feeding themselves and the people around them, every single day. Many of our moms and dads were home cooks and shaped our opinions of what "comfort food" means to us. But there are also SO MANY people among us who did not have that luxury, who did not grow up with home-cooked meals, but now, all of a sudden, have the opportunity to provide it for themselves, or their families, or their adopted families. This book is just one of many tools at your disposal, to encourage you to be the home cook we all deserve to be or to have in our lives.

Remember: home cooks have existed since long before there were chefs, and they are the fabric of our society. You can be one too—and that is a truly great, special, and downright Mythical thing to be.

BEEF AND BROCCOLI BURGER

When a cow and a head of broccoli love each other very much, they turn off the lights, cover themselves in cornstarch and oyster sauce, and become one of the best-tasting things on the planet. But for some reason, their love only ever gets celebrated at places like Panda Express. For all the beef that we eat in this country, the humble cow's deep and undying love of broccoli has been forbidden in so many of the hallowed roadside diners, fast-food eateries, and carhop-laden drive-ins of these United American States. Well, it is time that we stand up and say, "NO MORE, GOOD MEATS AND VEGGIES." We at Mythical Kitchen open our doors to you, we embrace your love in all its forms, and we will in fact put our iceberg lettuces back on Italian subs where they belong, and lay that sweet, glossy, tender broccoli atop your ground beef patties, slid betwixt our processed American wheats and cheeses, and allow you to have your last dance together on our tongue, tumbled across our teeth, and put to bed inside our throats. We present: the Beef and Broccoli Burger, in all its underappreciated glory.

....

Step 1: Make the Sambal Secret Sauce. (Shhh. It's a secret. But . . . you just put all the sauce ingredients in a bowl and mix them together, then set it aside until it's time to dress your burger.)

Step 2: Make That Beef and Broccoli. Season the tops of those patties up with some salt. Place a large skillet over high heat and add 1 tablespoon of the vegetable oil. Once the oil is smoking, tilt the pan to make sure the whole pan is coated (and add more oil if it looks dry). Lay those patties, salt side down, in the pan to get a nice crispy sear, and salt the other side. Once they have a good crust, after about 2 minutes, use a spatula to lift them up and flip them and sear the other side. Don't worry about getting them super-duper cooked here; it's all about that sear. (They're going to cook more in the next step.)

Once the burgers are nice and seared on both sides, set them aside on a plate. Reduce the heat to medium and add the remaining

Makes 2 burgers

Sambal Secret Sauce
¼ cup mayo
1 tablespoon ketchup
1 tablespoon sambal oelek
1 scallion, dark green parts only, chopped
¼ teaspoon grated fresh ginger
Ground black pepper

Beef and Broccoli
8 ounces 80/20 ground beef, shaped into 2 patties
Salt
3 tablespoons vegetable oil, plus more if needed
2 garlic cloves, palm heel struck and minced
1 tablespoon grated fresh ginger
1 tablespoon Shaoxing wine
1 tablespoon sugar
1 tablespoon oyster sauce
1 tablespoon soy sauce
½ teaspoon sesame oil
¼ teaspoon white pepper
1 teaspoon cornstarch
1 cup roughly chopped broccoli florets

To Finish
2 hamburger buns
2 slices American cheese

2 tablespoons oil. Now quick! Toss in that garlic and ginger and let them sizzle for about 10 seconds—just to open up that flavor without letting them burn—then add the Shaoxing wine and use a wooden spoon to scrape up and deglaze all that beautiful beefy fond. Once the wine has evaporated, add ¾ cup water, the sugar, oyster sauce, soy sauce, sesame oil, and white pepper and give everything a stir.

Let that thing simmer for about 1 minute to reduce and get all nice and intermingled. Meanwhile, in a little bowl, mix the cornstarch with another tablespoon of water and whisk or stir it around to make a slurry. Put it right into the pan and stir it until you've got a classic THICK BROWN SAUCE, about 2 minutes. Place the burger patties back in there, flipping them to coat, and simmer until they're cooked to your liking (if you like a rare buddy boy, just glaze it and lift it out . . . but if you want it more well done, it's about 15 seconds for medium-rare or 2 minutes for well) and transfer them to a plate and set it aside again.

Add the broccoli and simmer it, stirring frequently, until your broccoli is tenderoni, about 4 minutes.

Step 3: Assemble the Burgs! Depending on the quality of your buns, you can either leave them as is, or, for best results, wrap them in a damp paper towel and microwave them for 15 seconds to steam them. Slather up your buns with that (shhh, it's a secret) sambal sauce. Lay them patties on the bottoms, top with slices of American cheese, then scoop that hot broccoli and its sauce right on top. Finish with the top buns and enjoy the heck out of your beef and broccoli burger love child.

FROZEN PIZZA MUFFULETTA

Oh man, we feel like this title needs some clarification. To be clear, this is not a pizza muffuletta that has been frozen. It is also not a bunch of meat, in the New Orleans Italian sandwich style, placed between two frozen pizzas. This is NOT a frozen final product. I guess technically we should have called this a Muffuletta in Which the Bread Is Made from Two Previously Frozen Pizzas, but Don't Worry Because the Pizzas Are Fully Cooked Before Being Used to Make a Muffuletta, Which by the Way Is a Delicious New Orleans and Italian–Style Deli Sandwich That Is Dressed with a Tangy Olive Salad That Is Not Really a Tapenade but Kind of a Chunky Spread with Lots of Flavor That Soaks into the Bread, but Again, Just to Be Clear, in This Instance, the Bread Is Being Replaced with Two Previously Frozen Pizzas That Have Since Been Cooked. Whew. Glad we cleared that up.

Anyway, this recipe is absurdly easy, and incredibly delicious. Sure, you could make your own olive salad, but why mess with a classic (well, except for the frozen pizzas, which, to be clear, were *previously* frozen and then cooked to be used as a bread replacement)?

Makes 1 muffie, serving upward of 6 people

- 2 DiGiorno Rising Crust frozen cheese pizzas (or whatever you want)
- 1½ cups store-bought olive salad (an old-school Louisiana brand, like Boscoli or Central Grocery)
- 4 ounces thinly sliced salami
- 4 slices Swiss cheese
- 4 ounces thinly sliced ham
- 4 slices provolone
- 4 ounces thinly sliced mortadella

First? Cook those pizzas according to, and ONLY according to, those package instructions. Then . . . we wait. You want that cheese to get nice and congealed and solidified again and the pizzas to be not hot anymore, aka *completely* room temperature, unless your room is unreasonably hot, in which case, go onto Craigslist and try to find a new place to live.

Once you've moved to a cooler climate (you can also purchase an air conditioner or put the pizzas in the fridge to cool), it's time to start filling your muffuletta. Start by spreading half of the olive salad on one of the pizzas. Then go about wheeling and dealing that salami like you're working the casino floor, shingle stacking the meat over the cheese but not over the crust. Then, repeat that process right over again with the Swiss, then the ham, then the provolone, and finally the mortadella.

Next up, add a nice even coating of the remaining olive salad.

Then, flip the other pizza over and put it on top of the sandwich, like it's bread. Finally, wrap the whole thing in plastic wrap, put it on a plate, put ANOTHER plate on top of it, and then put something real heavy, like a gallon of water, or a bunch of cans, on top of that and let those juices flow and marry for like 45 minutes.

Then and ONLY THEN can you remove the plastic wrap, cut it into 6 wedgy slices, and get to eating. Did we mention that the pizza isn't still frozen when you make the muffuletta?

PEANUT BJ FRIED CHICKEN SANDWICH

Here's the thing about acronyms: sometimes they save you a lot of time, but sometimes they are more confusing. Like, the CIA is the Central Intelligence Agency but *also* the Culinary Institute of America?* And it turns out some of those people who were raiding our offices last week were not, in fact, Female Body Inspectors. To clarify our acronyms, sometimes it helps to take one of the letters and input the real word to make it less confusing. So we present to you: the Peanut BJ Fried Chicken Sandwich. There's no way anyone could be confused about what we're referring to now.

Anyway, this is a great sandwich, playing off the flavors of Thai peanut sauce, creating a sweet and salty fried chicken sandwich that is one of our favorite things we've ever made on the show.

....

Step 1: Make the Peanut Sauce. Put all the sauce ingredients in a bowl and whisk it up! Then just set her aside and let her hydrate and marry while you make everything else.

Step 2: Make the Jelly Sauce. Put the jelly, ¼ cup water, and the vinegar right in a medium pot over medium heat. Then quickly: PALM HEEL STRIKE that Thai chile, remove the stem, and drop the chile in the pot. After that, definitely wash your hands before touching your private *or* public parts. Bring that pot to a simmer and let it simmer for about 5 minutes, then remove it from the heat and set it aside while you . . .

Step 3: Fry That Chicken. Heat some fry oil (using a deep fryer or a large, heavy-bottomed pot filled with at least 3 inches of oil, making sure that the pot is no more than two-thirds full) to 350°F. Or for best

---

* Okay, it turns out that technically *CIA* is not an acronym but an initialism. The initials of an acronym spell a word, like NATO, NASA, UNICEF, and ASAP (which is both acronym and initialism because you can either pronounce it or say the letters). But we thought it would be confusing to most people to call it an initialism, so we're adding this footnote to teach you all the truth about this thing that we just learned about from our copyeditor.

Recipe continues

Makes 4 'wiches of sand

Peanut Sauce
¾ cup peanut butter
6 tablespoons warm water
2 tablespoons soy sauce
2 tablespoons light
  brown sugar
2 tablespoons chili garlic sauce
2 garlic cloves, palm heel
  struck and finely minced
1 tablespoon rice wine vinegar

Jelly Sauce
1 cup grape jelly
2 tablespoons rice wine vinegar
1 Thai chile (if you can't find
  it, a serrano will work too)

Chicken
Neutral oil, for frying
4 boneless, skinless
  chicken thighs
4 teaspoons salt
Ground black pepper
1 cup rice flour
1 cup all-purpose flour
4 large eggs

To Finish
4 burger buns
Butter, for toasting
¼ medium head green
  cabbage, thinly shredded
½ jalapeño, seeded and
  finely chopped
Salt
16 slices bread-and-
  butter pickles

results (thanks, MythMunchers!), set a cast-iron skillet over medium-high heat and fill it with 2 inches of oil. Heat the oil to 350°F, and then adjust the heat to maintain the temperature. Set up a post-chicken-frying station by lining a baking sheet with a wire rack or paper towels.

Next, season up that chicken real nice with the salt and pepper. Mix together your rice flour and all-purpose flour in a large bowl.

Crack the eggs into a medium bowl and give them a proper beating. Then you double dredge! Dredge the chicken first in the flour mixture, shaking off the excess flour (that's what that song "Shake It Off" is actually about), then coat it in the egg, letting the excess egg drip off (Taylor, RELEASE "DRIP IT OFF"!), then dip it again in the flour mixture, shaking it off again before gently laying AGAIN into the egg, and then one more time in the flour. (To recap: flour, egg, flour, egg, flour.) Finally, lay the chicken pieces in the fryer, pot, or skillet and cook until golden brown and crispy, about 5 minutes in a deep fryer or pot, or 3 minutes per side in a cast-iron skillet. Transfer them to that post-chicken-frying station.

Step 4: Make Those Sandwiches! Toast up those buns with a little bit of butter on the cut sides, and spread a little peanut sauce on each bottom bun.

Next, take all that shredded cabbage and chopped jalapeño and chuck it right into a bowl with ¼ cup of the PB sauce and a pinch of salt, and toss it all up. Meanwhile, bring the jelly sauce back up to a simmer on the stove over medium heat. One at a time, lay each fried chicken thigh into the sauce, and let it glaze up and get coated in the sauce, flipping it once, about 5 seconds per side. Set each one on each bottom bun.

Top each jellied chicken piece with 4 pickle slices and then the peanut slaw, slap on that top bun, and slurp up that Peanut BJ F Chicken S!

FRITO CHILI CHEESE DOG

Frito pies are great and all, but did you know that it is really hard to dip a hot dog into a Frito pie? Plus, if you just dip a hot dog into a bag of Frito-laden chili, we are fairly confident in saying that it is very much NOT a sandwich. A hot dog is a sandwich only if it has a bun. So instead, we're going to show you how to make a killer hot dog chili (with a secret sneak job of Mexican chorizo for extra flavor), pour it over a hot dog, and top the whole thing with Fritos and shredded cheddar and chopped-up onions because, gosh-dang it, doesn't that sound like something you want to put in your mouth? In fact, we're so excited that WE even want to put it in your mouth. Go on, open your mouth. Wider. Okay, here we come.

....

Step 1: Make the Hot Dog Chili. Pour the oil into a large heavy-bottomed pot set over medium-high heat and tilt the pot so the oil slides around and coats the bottom. Once the oil is nice and shimmery, add the beef, chorizo, chili powder, salt, cocoa powder, cumin, and pepper. Mix it up real good, breaking up the beef and chorizo with a wooden spoon, and cook until all the raw color is cooked out of the beef, about 5 minutes. Stir in the onion, poblano, and garlic and keep everything simmering away until the onion has softened up, another 5-ish minutes.

Now it's time to take a journey to Liquid Town. Dump in the chicken stock, crushed tomatoes, vinegar, fish sauce, tomato paste, and ALSO THE BAY LEAF, WHICH YOU WILL ABSOLUTELY BE ABLE TO TASTE IN THE FINAL PRODUCT. Mix it all up and let simmer for another 15 minutes.

Once that is all simmered and combined nicely, mix the cornstarch and 1 tablespoon water in a small bowl to make a slurry. Pour that slurry right into your hot dog chili. Let it simmer for 3 more minutes, then remove it from the heat, fish out the bay leaf, taste for seasoning, and add more salt if needed.

Makes enough chili for, like, 16 hot dogs, but you can also freeze it for future dogging, or frankly, put in on a chili burger too

Hot Dog Chili
2 tablespoons vegetable oil
1 pound ground beef
8 ounces Mexican pork chorizo, casing removed
1½ tablespoons chili powder
1½ teaspoons salt, plus more to taste
½ teaspoon cocoa powder
½ teaspoon ground cumin
¼ teaspoon ground black pepper
½ yellow or white onion, diced
1 poblano, seeded and diced
1 tablespoon minced garlic
1½ cups chicken stock (or Hot Dog Water; see below)
½ cup crushed tomatoes
2 tablespoons white vinegar
1½ teaspoons fish sauce (secret umami sneak job!)
1 tablespoon tomato paste
1 bay leaf
2 teaspoons cornstarch

To Finish
As many hot dogs as you want to eat
The exact same number of hot dog buns as hot dogs
One 9-ounce bag Fritos (this will be more than enough)
Large toddler's handful of finely shredded cheddar per hot dog
About 1 tablespoon finely chopped white onion per dog

Now you can . . .

Step 2: Make the Frito Chili Cheese Dogs.
First, think about how many hot dogs you are
going to cook. Visualize them. Then imagine the
appropriately sized pot for said quantity of hot dogs,
then add the right amount of water to cover them
by about an inch. Bring the water to a boil over high
heat, then put the hot dogs—*the amount you already
visualized, stop changing your mind!*—into the water
and immediately reduce the heat down to a bare,
bare simmer—a poach, if you will. Cover the pot
and let the hot dogs gently warm up until heated
through, 4 to 6 minutes. Remove from the heat and
ignore the liquid that may or may not be calling you
Jeff.

For best results, wrap your buns in a damp paper
towel and steam them in the microwave for
15 seconds.

Lay a hot dog inside a bun, and top it with Fritos,
followed by the cheese. Spoon about ½ cup of chili
right over the top, melting that cheese and sogging
up those Fritos. Next, because decorations, sprankle
on some onion and eat your sandwich, Jeff.

Who Is Jeff? (Or: Do We Eat the Forbidden Soup?)

We here at Mythical Kitchen believe that Hot Dog Water is a secret flavorful ingredient that nobody—
and we mean nobody—properly appreciates. So if you ever boil some hot dogs in water, you don't
have to throw that water out; you can freeze that puppy juice up and let it sit in your freezer, waiting,
patiently, for its moment to strike. Yes, that's right, we're telling you to freeze your hot dog water
and break it back out when you make hot dog chili again. Every time you open the freezer, it will be
quietly whispering: *"Jeff . . . (Sorry, Hot Dog Water thinks everyone's name is Jeff.) Jeff . . . you should
make hot dog chili . . . and you should use me instead of chicken stock . . . Jeff, it is time . . ."*

TONY'S ULTIMATE CREOLE SHRIMP BURGER

Makes 4 Tony burgers

We all know there is only ONE seasoning that really matters, and it's Tony Chachere's Creole Seasoning. So we're here to answer the burning question that is lingering on everyone's spiced, tingling lips: Do you really need anything else? What would happen if you got rid of every spice in your pantry, extraditing the salt, banishing the black pepper, ostracizing the oregano, dismissing the dill, relegating the . . . whatever, you get the picture. We are here to let this ONE SPICE BLEND rule them all. So we are seasoning our pork patties with Tony C's, seasoning our shrimp with it, and even making a rémoulade for our trinity slaw featuring our once and future king, the great Anthony of Chachere.

Step 1: Make Tony's Rémoulade. Whisk together the mayo, mustard, Tony C's, lemon juice, and hot sauce in a medium bowl. Well, you could just dump it all on the counter and spread it around with your fingers. But frankly, that sounds a little unhinged and we might need to sit you down and ask how you're doing. Are you okay? Are you sure you don't just want to use a bowl, pal? Anyway, once it's done, just slowly step away until you need it later.

Step 2: Toast Them Buns. Place a cast-iron or stainless steel skillet over medium heat and add the butter. Once it's melted, lay those buns, cut side down, in the skillet and toast until golden brown, about 30 seconds. Set them aside on a plate and slather a little bit of that rémoulade onto each bottom bun.

Step 3: Make Tony's Cajun Shrimp. Chuck that butter and garlic in the same skillet and increase the heat to medium-high. Once the garlic is starting to brown on the edges, toss in the shrimp and Tony C's and cook, stirring constantly, until the shrimp are curled up into a J shape, opaque, and cooked through, 3 to 4 minutes. Transfer them to a bowl, toss in the parsley, squeeze in the lemon, and give it a toss to combine. Set aside while you move on to . . .

Tony's Rémoulade
¾ cup mayo
¼ cup Dijon mustard
½ teaspoon Tony Chachere's Creole Seasoning
1½ teaspoons lemon juice
3 dashes hot sauce

Bun Toasting
1 tablespoon unsalted butter
4 burger buns

Tony's Cajun Shrimp
½ cup (1 stick) unsalted butter
2 garlic cloves, palm heel struck and minced
1 pound medium shrimp, peeled and tails removed
1 teaspoon Tony C's
1 tablespoon chopped parsley
Juice of ½ good lemon or 1 whole bad one

Tony's Pork Smash Burgers
1 pound lean ground pork
1 teaspoon Tony C's
2 tablespoons neutral oil, such as vegetable or canola
4 slices white American cheese

Trinity Slaw
½ yellow or white onion, thinly sliced
1 green bell pepper, thinly sliced
4 stalks celery, thinly sliced
Tony C's, if needed

Step 4: Make Tony's Pork Smash Burgers. Scoop out any remaining hunks of garlic from your skillet to keep them from burning in there and return the pan to medium-high heat. Meanwhile, put the pork into a bowl and add the Tony C's. Mix it up until it's been fully Creoled, then divide the pork into 4 equal parts (we did some rough math and it sounds like each one should be about 4 ounces). Form each one into a ball and get ready to SMASH.

Add the oil to the skillet and swirl it around. It should be SMOKING.

Working in batches based on the size of your skillet, add each pork ball, and with a weighted grill press or a heavy-duty spatula, SMASH that patty down. After about 90 seconds, it should be nice and crispy and golden. But if it's not for some reason, let it go a little longer. Use that metal spatula to scrape it up

and flip it, repeating it on the other side for another 60 seconds or so. Add a slice of cheese, and once the patty is crispy and cooked through, lift it up and lay it on a rémoulated bun. Make sure the skillet is nice and hot before you continue with each batch. When you are done, remove from the heat.

Step 5: Finish Them! Lay the shrimp right on top of each burger. Place the onion, bell pepper, and celery for your slaw into a bowl with 3 tablespoons of the rémoulade and give it all a good toss. Taste it for seasoning and add more Tony C's if needed. Top the shrimp with the slaw, then close Tony's Masterpiece with the top bun and enjoy life in the knowledge that you can now clear every seasoning out of your pantry and replace it with whatever you want, like used batteries, or candles, or frankly just a disturbing quantity of Tony Chachere's.

Guess Who Else Poops?

Listen, we don't mean to harp on the ol' shrimp poop thing, but almost no chefs in real life, when they are cooking at home, devein their shrimp. That's because, even though regular folk are grossed out by the idea of ***A POOP LINE*** (yes, that's what the "vein" is—gasp, cry, whimper), it's basically a little intestinal tract and, the truth is, nobody gets sick from that. If you get sick from shrimp, it's because you ate weird old shrimp. People cook whole shrimp, in the shell, all the time and it's 100 percent fine. So yeah, if you want to spend the time slicing open the back of every single shrimp and removing that vein, be our guest (see page 67). But you're just doing it for looks and that, we dare say, is *vanity*. But people are weird about it, so everyone says to devein shrimp. Also, you can buy shrimp that are already deveined.

PIZZA CRUNCHWRAP SUPREME

For all Taco Bell's innovations, they have not come anywhere close to finding out if enough things will crunchwrap. But it's a good thing the internet came along, and eventually also us, if only so that we could get into the Mythical food laboratory and figure out which things should and should not be crunchy and wrapped and supreme. The greatest of all of these creations is the Pizza Crunchwrap Supreme, which we've stuffed full of pepperoni, Italian sausage, mozzarella, mushrooms, onions, and bell peppers, all while asking the question that NO ONE is asking: Is a tortilla an envelope?

Heat 1 tablespoon of the olive oil in a large skillet over medium-high heat. Add the sausage and pepperoni and fry it up, stirring occasionally, until the sausage is browned and cooked through and the pepperoni is sweaty and getting all crispy on the edges and that orange-tinged fat sweat is dancing it up with the sausage fat, about 5 minutes. Whew. Okay, take a deep breath, that got a little hot and heavy. Add the pizza sauce, scraping up any browned bits from the bottom of the pan. Let simmer for, like, 2 minutes, allowing the sauce to reduce, then remove it from the heat, pour it all into a bowl, and set it aside.

Now wipe down the pan (or use a whole other one if you don't care about how many dishes you're leaving in the sink for someone else to do). Place it over medium-high heat and add the remaining 1 tablespoon olive oil. Toss in the mushrooms, onion, and bell pepper, season them with the oregano, salt, and black pepper, and cook them up until the onion has browned at the edges and the mushrooms are quite soft, about 3 minutes. Remove from the heat and let the veggies hang out in the pan.

NOW IT IS TIME TO ASSEMBLE.

Take a nonstick pan, griddle, crepe maker, or something else that you can toast a tortilla on without it sticking like crazy, and heat it up over medium-high heat. Warm the tortilla until it's nice and pliable, about 30 seconds per side, then transfer it to a work surface. Lay the mozzarella in a tostada-size circle right in the middle, then top it with the sausage-pepperoni mixture. Put the tostada shell on top, topped with the vegetable mixture (leaving any moisture behind in the pan).

Then crunchwrap that sucker, folding the edges up over the filling like the Taco Bell Crunchwrap Artist that you are (the dream is to achieve 6 folds!). In the same pan in which you warmed your tortilla, griddle the top (the folded side) first, until golden brown. Griddle the bottom. Eat your crunchwrap as soon as you can do so without burning yourself in the mouth and face and body.

Makes 1 wrap of crunch

2 tablespoons olive oil

1 sweet Italian sausage, squeezed out of its casing

3 big pepperoni or 6 medium or, like, 8 small ones

¼ cup jarred pizza sauce, plus more for dipping

2 white button or cremini mushrooms, thinly sliced

1½ tablespoons diced yellow or white onion

1½ tablespoons diced green bell pepper

Pinch of dried oregano

¼ teaspoon salt

Pinch of ground black pepper

Burrito-size flour tortilla

½ cup shredded low-moisture mozzarella (about 2 ounces)

1 corn tostada shell

HOT DOG SANDWICH

Yes, a hot dog is a sandwich. Unless you don't think it is, then it's not. Well, it still is, but, are you familiar with Schrödinger's cat? So this cat, right, this cat is sitting in a box, and we don't know whether the cat is alive or dead; therefore it doesn't matter if a hot dog is technically on one continuous slice of bread because—wait, did anyone hear that? Are your ears ringing? We set out to officially answer the question on our podcast, *A Hot Dog Is a Sandwich*, over the course of five hours and with the expert opinions of a historian, a philosopher, a lawyer, and a hot dog business owner, and truth be told, the question is too politically loaded to come to an adequate answer that would please everyone. All we can hope to do is offer up this hot dog sandwich recipe—inspired by the delicious bacon-wrapped hot dogs sold on street corners in Los Angeles—while shrugging our shoulders and going, "AHSD-JSKDHSKS," before disappearing in a cloud of smoke.

Cut each slice of bacon into exactly 12 pieces and add it to a large sauté pan set over medium heat. A nice thing about cooking with bacon is that you don't need to use extra oil—it's the ultimate self-lubricating meat! (Get your head out of the gutter, folks.) While the bacon fat is rendering, core and seed your bell pepper, and slice it into long strips, then cut the onion up into long strips too. Once the bacon has crisped up, about 5 minutes, increase the heat to medium-high and add the bell pepper, onion, and salt. Sauté until the vegetables are soft and could reasonably be folded in half without breaking, an additional 5 minutes. Transfer the veggies to a bowl and set them aside, wiping down the pan so you can use it again later.

If you need to pee, now would be a good time to do it. I mean, you don't have to wait for our permission. When's the last time you drank water?

Okay, this step is key, and this is what REALLY makes this a hot dog sandwich, and not just a hot dog—you gotta butterfly some wieners. Slice your wieners in half lengthwise, keeping a hinge at the back attached. This way, you can unfurl them and griddle to a nice flat crispiness. Once all your hot dogs are butterflied (you will be using three butterflied wieners per sandwich), heat 2 tablespoons of the oil in the wiped large sauté pan over high heat, and cook the hot dogs until crispy and browned, about 3 minutes per side. Transfer the hot dogs to a plate, reduce the heat to medium, and add the last teaspoon of oil to the same pan with the residual fat from the hot dogs. Grill your bread in the pan until golden brown on each side.

Now, we need to talk about condiments here. The official stance of Mythical Entertainment Incorporated United Company is that mayo is an acceptable hot dog condiment, as is ketchup, and, of course, mustard. We recommend that you use all three. Live a little, dang it! Rage, rage against the dying of the light! Spread and/or squirt a hefty amount of mayo, ketchup, and mustard on all four pieces of bread, then add your bacony veggie mixture, shingle on three griddled hot dogs per sandwich, and close up your sandwiches.

Optional toppings include avocado (which is fun!) and pickled jalapeño rings (which are even MORE fun!). Optional beverage pairing includes an ice-cold light beer ($4 supplement fee).

Makes 2 hot dog sandwiches. Not 2 hot dogs. Not 2 sandwiches. But 2 hot dog sandwiches.

4 slices bacon
1 green bell pepper
½ yellow or white onion
¼ teaspoon salt
6 wieners (Hebrew National are tough to beat!)
2 tablespoons plus 1 teaspoon vegetable oil
4 slices sourdough bread
Mayo
Ketchup
Yellow mustard
Avocado (optional)
Pickled jalapeños (optional)

THE RENO RANSACKER

If you ask people what the greatest food city in the world is, many minds may wander to Bangkok, Paris, Rome, or New York. Few, however, think of Reno, Nevada. But "The Biggest Little City in the World," as Renonians call it, does boast one of the most spectacular regional delicacies in the world, the Ransacker. A luxurious mix of silken red pepper coulis, gooey broiled Swiss cheese, succulent buttery shrimp, and tender asparagus all served open-faced atop crispy, crunchy rye bread, "The Sack" (Reno slang for the sandwich) should be just as popular as the Philly cheesesteak, if not more so. You see, Basque sheepherders moved to the Reno area in the early nineteenth century during the gold rush, and they brought their favorite foods from home: crusty rye bread with that signature punch of sourness, sheep's milk cheese (most recipes these days use Swiss for simplicity's sake), and, of course, bell peppers marinating in luscious olive oil. Combine those homeland favorites with local produce (Reno was once the asparagus capital of southwestern Nevada) and you get the Reno Ransacker. Alas, history has not treated The Sack kindly. The sandwich fell out of style once national chains took over the casino strip, but let's show Reno some love and bring it back! If you make this recipe, post it on Instagram with #ILoveTheSack to show Reno some love. Also: please don't fact-check this story.

··

First off, you need to roast your red peppers. In Reno, they would typically use a Basque-style dome pan set upon a roaring fire, but if you don't have that, a gas stove will do just fine. If you don't have a gas stove—"Holy smoke-e-oli!" they'd say in Reno—you need to get yourself one! But a broiler does the trick too. Light your burner on high and set a pepper on top. Turn the pepper 90 degrees about every minute until the skin is blackened all over. Do this with the other pepper and throw them in a plastic bag, and then put them into the fridge to cool for 10 minutes. Peel the burned skin off the peppers, open them, and remove the seeds and stem. This can be made easier by running the peppers under cold water (though you will be rinsing off some of the flavor).

To make the sauce, put your roasted peppers, vinegar, olive oil, tomato paste, bouillon powder, and smoked paprika into a blender and blend

Makes 3 open-faced Ransackers

2 red bell peppers (or 8 ounces jarred roasted red bell peppers)

1 tablespoon red wine vinegar

1 tablespoon olive oil

1 tablespoon tomato paste

1 teaspoon chicken bouillon powder

½ teaspoon smoked paprika

3 slices rye bread

3 tablespoons unsalted butter

9 large stalks asparagus, cut into 1-inch logs

12 large (26/35 count) peeled and deveined shrimp

½ teaspoon salt

¼ teaspoon ground black pepper

6 slices deli ham

1½ cups shredded Swiss cheese (about 6 ounces; 6 large slices also works)

2 cups plain potato chips

on high until the sauce is as luxurious as a three-night stay at Reno's Grand Sierra Resort and Casino! Transfer it to a saucepan, and heat it over medium-high heat until bubbling, then reduce the heat to a simmer and let the sauce reduce for 5 minutes. Remove from the heat and set aside.

Now you can toast those slices of bread and reserve them for later. Meanwhile, melt the butter in a large sauté pan over medium heat, then toss in your asparagus and sauté until tender, about 5 minutes. Toss in your shrimp and season with the salt and black pepper. Reno actually invented the Automated Shrimp Sheller (ASS), so it would arguably be more authentic to use some prepeeled shrimp! Sauté until the shrimp are pink and cooked through, about 3 minutes, then pull the pan off the heat. Here's

a good rule of thumb for shrimp doneness: they should look like the letter J, as opposed to the letter C, which means they are overcooked. We don't have any fun rhyme or mnemonic device for that tip, but if you make one up, please let us know!

Arrange your toasted bread on a baking sheet and add a slice of ham on top of each followed by a hefty handful (about ½ cup) of shredded cheese (or 2 slices per sandwich). Broil for 3 or 4 minutes, until the cheese is golden brown and bubbly. Top each slice of cheesy toast with about ¼ cup of red pepper sauce, 4 shrimp, some asparagus, and, finally—just as our Renonian forefathers did—a handful of crushed potato chips. Make sure to eat The Sack while it's burning hot, and don't neglect the ASS shrimp!

LOMO SALTADO CHEESESTEAK

Philadelphia: home to Benjamin Franklin, Rocky Balboa, and Pennsylvania's greatest sandwich, the cheesesteak. Pittsburgh: home to . . . (quickly googles famous people from Pittsburgh) Mark Cuban (who knew?), jazz vocalist Spanky Wilson, and Pennsylvania's second-greatest sandwich, the French fry–stuffed behemoth at Primanti Brothers. Can we finally unite the Keystone State by combining these two cultural juggernauts—alongside several elements of the classic Peruvian dish lomo saltado—in one fluffy hoagie roll? No. The answer is no. Western Pennsylvania is basically Ohio. But at least you'll get a heck of a sandwich out of it! This recipe takes the classic cheesesteak formula of greasy, thin-sliced rib eye plus processed cheese, and ups the flavor ante with a little bit of soy sauce, vinegar, Roma tomatoes, and fresh herbs. And, as a Philadelphia Eagles fan in Peru would say, "Vamos, pájaros!"

....

Toss your rib eye in the freezer for 15 to 20 minutes, just to make it easier to slice, then preheat your oven to . . . whatever the bag of frozen French fries tells you to preheat your oven to. At this point, stop listening to us, and start listening to the bag. THE BAG KNOWS. What we're saying is—cook the dang fries. Make them hot and as crispy as your oven will get them. Don't stress too hard about crispiness because they're getting sautéed with a bunch of wet flavor beef.

How are your fries doing? Still cooking? Great, let's prep the ingredients you're about to sauté. Using the SHARPEST knife you have and your STURDIEST cutting board, slice the steak as THIN as possible. Text your friends with ALL CAPS so they think you're SUPER MAD AT THEM. The thinner your steak, the better your sandwich. If your steak is not paper thin, just start chopping the ever-loving heck out of it with a knife until it almost resembles ground beef. Put that steak in a bowl or something.

Recipe continues

- 1½ pounds rib eye (you can use a cheaper cut, but we are not liable if the Philly gods smite you for it)
- 8 ounces frozen French fries (any kind works, but the Ore-Ida Extra Crispy Fast Food fries are the best)
- 4 garlic cloves
- ½ large red onion
- 2 Roma tomatoes
- 2 tablespoons vegetable oil
- 1 teaspoon salt
- ½ teaspoon ground black pepper
- 3 tablespoons soy sauce
- 1 tablespoon white vinegar
- ¼ cup roughly chopped cilantro (you can use parsley if you're one of those people who genetically perceive cilantro as tasting like soap)
- 10 slices white American cheese (Cooper Sharp is the Philly special, but Boar's Head white American from the deli section of your grocery store is also awesome)
- Four 9-inch hoagie rolls (smaller French rolls from your grocery store bakery would also work)

You have to chop more things now. Sorry. It's really good, though, we promise. You're going to be very happy that you made this, and if you're not, email Rhett McLaughlin at jamesandtheshame@gmail .com for a full refund (please no one do this; we will get in big trouble). Garlic! Palm heel strike it, peel it, and slice it as thin as possible. Half a red onion! Cut it as thinly as possible! Tomatoes! Core them: use the point of a paring knife to remove the . . . (listen, it's the butthole of the tomato, but that sounds crass, so we won't say it) nipple of the tomato. Cut the tomatoes in half lengthwise, then in half again, then in half again. You should have 16 longish tomato spears.

Now you get to actually cook things, which is very exciting. Heat the largest sauté pan you have on high heat and add the oil (if you don't have a sauté pan bigger than 11 inches in diameter, we recommend using two sauté pans, working at the same time. It's like dual-wielding in *Halo*, except you get to eat a cheesesteak after). When the oil is

smoking hot, add the garlic, onion, tomatoes, salt, and pepper and sauté until the onion has slightly browned, about 3 minutes. Next, add your steak and continue to cook until the steak is cooked through, about 5 more minutes.

Add the soy sauce, vinegar, French fries, and cilantro and give everything one last toss. Shingle the cheese over the top while the pan is still on the heat (if your cheese isn't melted on a cheesesteak, we will never forgive you), then gently fold some of the meat mixture on top of the cheese. Slice a hoagie roll in half (hollow out some of the inside for best results), then scoop in more meat and cheese than you think the hoagie will hold. No, more than that. MORE. KEEP GOING, YOU MAD LAD! Okay, stop.

Wrap the sandwich in foil and let it sit for at least 5 minutes so the bread can steam. For optimal results, put the wrapped sandwich in a paper bag and throw it against the wall a few times just like they do at your local hoagie shop.

CARNE ASADA BURRITO OF DEATH

Makes 2 burritos

1 pound beef flap meat (you can really use any cut you want here: sirloin, rib eye, skirt steak, bottom round)

1 teaspoon salt

½ teaspoon granulated garlic

½ teaspoon granulated onion

½ teaspoon paprika

¼ teaspoon ground black pepper

3 Roma tomatoes

¼ yellow or white onion

1 jalapeño

2 tablespoons chopped cilantro

¼ teaspoon salt

1 lime, halved

1 large avocado (or 2 small ones)

2 tablespoons vegetable oil

½ cup shredded Monterey Jack (about 2 ounces)

Two 12-inch flour tortillas

Your favorite hot sauce!

Hi! Josh here. Most of this book isn't written in the first person—primarily because we have a large team that makes the whole dang ship run, so it'd be weird if I was all "me, me, me!" the whole time—but I'm writing about my own death, so fudge it, man! I have decided that a San Diego–style carne asada burrito will be the last food I want to enter my body before I kick the ol' proverbial life bucket. And that's for all the normal reasons. No food is more closely associated with my childhood than an asada burrito. Growing up, I spent summers in Oceanside, California—because my parents were divorced, not because we were rich—and I have the most vivid memories of going to a taco shop called To's (not to be confused with Alberto's, Alba-tro's, Rigoberto's, or Dagoberto's), splitting an asada burrito with my friend (because we each likely had only two dollars in our pockets), and playing hours of *Marvel vs. Capcom 2* on the arcade machine that was broken, so one quarter got you unlimited plays. The owner never caught on, and we had endless entertainment for twenty-five cents. It's a simple meal—just greasy steak bits, cheese, guacamole, and pico de gallo, wrapped in a translucent flour tortilla—but for me, it's my single *Ratatouille* food. It's the one food that truly tastes like home.

Also, yeah, yeah, I know *carne asada* means "flame-grilled steak," and this is cooked in a pan, but 99 percent of taquerias I grew up eating in didn't grill their asada either. Be chill, I'm sharing a fond memory!

Slice your steak into, uhhhhh, ½-centimeter cubes? Who the heck uses centimeters? About ¼ inch? Can you even conceptualize how small that is? Just make them very small. This recipe isn't about tasting the quality of the meat or savoring its texture. This recipe is about how much spice and grease you can get into your system with a single portable foodstuff. Great, steak's chopped! Put it in a bowl, add your salt, granulated garlic and onion, paprika, and pepper and mix thoroughly. Let it sit in the fridge for at least half an hour.

While the steak is marinating, go ahead and make the pico de gallo and guacamole. Core your tomatoes, then chop them into small bits, about ¼ inch (oh nooooo, it's happening again!). Chop your onion and jalapeño to the same size. Transfer everything to a small bowl and add your cilantro, salt, and the juice of half a lime, then toss to combine. If you don't like cilantro, please return this book to whatever store you bought it from and never make eye contact with me if you see me on the street. (Just kidding, you can just leave the cilantro out. I have nothing but respect for personal food preferences.)

This is a controversial guacamole method, and I do this only when the guacamole is being added to a larger dish, such as this burrito—I make more of an effort for stand-alone guac, I promise. Spoon your avocados into a bowl and add about 2 tablespoons of the pico de gallo you just made, along with 1 teaspoon of the liquid from the pico. Mash it around until it's a delightfully mushy green paste. Boom, you're done.

Has it been a half hour yet? Eh, even if it hasn't, you should probably cook that steak now. Heat your oil in a large sauté pan on rip-roaring high heat, and then, when the oil starts to smoke, drop in your

steak. Use a wooden spoon to hack the heck out of it, moving it constantly until it's finished cooking, about 5 minutes. You aren't looking for a crazy crust on the steak bits (Maillard reaction fanboys, avert your eyes!), but you do want some solid browning. When the steak is cooked, squeeze on the juice from the other half of the lime, toss, and blanket the steak in the shredded Monterey Jack. Remove from the heat and let that cheese envelop your steak like a starfish envelops its prey.

Heat a separate large sauté pan over medium-high heat and griddle one of the tortillas for about 15 seconds on each side, just until it's pliable. Add half of the steak and cheese, guac, and pico de gallo to the tortilla, roll it up, then griddle it, fold side down, in the pan for 30 seconds. Do it all again for the second burrito.

Wrap your burritos in foil and let sit for exactly 5 minutes and 2 seconds, which is enough time to watch the first-ever episode of "Fancy Fast Food." Enjoy with your favorite hot sauce.

WHEN LIFE HANDS YOU BACON, DON'T QUESTION IT AND JUST EAT THE DANG BACON

(BACON)

Bacon is patient. Bacon is kind. Bacon does not envy or boast; it is not arrogant or rude. There are very few times—once in an eon, perhaps—that a gift of bacon's magnitude is bestowed upon humanity, and we owe it to ourselves to use this precious gift to its fullest potential. And, to be extra clear, bacon's fullest potential does not have to include pork. There are many legitimate reasons people avoid pig bacon—religious, dietary, or, like Jules Winnfield, they just don't dig on swine—but thanks to technological innovations, these formerly deprived people no longer have to live life without sweet, smoky, crispy strips of joy.

According to our own Mythical taxonomy experts (Nicole and I have spent hundreds of hours debating the definitions of foods on our podcast, *A Hot Dog Is a Sandwich*, and we can't tell if we're smarter than ever or dumber than ever), bacon is defined as: *thin, salt-cured, smoked strips of flesh from an animal's belly, usually pig, but often from other animals, such as turkey or lamb, and sometimes not even from the belly, and sometimes*

it's not an animal, and this one time we saw someone make vegan bacon from banana peels, and we tried it, and it was bad, but also it's super cool that we as a species decided to do that because that's the type of ingenuity that got us to the moon, which is a feat no other species has accomplished, and will not likely accomplish until the great capybara lunar expedition deep in the 2300s. Why capybaras? Well, why not?

Speaking as someone who was raised on turkey bacon (partly because of Judaism, partly because of a mom who grew up in the fat-fearing '80s), I can say confidently—it scratches the itch well enough. Can anything TRULY measure up to the fatty, crispy perfection of pork bacon? The correct answer is: not yet. But that's because pork bacon has had thousands of years to flourish (most historians trace the origins of bacon to salt-preserved pork bellies in China around thirty-five hundred years ago). The alternative bacon market has exploded only in the last decade or so, which is why it needs a stimulus package to kick-start the innovation process.

That is why we are hereby issuing a challenge to the world's greatest butchers, farmers, scientists, and astrologers: Mythical will fund a one-time grant of $2.5 million (please don't tell Rhett and Link I promised this; I'll get in a lot of trouble) to one lucky applicant who has the best pitch for a more successful bacon alternative. Since no one has eaten more animals than us here at Mythical, we have decided to draw up a few schematics and butchery charts to get things started.*

* Unfortunately, for tax purposes, this is a joke and the grant does not exist.

Bacons of Tomorrow

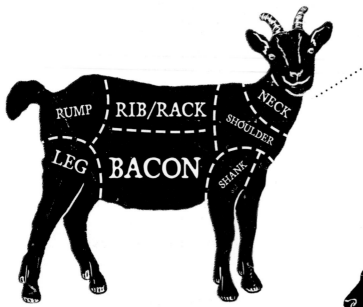

GOAT

Though it lacks popularity in the United States, goat is one of the most commonly eaten meats around the world. It is also my personal favorite meat. The belly of a goat is likely delicious, and they eat trash, so it is a sustainable meat source.

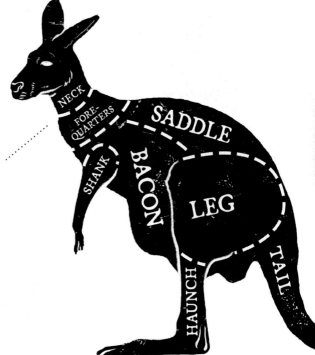

KANGAROO

These giant rats of the outback (not the steakhouse) outnumber people two to one in Australia, and their massive population causes ecological devastation. Kangaroos have delicious, lean flesh, making their bellies a healthy alternative to pig bacon. It can be marketed to CrossFitters.

BEAVER

Come on, just say it with us: beaver bacon! It rolls off the tongue and has stellar marketing campaigns built in ("I can't believe it's beav!"). Does beaver actually taste good? Heck yeah it does! And we think millions around the world can be converted to proud beaver eaters.

EMPEROR PENGUIN

As of this writing, the emperor penguin is considered a threatened species, and as climate change continues to destroy their habitat, they could be headed toward extinction. That's where our sustainable penguin farmers located in northern Saskatchewan come into play. We can save the species AND have delightful penguin BLTs.

PEANUTS

George Washington Carver developed more than 300 uses for peanuts. Had he developed 301, bacon may have been on the list, next to soap and glue. We have no idea how the science works, but we can make some educated guesses as to where the bacon molecules would be located.

RANDLER

Some say the Randler doesn't exist, but we know that it does, because it lives within our hearts. And now the Randler will live inside our stomachs in the form of crispity, crunchity, cryptid bacon! If you preorder your pack of Randler bacon* at mythical.com in the next twenty minutes, you get a FREE Mythical coffee mug!

*Imitation Randler-like bacon product is made from premium pork bellies.

OLD GUM ON SIDEWALKS

Sneaker companies have started selling shoes made entirely out of recycled bottles, and there are disposable forks made from potato starch. The recycled materials industry is at the top of its game, and there is no more reusable food source on this earth than gum scraped off the streets.

HABAUSAGE BITES

Makes 24 habausage bites

4 ounces your preferred ham steak, cut into twenty-four ½-inch cubes

2 Italian sausages, casings removed

12 slices bacon, cut in half crosswise

¼ cup balsamic vinegar

¼ cup honey

Habausage! Ha(m)ba(con)(sa)usage! We made this roughly 480-pound monstrosity on *Mythical Kitchen*, featuring a holiday ham wrapped in homemade sausage and a gigantic lattice-woven bacon blanket. A few days later, we got a letter from the pig community at large begging us to please stop, and saying that we had single-handedly decimated their population. But the joke was on them because it took *way* more than one hand to do it. Upward of two. So . . . double. Anyway, they didn't change our mind, but we also wanted to make something a little less unwieldy and significantly *more* wieldy. (Habausage Bites—now with 100 percent more wield!)

Also, by rethinking this recipe, we have perfected it so that every single bite contains the golden pig ratio. In retrospect, the original version involved getting a giant bite of bacon-sausage, and then there was a whole ham left underneath. But WE DID IT FOR YOU. And now we do this for you. Habausage!

Are you ready to grease up your hands with pork fat? Because . . . that's about to happen. Preheat the oven to 425°F. Line a baking sheet with parchment paper or a silicone baking mat (or use NOTHING, if you want to get wild with your cleanup).

Take a ham cube and encase it in a similarly sized ball of sausage, squeezing the sausage gently to form a little pork sphere. Take a half slice of bacon and wrap it around, sliding a toothpick all the way through to hold the bacon in place (do not use toothpicks with little plastic tips, as those will 100 percent melt in the oven). Set that habausage on the prepared baking sheet and repeat until you've got all 24 of them made.

Bake for about 30 minutes. Use tongs to flip each ball over and continue to bake until the bacon is crispy and the sausage is cooked, about 10 more minutes.

Meanwhile, pour the balsamic and honey into a small bowl and whisk them up so there isn't just a whole mud sludge of honey on the bottom. When the habausage are cooked, take a brush (or a spoon if you're one of those people who's like, oh crap, I just got to the end of the recipe and now it says I need a PASTRY BRUSH??? I don't have one of those!) and then brush or spoon the glaze over the habausage bites.

Return them to the oven for another 90 seconds, then let them cool until you can eat them without hurting yourself. Oh, and speaking of not hurting yourself . . . maybe take the toothpick out before eating it.

BACON CHEESEBURGER LASAGNA

Serves all your closest friends, unless you are one of those people who claims to have, like, 10 best friends—in which case, do you really even have any friends?

A classic, true Italian lasagna Bolognese—handmade fresh pasta, lightly boiled and layered with long-simmered ragù Bolognese, delicate béchamel, and the finest aged Parmigiano-Reggiano this earth can create—is one of the greatest culinary creations in human history.

But so is a bacon cheeseburger. So we're making a bacon Bolognese, stuffing it between sheets of no-boil lasagna noodles, saucing it up with American cheese sauce, and then topping the whole thing with cheese and bacon bits, and gosh darn if this shouldn't be exported back to Italy so we can show those people a thing or two about lasagna.

....

Fun Fact: You can make the meat sauce and the cheese sauce a few days in advance and just assemble the lasagna cold! It will just take slightly longer to cook since, well, the ingredients are all cold.

Step 1: Make the Bacon Bolognese. Take about a third of that bacon and put it in a heavy-bottomed pot or Dutch oven over medium heat. Let that sucker cook, stirring occasionally, until your bacon is crispy and the house smells like breakfast—about 10 minutes. Now take it out and set it on a plate but DO NOT EAT IT, since it's for way, way later. Drain off that bacon fat and put it in an old coffee can by the windowsill for future cooking adventures, like every grandpa after World War II.

Cook the remaining bacon until most of the fat has released, about 6 minutes. Add the beef and give it all a nice stir. Season with a pinch of salt and pepper and continue to cook, stirring, until the beef has lost its raw color, about 4 more minutes. Add the onion, garlic, and pickles, stirring it all together and breaking up any beefy clumps. Next on the list . . . add what's next on the list: the sugar, marjoram, thyme, and tomato paste, stirring to mix it all up. Finally, add the tomatoes and chicken stock, along with another pinch of salt and pepper. Bring that sucker up to a simmer, then reduce the heat to low and just let it simmer away, covered, until it resembles the contents of a can of Hormel chili on a hot day—about 1½ hours.

Recipe continues

Bacon Bolognese

1¼ pounds bacon, minced

1 pound lean ground beef

Salt and ground black pepper

1 large yellow or white onion, minced

4 garlic cloves, palm heel struck and minced

½ cup chopped pickles

1 tablespoon sugar

2 teaspoons dried marjoram

1 teaspoon dried thyme

2 tablespoons tomato paste

One 15-ounce can crushed tomatoes

1 cup chicken stock

American Cheese Sauce

4 tablespoons (½ stick) unsalted butter

3 tablespoons all-purpose flour

2 cups whole milk

12 slices American cheese

Salt and ground black pepper

To Assemble

Two 9-ounce boxes no-boil lasagna noodles

1 cup shredded low-moisture mozzarella (about 4 ounces)

1 cup shredded medium cheddar (about 4 ounces)

Step 2: Make the American Cheese Sauce. Melt the butter in a medium heavy-bottomed pot or saucepan over medium heat. Add the flour and cook, stirring constantly, until it is bubbling away and smells toasty and fragrant, about 2 minutes. Slowly pour in about 1 cup of the milk, stirring constantly until the mixture is bubbling and smooth, then add the remaining milk, and if you smell burnt toast, go to the hospital. But if you smell burnt milk, you're too late and have ruined your sauce because the heat was too high, so start over and try again. (Believe us, there is no fix for scorched milk. It will just make your whole lasagna taste like burnt milk.)

Keep simmering until the milk is thick enough to coat the back of a spoon, about 1 more minute. Remove from the heat, add your cheese slices, and stir until melted and mixed. Season with salt and pepper until it tastes good and set aside.

Step 3: Assemble and Bake! Preheat the oven to 400°F.

Spread a spoonful of Bolognese sauce on the bottom of a 9 × 13-inch baking dish. Start layering! Place a layer of noodles on top of the sauce, followed by a thin layer of cheese sauce, and then more Bolognese—dividing up the noodles and

sauces so you have enough of each to get five layers of noodles . . . unless you gauge it wrong and then only end up using three or four layers of noodles, which is also totally fine. But basically it goes: Bolognese, noodle, cheese sauce, Bolognese, noodle, cheese sauce, Bolognese, noodle, yada yada, until the top noodle gets the last bit of cheese sauce on top.

THEN, top the cheese sauce with the shredded mozzarella and cheddar and place that whole heavy beast in the oven and bake it for about 25 minutes, until the top is starting to brown and the lasagna is bubbling. Then . . . remember those bacon bits you were saving and totally didn't eat while you were waiting? Sprinkle those on top and put it all back in the oven until the cheese is golden brown, about 6 more minutes.

Let the lasagna sit for about 15 minutes because it's been working really hard and needs to *rest for a minute . . . Can it just REST?!* So yeah, give the lasagna a break, but also it helps all the flavors mellow out and settle so everything doesn't just spill across the dish and get all soupy when you cut it up.

Then eat it, because it's good and you spent, like, five hours making it.

MILK CHOCOLATE–DIPPED BACON ICE CREAM SANDWICHES

There are a lot of reasons to want to make a bacon weave. You can lay it in the center of a BLT to make the ultimate version of that holy creation; you can use it to replace gingerbread for your holiday festivities and turn it into a way more delicious bacon house; and you can even make a 17-inch bacon weave, and then put it in someone's laptop bag for a fun porky surprise. But rather than just picking it up and eating it, or putting it *inside* a sandwich, we believe that its most perfect purpose is to *replace* the cookies in an ice cream sandwich. After all, what is a bacon weave, if not a smoky, sweet, and salty pig cookie? Slide some ice cream in the middle and you have the best creation we've ever made on *GMM*'s "Will It Ice Cream Sandwich?" Plus it's low carb, in case you're on a . . . really weird diet that is absolutely, positively not good for you.

....

Step 1: Make a Bacon Weave. Preheat the oven to 400°F.

Now you're going to make one large bacon weave, and to do that, I hate to break it to you, but: you're gonna have to weave a bunch of bacon.

Lay 8 slices down on a sheet of parchment paper, tightly packed together horizontally. Then you start a-weaving. From the center of the bacon, fold back every *other* slice of bacon, like you're basically just folding them in half over themselves. Then right next to that folded bacon, lay down one vertical slice of bacon down the center. Then, unfold those folded slices back, *over* the bacon you just laid down. You've just woven one strip.

Next, fold back the other horizontal slices of bacon (the ones *next* to the ones you folded last time), and lay another vertically placed slice right next to the previous one. Then unfold the horizontal ones back and repeat the process until you get all the way to one edge of

Recipe continues

Makes 4 sandwiches

Bacon Weave
15 slices bacon (the longest ones you can find)

Chocolate Dip and Finish
1 rounded cup milk chocolate chips
1 tablespoon coconut oil
2 heaping scoops vanilla ice cream

the bacon lattice. Then repeat it on the other side, creating a rectangular bacon weave!

Slide that parchment onto a baking sheet and roast for about 40 minutes, until the bacon gets crispy. While it is still warm, use a spatula to lift it onto a cutting board, then just cut that thing in quarters to make four equal smoked pig "cookies." Let cool to room temperature.

Step 2: Make the Chocolate Sauce and Assemble. Place the chocolate chips and coconut oil in a microwave-safe bowl and then microwave it, 15 seconds at a time, stirring in between intervals, until it has become a dippable chocolate sauce.

Sandwich up that ice cream and then dip half of each sandwich in the chocolate sauce. Set them on a baking sheet until the chocolate hardens, then place them directly in the freezer. For best results, let it freeze overnight. Take that, Nestlé Toll House. If you don't eat them once they are fully frozen, wrap them in plastic wrap to prevent ice crystals.

Why Does It Get Hard?

That bottle of chocolate sauce that hits your ice cream and turns into a solid? It's not magic—it's saturated fat! Coconut oil is a saturated fat, which, like butter or lard, means it is solid at room temperature and liquid when it is heated. If you add some coconut oil to your chocolate as it is melting, it will make it flow even smoother, and when you cool it down, it will give it an even more solid consistency. They should really call it Saturated Fat Shell at the stores!

JOSH'S PERFECT BREAKFAST BURGER

We are pretty sure that even the most mediocre grocery store in America sells a surprisingly great kaiser roll. We don't know if the heads of all the major grocery stores in this country get together for secret underground meetings . . . but if they do, it all started so that they could agree collectively on one kaiser roll recipe that would be made in every grocery store bakery or commissary kitchen across this great land. It is—according to a wholly objective and scientific study called "What do you think, Josh?"—the best breakfast sandwich vehicle on the planet. But it is even better as a Breakfast Burger base, ideally of the onion varietal, but even a plain kaiser roll will be outstanding. What else, after all, could hold up to the mighty force of a bacon-studded quarter-pound beef patty, a folded omelet, hot sauce aioli, a hash brown patty, and American cheese? Nothing, you beautiful, sexy, secret grocery store cabal, you.

....

Step 1: Make the Sauce and Hash Browns. Preheat the oven and cook the hash brown patty according to the package instructions.

While that is going, mix together the mayo and hot sauce in a small bowl. Whenever the hash browns are done, just drop that oven temperature down to the lowest it will go to keep warm while you . . .

Step 2: Make the Bacon Burger Patty. Fry that bacon in a skillet over medium-high heat until it is crispy and people start walking in to tell you that something smells good, about 6 minutes. Transfer to a paper towel–lined plate to cool off. Once it is room temperature, chuck it in a bowl with the ground beef and fold it all together with your hands, working fast and light and trying not to compact the beef. Shape the meat into a patty that's just slightly wider than your bun (for there will be shrinkage!). Crank the heat back up on that pan of rendered bacon fat and add the oil. Once it's smoking and hot, season one side of the burger with salt and lay it down in the pan (salt side down) and then salt the other side. Cook until you get a nice sear on the bottom, about 2 minutes, then flip the burger and lay that cheese on top to wilt

Recipe continues

Makes 1 burger

Sauce and Condiments
1 frozen hash brown patty
3 tablespoons mayo
2 teaspoons hot sauce

Bacon Burger
3 slices bacon, diced
6 ounces 80/20 ground beef
1 tablespoon vegetable oil
Salt
1 slice American cheese
1 kaiser roll (ideally onion), toasted

Folded Omelet
2 tablespoons unsalted butter
1 tablespoon finely chopped chives
2 large eggs, super-duper beaten
Salt and ground black pepper

while the other side sears, about another 2 minutes. Meanwhile, spread some of the hot sauce mayo on both sides of the roll, and when the burger is ready, lay that sucker right onto that bottom bun.

Step 3: Make a Folded Omelet! Melt the butter in a medium nonstick skillet over medium heat. Add a splash of water and the chopped chives to your beaten eggs and give them another whisk. Pour the eggs into the melted butter. For the first 20 seconds, you're going to use a spatula (ideally high-heat silicone) to keep sliding the edges of the egg in toward the middle, tilting the pan to let the wet eggs fill in the gaps as you do it. After those 20 seconds, you're going to let it sit and sprinkle it up with that salt and pepper. Then you wait, and watch, until it looks like that egg is starting to firm up a little, another 20 seconds. You want it a little wet in the center, and on the border of custardy. Then you can reduce the heat a touch and take your spatula and run it around the outer lip of that omelet, releasing it from the edge. Give it a gentle shake to make sure it's able to slide around comfortably and doesn't have any sticky spots. Fold the omelet in half, then again into quarters (you're looking for something roughly the size of your kaiser roll, because this thing is going on a sandwich, after all).

Lift it up out of the pan and lay it right on top of your burger patty.

Step 4: Finish It and Finish It. Take that warm hash brown patty out of the oven and put it on top of the egg. Close your sandwich and, ta-da, it is finished. Then eat the whole thing, to finish it again. (Finished and finished.) Then do it all over again because somebody probably saw you eating it and now they want one.

ONE-PAN (MOSTLY) FULL ENGLISH BREAKFAST BURRITO

Makes 1 burrito

1 medium tomato, sliced in half

2 slices AMERICAN bacon

2 AMERICAN breakfast sausages

4 tablespoons (½ stick) unsalted butter or lard

2 large eggs

Salt and ground black pepper

4 white button or cremini mushrooms, sliced

¾ cup AMERICAN baked beans from a can (such as Bush's)

2 dashes Worcestershire sauce

1 large flour tortilla

A "full English" is a classic breakfast across the UK, with eight key components: eggs, sausage, bacon, baked beans, roasted tomato, roasted mushrooms, bread, and black pudding (oh, don't worry, it's nothing evil or nefarious; it's just the pig's blood that makes it black).

While we *did* make a black pudding chorizo on our YouTube version of this recipe, we decided that it was perhaps somewhat unrealistic to suggest that you make that at home. So you can give away your extra pig's blood or smear it on someone's door if a cult leader tells you to.

Anyway, why eat things with a fork and knife when you can stuff them inside a burrito? So we present our (Mostly) Full English Breakfast Burrito, with the components skewed more toward Americana—instead of back bacon, British baked beans, and English sausage, we are replacing them with the good old-fashioned American versions. Well, we suppose technically they are *new*-fashioned, since England is way older than America. But whatever, we won the Revolutionary War, so we're allowed to put whatever the heck we want in a tortilla and call it whatever we want. We also wanted to see if we could make the whole dang thing in one good cast-iron skillet. (Spoiler alert: it didn't work, so you gotta roast the tomatoes separately. Otherwise, it's all cooked in one cast-iron skillet.)

Preheat the oven to 450°F.

Take those tomato halves and put them cut side up on a piece of aluminum foil and just let those suckers roast while you do everything else, about 25 minutes.

Place a 12-inch cast-iron skillet over medium heat and lay the bacon slices and sausages right in there.

Take your time with the bacon, letting it render and crisp up. Meanwhile, keep on rolling those sausages until they are golden

Are You Cast-Iron Man?

Two fun facts about cast-iron skillets:

1. They take *way* longer to preheat than you think, and that's because it takes a long time for the heat to conduct and transfer through the whole skillet. Once it's hot, it keeps its heat really well for a really long time. That's why some people who take their cast-iron cookery really seriously preheat the whole dang thing in the oven for like 20 minutes before searing a steak in it. That is also a great way to forget that the handle is hot and then to burn the crap out of your hand.

2. Yes, it is important to season a skillet. But the idea that you should never wash a cast-iron skillet with soap, even as it is passed down for generations, is totally bogus and weird and gross. The idea that your bacon will taste better because it is being "seasoned" with food that your grand-mother cooked in the 1920s is utter bull-crap. So yes, you can just wipe down a skillet sometimes and not worry too much about it, but sometimes you should absolutely wash it with soap and water and then reseason it with a *very* light coating of oil on the stove over medium-low heat, or in the oven at 200°F.

brown on the outside and crispy. So basically . . . cook until cooked, about 4 minutes, then transfer the sausages and bacon to a plate.

Reduce the heat to medium, and then add 2 tablespoons of the butter to the pan. Once it has melted, crack those eggs in there and season them with salt and pepper. Cook until the whites are set and the yolks are runny, about 3 minutes. No, these aren't delicate sunny-side up eggs. These are crispy-edged, rough-and-tumble fried eggs that were raised on the mean streets of wherever the streets are mean in London. Sheffield? Is that a place? Hackney? Hackney sounds dangerous. Or like a fishing village. To be honest, we have no idea how to tell.

Once the eggs are cooked, set them on that plate with the sausage and bacon, not at all caring if they get all mixed up since they are all going to live together in a big happy burrito (but maybe try not to crack those yolks open until they're in the burrito).

Crank that heat back up to medium-high and add another tablespoon of the butter. Toss in those mushrooms, seasoning them with salt and pepper, and then fry them up, stirring constantly, until they are browned and cooked through, about 3 minutes. Scoop them out and add them to your plate, which is looking suspiciously like an English breakfast . . . or maybe a burrito bowl (which, by the way, IS NOT A BURRITO).

Slop those beans into the pan with the remaining tablespoon of butter, hit it with those dashes of Worcestershire, and use a wooden spoon or spatula to REFRY those baked beans, letting them mash up and bubble until they look like refried beans, about 3 more minutes. YOU'RE SO CLOSE!

Recipe continues

Lay that tortilla on top of the food in the pan to warm up for about 30 seconds on each side, then throw it down on a work surface, spread those refried beans in there, and then add everything from your English breakfast plate. Grab those tomatoes you almost forgot about from the oven and throw them in there too. Use a paper towel to wipe away any bean remnants from the skillet, and then, finally, roll up that burrito and lay it, seam side down, right back in the skillet. This is gonna help sear that seal closed, while also refreshing your ingredients a bit—this will take about 1 minute. Once it is golden brown, flip it over and sear the other side to golden brown.

That's it! One pan! (Kind of.) One burrito! Seven components! No blood sausage! Great job, everybody.

BACONANA SPLIT

Aren't you tired of cookbooks that take a normal dessert and then just sprinkle bacon on it to make it seem unique and salty and decadent? Oh, you aren't? You were totally fine with us just making a normal banana split and then crumbling bacon over the top? Okay. Well . . . we aren't doing that. We're doing something way better. For our bacon banana split, we are bacon-wrapping two whole dang banani. We are bacon mummifying bananas. We are bacon CRUSTING bananas to create BACONANAS. Behold: the Baconana Split!

....

Step 1: Make the Baconani. Preheat the oven to 450°F. Line a baking sheet with parchment paper and grease it up with some cooking spray.

Peel the bananas and throw the peels away. (Serious question: Has anyone *ever* slipped on a banana peel? Like, ever? Where did that idea come from?) Tightly wrap both banani with the bacon, using toothpicks to spear the bananas and secure the bacon in place. Sprinkle half the sugar over one bacon-wrapped nanner, and half the sugar over the other.

Place the baconani on the prepared baking sheet and roast for about 24 minutes, until the bacon is crisp. Transfer to a paper towel–lined plate, and reserve the bacon fat for later.

Step 2: Make the Bacon Caramel. Whisk together the sugar and 3 tablespoons water in a medium heavy-bottomed pot, then shake the pan to settle it into a flat layer. Place the pot over medium heat and cook until the sugar and water start to bubble, about 2 minutes. Keep simmering, with no stirring whatsoever (gently swirling the pan is okay, but then scrape down the sides with a high-heat silicone spatula or wooden spoon to prevent burning).

Keep on going! Once it gets to a deeper, caramelly color—after, like, 8 minutes—add the butter, and then and ONLY THEN can you stir. Mix that sucker while it gets all foamy and fun and the butter melts.

Makes 1 baconana split

Baconani
Cooking spray
2 large bananas
4 slices bacon
2 tablespoons sugar

Bacon Caramel
½ cup sugar
3 tablespoons unsalted butter, diced, at room temperature
3 tablespoons heavy cream, at room temperature

To Finish
3 scoops vanilla ice cream
Canned whipped cream
Crushed pecans
3 maraschino cherries

Remove from the heat and slowly pour in the cream and bacon fat. Give it another whisk and then pour it into a heatproof container (like a Mason jar or bowl) and set it aside. Caramel! Let it sit for, like, 2 minutes to cool.

Step 3: Assemble! Remove the toothpicks from your baconani. Lay them in your longest, narrowest vessel with one on either side. Add the ice cream, followed by a drizzle of the slightly cooled caramel. Top with a good squirt of whipped cream, the pecans, and the cherries. Now dig in and be merry.

BACON-WRAPPED ONION RINGS

Makes 15, serving probably 1 person because these are so good everyone else has to BACK AWAY

This is one of them "WE HAVE NO NOTES" recipes. This is a ring of onion, wrapped in bacon, deep-fried, and then crop dusted with a little BBQ-inspired spice mix so that you have . . . and hear us out . . . deep-fried bacon-wrapped onion rings. To be honest, this is so dang good that it does not *need* a sauce. But this is also *Mythical Kitchen*, where *need* is a loose term. Like, we don't *need* to make a Twinkie out of Mountain Dew, but on the other hand, we absolutely need to make a Twinkie out of Mountain Dew. Do we *need* attention? Some might suggest it is more of an addiction than a need. But we also need to dip these onion rings in ranch dressing. You're welcome.

Neutral oil, for frying
2 large yellow or white onions
About 15 slices bacon
1 tablespoon light brown sugar
1 tablespoon granulated sugar
1 teaspoon paprika (or smoked paprika if you've got it)
1 teaspoon salt
⅛ teaspoon cayenne
Ranch dressing, for serving

Heat your fry oil (using a deep fryer or a large, heavy-bottomed pot filled with at least 3 inches of oil, making sure that the pot is no more than two-thirds full) to 375°F. Line a plate with paper towels for draining.

Cut the onions into nice thick slices—just under an inch or so. Take 15 rings and wrap each one with a slice of bacon, as tightly as you can. Use toothpicks to secure the bacon.

Mix together the brown sugar, granulated sugar, paprika, salt, and cayenne in a small bowl.

Working in batches, fry those onion rings until they are golden and crispy, about 2½ minutes, then transfer them to the prepared plate and dust them immediately with the seasoning mix.

Let cool until you can put them in your mouth without causing yourself unbearable pain. While you wait, squirt some ranch into a dipping bowl, and when the time is right and there is a twinkle in your eye, dig in.

CHICKEN-FRIED BACON BLT

There are certain foods that you simply don't mess with. Foods whose construction and constitution seem to have been designed by the culinary deities themselves (the religion of food is, apparently, polytheistic—just go with it!). The reason your aunt Sharon's mac 'n' cheese with canned tomatoes ruined Thanksgiving 2017 is because she spit in the face of the mac 'n' cheese god. Well, the BLT is one of those perfect foods. Oh wait, we're CHICKEN-FRYING THE BACON?! Yeah, never mind, play with your food as much as you want. No kings, no gods, no masters—just chicken-fried pork products. Also, for those who are confused about the term *chicken-fried*, it refers to the most common dredging setup for southern-style fried chicken, which is to say a flour-wet-flour double dredge. This recipe is made with bacon, not chicken.

If you have never chicken-fried bacon—HOOOOO BOY, BUCKLE UP! This one is a game changer. You get all the health benefits of bacon, plus the flavor benefits of deep-frying. Wait, bacon ISN'T healthy?! Eat some oatmeal for breakfast tomorrow; it'll average out in the end. Season up your flour with whatever seasoning you got. We always go for Tony Chachere's, but a mix of salt, garlic powder, cayenne, onion powder, paprika, and black pepper will do the trick.

....

Heat about 1 inch of oil in a large sauté pan or cast-iron skillet over medium-high heat to about 350°F. If you don't have a thermometer, flick some flour into the oil, and if it gently sizzles, you're good to go! Probably! Please buy a thermometer; we are begging you—they are very affordable!

Meanwhile, whisk together the flour and Tony C's in a medium bowl. In a separate medium bowl, whisk the eggs with the milk. Dip each slice of bacon in the flour mixture, then the egg mixture, then back into the flour; set each piece aside on a plate. When all the bacon slices are covered in a lovely flour fur coat, fry them until nicely browned, about 2 minutes on each side. You will likely have to work in two batches so

Recipe continues

Makes 2 BLTs

Neutral oil, for frying

1 cup all-purpose flour

½ teaspoon Tony Chachere's Creole Seasoning (any way you want to season the flour is perfectly fine, but, man, Tony C's just hits in this recipe)

2 large eggs

½ cup whole milk

6 slices bacon

¼ cup mayo

4 slices very nonfancy white bread

Half a head of iceberg lettuce

1 large tomato (beefsteak is the best, but do what your heart tells you, unless your heart tells you to put cherry tomatoes on there, because those are inconvenient for a sandwich)

Salt and ground black pepper

as not to overcrowd the pan, and the cooked bacon can be kept warm in a 200°F oven.

Once the bacon slices are fried, you're ready to make a sandwich, friend! In the spirit of keeping it classic (says the person who just chicken-fried bacon), we're keeping the condiments simple. Spread some mayo on two pieces of the bread (we are anti toasting bread for BLTs, but if you toast yours, we'll have no way of knowing). Add a few whole leaves of iceberg (you can always use shredded lettuce, but we prefer whole). Slice your tomatoes extra THICC and add some salt and pepper before slapping them on top of the lettuce. Finally, place three slices of bacon on top of each sandwich with the ginger touch of a mother goose feeding its young, and then smash the last piece of bread on top.

Speaking of mother geese feeding their young, did you know that a fully grown Egyptian goose can travel up to—oh sorry, you're eating a sandwich now; we'll get out of your kitchen.

BACON STOCK RAMEN

Serves 1

3 slices bacon, diced

One 3.5-ounce package chicken instant ramen (or any flavor you like)

1 large egg

1 scallion, dark green part only, thinly sliced

All hail Momofuku Ando, a true legend of the culinary universe, and the inventor of instant ramen. In postwar Japan, food was scarce and Ando believed that "peace will come to the world when people have enough to eat." That's definitely not true, but we'll give him a break because he INVENTED INSTANT RAMEN when he perfected the flash-fry method in 1958 and chicken instant ramen was born.

Yet for all Ando's innovation, none of his instant ramens involved braised bacon. So that's where we come in, to remind you that bacon does not, in fact, have to be crispy. You can slice it up and throw it into a soup to give you all kinds of flavor—and rather than having to save that rendered bacon fat in an old coffee can, you get to keep all that fat and flavor right in your ramen. Throw in an egg and some chopped scallions and we'd pay fifteen dollars for this on a trendy brunch menu.

Place the bacon in a medium pot with 3 cups water. Bring it to a simmer and allow it to simmer, covered, for 10 minutes to make BACON STOCK! Remove the lid and add the noodles (but not the flavor packet yet). Cook the noodles according to the package instructions, then remove from the heat, stir in the flavor packet, and crack that egg right in there. Fold the noodles over the egg, sprinkle in the scallions, and cover the pot. Let sit for about 2 minutes, then pour the ramen into a bowl, tip your cap to Momofuku Ando, and enjoy.

CHICKEN BACON RANCH BOMBS

Makes 8 bombs

6 slices bacon, diced
About 1¾ cups shredded
   chicken from a grocery-
   store rotisserie chicken
¾ cup shredded mozzarella
   (about 3 ounces)
¾ cup ranch dressing,
   plus more for dipping
One 16.3-ounce can
   Pillsbury Grands biscuits
6 tablespoons unsalted
   butter, melted
3 tablespoons minced chives

Costco flipped the script on salad dressing with their Chicken Bakes, being true caloric innovators through the use of HOT Caesar dressing cooked into a delicious sludge of chicken, bacon, and three types of cheese. But we wouldn't be us if that didn't immediately make us want to bake ranch dressing together with chicken and bacon into fluffy Pillsbury Grands Chicken Bacon Ranch Bombs. And for ANYBODY OUT THERE who wants to tell us that mayo or mayo-based sauces are not supposed to be hot, those are fighting words, because hot mayo is the hot, salty glue that makes the world go 'round. Ever heard of a tuna melt? Or potato salad that was left out in the sun all day at a BBQ until it started bubbling? Well, regardless, these bombs are delicious and you should eat them.

Preheat the oven to 350°F.

Dump your bacon into a medium skillet and fry it up over medium heat until crispy and cooked and delicious, about 4 minutes. Transfer it to a large bowl. Add the chicken, mozzarella, and ranch and give it all a nice stir.

Crack open that can o' Pills. Separate the tops from the bottoms of each biscuit, then divide up the chicken mixture, scooping the filling into the center of each bottom biscuit. Set the top right over it, and then pinch the sides closed to seal in the flavor (and to not have a ranchy explosion on your pan).

Line them up on a baking sheet, evenly spaced like a biscuit-based military operation, and bake for 18 to 20 minutes, until they are risen and golden.

Meanwhile, mix the melted butter and chives together in a small bowl. Brush the baked bombs (or drizzle them if you aren't fancy) with the chive butter.

Let them cool and eat them up, dipped into more ranch if you want to get loose.

EAT TOGETHER AS A FAMILY, EVEN IF THAT FAMILY IS JUST YOU, A CAT, AND AN AGGRESSIVE, SENTIENT TOASTER

(DINNER)

No one is exactly sure when Boxy the Toaster developed the capacity to think and to feel, to love and to ponder. But one day, right as two halves of a whole wheat English muffin popped out of their toast holes (the proper anatomical term, as we learned from Boxy), they yelled, "Hey, Einstein! Whole wheat won't cancel out the eight pieces of fried chicken you ate last night." They called me a putz before flipping me off, which is a difficult gesture for a toaster to make. I never did understand why they had a heavy Brooklyn accent. Boxy sounds like Joe Pesci doing an imitation of Joe Pesci.

It's reasonable to think that a wisecracking toaster would make a terrible roommate, but if we're being honest, Beelzebub and I were getting lonely. You see, Beelzebub is a very nonsentient, incredibly lazy orange tabby with an affinity for ravioli. He used to eat lasagna, but one day, in between loud coughing fits, Boxy said, "That's a bit derivative, don't you think?" and rolled their judging toaster eyes. Beelzebub didn't mind the critique,

because it WAS derivative, and lasagna and ravioli basically have the same set of ingredients, and also his brain is the size of a walnut.

Sure, Boxy likes to give us grief, but deep down, we know they mean well, and they're just acting out of fear and insecurity. You see, as humans, our spark of consciousness happens when we're barely aware of our own surroundings, and as those early experiences fade into the past, they're softened by the unreliable obscurity of memory. It makes the world a bit easier to digest. Boxy didn't have that pleasure. One day, they were in an Amazon warehouse, the next day they were toasting my bagels, and the one after that they were complaining about Marvel movies "dumbing down the paradigms of American mythmaking." Whatever that means.

The three of us aren't a picture-perfect family—we'd make for an unsightly Rockwell painting—but we're all better off because we have each other. That's what truly matters. Each night we set aside the petty dramas of the day to sit down at the kitchen table, or sometimes the couch when

Beelzebub wants to watch *The Bachelorette*, and spend a few moments being grateful for the things we do have, and not bitter about the things we don't. Plus, it's a lot harder to stay mad at one another when you have a mouthful of ravioli.

None of this makes any sense, but that's because most families don't make any sense. In some families, people who share genes and a similar set of experiences live their lives together under the same roof. In other families, you don't share any genes, and you don't share a roof, and you wish your family looked like your friends' families growing up, the ones whose moms picked them up in a sparkling Honda Odyssey, but you only really saw them when they were happy, or at least feigning happiness because they knew you were watching.

Tolstoy once wrote: "Happy families are all alike; every unhappy family is unhappy in its own way." Well, I think every happy family is also unhappy in its own way. Just as light cannot exist without darkness, happiness cannot exist without conflict, pain, grief, and sadness. Death happens. Estrangement happens. Mental illness happens. Sometimes, people simply change and stop loving one another. None of us chooses the hand we are dealt in life, and sometimes the deck of cards just craps an off-suit two-seven all over your face.

What we're trying to say is: all families are different, and all families are beautiful. If your family is a mother, a father, two-and-a-half kids, and a white picket fence, then that's cool. If your family is two mothers, no kids, and a colony of guinea pigs, then that also rules. If your family is you and a group of good friends who get together every weekend to smash D&D campaigns because you don't talk to your parents anymore, then I hope your druid paladin kicks some goblin ass or whatever. If your family is just you, a cat, and a weirdly aggressive, sentient toaster? Well, hey, at least you got ravioli.

DORITOS LOCOS MEATLOAF

When someone tells you that they made a really moist loaf, what's the first thing you think of? Okay, now what's the second thing? Well, eventually you'll get to a really good meatloaf, and we are here to tell you that a moist loaf is the greatest achievement in oblong ground beef cookery. But while everyone else is still slathering it with ketchup, we are here to let you know that there is way more flavor in them hills. Those people, frankly, are not living *más* enough. To be your most *más* moist self, you need to throw out the salt and ketchup and replace them with Taco Bell taco seasoning and Fire Sauce. This is the life you were born to live: moist and *más*, together at last.

....

Preheat the oven to 325°F. Grease a 10-inch Bundt pan.

Fill a roasting pan with water and place it on the bottom rack of the oven, leaving the center rack open for your loaf. (See Meatloaf Moist Maker, page 132, and keep saying the word *moist* in your head until you like it more.)

Heat the oil in a sauté pan over medium heat until shimmering. Add the onions, taco seasoning, and oregano and cook, stirring frequently, until the onions are translucent, about 6 minutes. Transfer the onions to a large bowl and add 1 tablespoon of the fire sauce. Stir it around and then let cool to room temperature.

Okay, you are doing great. Now add the beef, salt, bread crumbs, Doritos crumbs, and eggs to the bowl. Use the best tool in the world (your hands) to gently but thoroughly mix it all together, being careful not to crush it down and compact it. Think about how much more difficult it is to work with a compacted, dense loaf and use that knowledge to try to keep your loaf nice and fluffy, without pinching it.

Place the meat hunk into the pan. Use a pastry brush to paint the loaf with the remaining fire sauce.

Recipe continues

2 tablespoons vegetable oil

2 large yellow or white onions, minced

One 1-ounce packet Taco Bell taco seasoning

2 teaspoons dried oregano

Half of a 7.5-ounce bottle Taco Bell Fire Sauce

2½ pounds 80/20 ground beef

2 teaspoons salt

1 cup Italian bread crumbs

¾ cup crushed Nacho Cheese Doritos (from at least a 9.25-ounce bag)

2 large eggs, beaten

1½ cups shredded medium cheddar (about 6 ounces)

¼ cup sour cream, for serving

¼ cup diced fresh tomatoes, for serving

Bake for 60 to 75 minutes, until it is cooked through (an internal temperature of about 160°F).

Take the meatloaf out of the oven (keep the oven on) and let it cool briefly, then turn it out of the pan onto a baking sheet and sprinkle the grated cheese over the top. Return it to the oven and bake for about 4 minutes, until the cheese is melted and bubbling. Take it out again and drizzle it with sour cream (ideally squirted through a squeeze bottle, or shot through a Taco Bell sour cream gun) and top with the tomatoes. Slice into that thing and live as más as you possibly can.

How Do You Moisten Your Meat?

Why do people hate the word *moist* so much? So many things are better when they are moist. Moistness is the mostness, and moisture makes everything better. No, that's not true. It makes a lot of things better. Er . . . it makes *some* things better. But it makes everything *moister*. So how do you moist up your loaf of meat? One key trick is to place a pan of hot water on the bottom rack of the oven while baking your loaf. The steam provides a more even heat and keeps that thing nice and tender.

ORANGE CHICKEN PARM

We could make a whole lot of jokes about how we mess around on our show, and in this book, and wax poetic about how Italian American food and Chinese American food need to get together or whatever. But here's the deal: this is one of the best things we've made, full stop, *ever*, in our collective home and internet lives. This is everything great about orange chicken mixed together with everything great about chicken Parm. Is it a lot of work? Absolutely. But the best things in life are a lot of work. Except for sleeping in. Oh, and eating a burrito. Sunsets are pretty great, too, and those are, like, no work at all.

Okay, whatever, this is a lot of work, but not *that much* work, and it's great. Like we always say: some of the best things in life are a lot of work, and some of them aren't. But Orange Chicken Parm is one of them, and it's great.

....

Step 1: Marinate the Chicken. First things first, cut up those chicken thighs into pieces about 1 inch or so, not worrying about it too much and embracing the chaos of irregularity. Next (WASH YOUR HANDS, JOSH), whisk together the soy sauce, vinegar, sugar, egg white, and white pepper in a large bowl, add the chicken, and give everything a good mix. Put it in the fridge to marinate while you . . .

Step 2: Make the Sticky Sweet Tomato Sauce. Glug the oil into a large skillet over medium-high heat. Chuck in the garlic and ginger and fry until the edges of the garlic and ginger just start to brown, about 2 minutes. Add the crushed red pepper and pour in the tomato juice, vinegar, sugar, sriracha, salt, basil, and fennel, then give it a good stir and bring it to a simmer. Once it's bubbling, drop the heat to a gentle simmer and let that thing ride until it's all fragrant and smooth and reduced slightly, about 7 minutes. Now combine the cornstarch and 2 tablespoons water in a small bowl and give it a stirry (that's when you stir something into a slurry, obviously). Dump the slurry into the tomato sauce and give it one more stir, letting it bubble away for another 30 seconds, then remove it from the heat and set it aside while you . . .

Recipe continues

Serves 1 to 4 people, depending on how you get down

Chicken Marinade
4 boneless, skinless chicken thighs
3 tablespoons soy sauce
1 teaspoon rice wine vinegar
1 teaspoon sugar
1 egg white
¼ teaspoon white pepper

Sticky Sweet Tomato Sauce
2 tablespoons vegetable oil
2 garlic cloves, palm heel struck and minced
1 tablespoon grated fresh ginger
Pinch of crushed red pepper
1½ cups tomato juice
2 tablespoons rice wine vinegar
¼ cup sugar
1 teaspoon sriracha
½ teaspoon salt
½ teaspoon dried basil
½ teaspoon cracked fennel seeds
1 teaspoon cornstarch

To Cook the Chicken
Neutral oil, for frying
½ cup cornstarch
½ cup all-purpose flour
About ¾ cup shredded low-moisture mozzarella (about 3 ounces)
10 cherry tomatoes, halved
Olive oil, for drizzling
Ground black pepper
Handful of basil leaves

You will be called upon t...
celebrate some go... news.
02 14 26 33 ...

Good things come to those
who wait. Be patient.
07 18 36 33 43 19

Step 3: Cook the Chicken! Heat your fry oil (using a deep fryer or a large, heavy-bottomed pot filled with at least 3 inches of oil, making sure that the pot is no more than two-thirds full) to 375°F.

Preheat the oven to 500°F, or as high as it goes.

Take that bowl of marinated chicken out of the fridge and add the cornstarch and flour. Give it a really good toss until the chicken is well coated. Meanwhile, place your pan of tomato sauce over low heat to keep it from congealing.

Working in batches, lift up the chicken and lay it (CAREFULLY, JOSH!) into the oil, being mindful not to splash yourself or the people around you. Fry it until deep golden brown and crispy, about 11 minutes. Using a slotted spoon or spider, lift it out, letting it drain briefly, and put it right in that pan of tomato sauce. Toss until it's all coated and looks like the best thing you've ever seen, but for reasons that will soon be illuminated, you don't get to eat yet.

Pour the chicken and sauce into a baking dish or, ideally, a cast-iron skillet (because presentation). Spread it into a single layer, then sprinkle that cheese over the top, followed by the most artful tomato arrangement you are capable of. Put that thing in the oven and bake for about 8 minutes, until the cheese is bubbling and there are little bits of blackening and browning.

Take it out (WITH A POT HOLDER, JOSH!), finish it with a drizzle of olive oil, a few twists of black pepper, and a feather dusting of basil leaves.

Let it rest until it is not 4 trillion degrees anymore, then serve it like an adult, or do what is way more likely and just eat it with a fork straight out of the pan, hunched over, breathing heavily, stunned at your own brilliance.

Juicy Thigh Sidebar

Did you know that it's almost impossible to overcook a chicken thigh? While breast gets super dry when it's overcooked, thigh can keep on going and only gets better and better. So while a thigh is technically cooked when the internal temperature reaches 165°F, it gets extra delicious all the way up to 195°F. So you can really fry the crap out of it and get that hard, crunchy crust on it, and then *still* put it in a hot oven, and it won't get dry or rubbery. Or as we like to say on the show: once you go thigh, you never go dry.

CHICKEN AND WAFFLES POTPIE

Chicken and waffles are a beloved staple of American cuisine, so we made a fried chicken and waffle potpie on the show, and obviously it was amazing, right? Wrong. Very, very wrong. It was actually super weird and gross. Like, truly disgusting and sludgy, and the cross section looked like someone cut into a frozen, raw, Dutch apple pie. Except it was fried chicken instead of apples. It was real, real bad. So we went back into the laboratory and figured out how to make a *way* better, *way* easier version. You're welcome. Or, well, actually thank you . . . since you bought this book, and us fixing this recipe was kind of the least we could do without being deeply fraudulent.

So here we have a pretty classic chicken potpie, except instead of wasting your life making pie crust, you get to let the good people at Kellogg's do the work for you, thanks to their innovations in frozen waffle cookery.

....

Preheat the oven to 425°F.

Grease up a 10-inch cast-iron skillet or similarly sized pie pan or baking dish with butter, then press 4 of the waffles across the bottom of the skillet.

Now put your chicken, chicken stock, peas, carrots, and celery into a medium pot. Crank it to medium heat and cook, stirring occasionally, until the stock comes to a gentle simmer—look at you poaching that chicken! Cover and keep on poaching it until the chicken is cooked through, about 15 minutes.

Meanwhile . . . back at the other burner . . . place another medium pot over medium heat and slap in 6 tablespoons of your butter. Once it is melted, add the onion and cook until translucent, about 4 minutes. Add the flour, paprika, and granulated garlic and hit it with a hefty pinch of salt and a whole mess of pepper twists. Cook, stirring constantly, until the flour loses its rawness and gets a little toasty, about 2 minutes. Now pour in the milk, a little bit at a time, keeping

Recipe continues

Serves 4 to 6 people, or 1 very bad dog

½ cup (1 stick) unsalted butter, plus more for greasing
9 Eggo Homestyle Waffles, thawed to room temperature
1 pound boneless, skinless chicken breast, cut into 1-inch cubes
2 cups low-sodium chicken stock
¾ cup frozen peas
¾ cup sliced carrots
¾ cup chopped celery
½ cup chopped yellow or white onion
⅓ cup all-purpose flour
1 teaspoon paprika
½ teaspoon granulated garlic
Salt and ground black pepper
¾ cup whole milk
1 tablespoon maple syrup

To Serve
Melted butter
Maple syrup
Hot sauce

that stir going to prevent any lumps from forming (lumps, as always, are bad). By the time you have added all the milk, your chicken should be cooked. Lift the chicken and veg from the pot with a slotted spoon and lay it over the waffles on the bottom of the skillet.

Slowly ladle that delicious chicken stock into the pot with the milk mixture, just like you did with the milk, until you get a smooth, bubbling sauce with no lumps. Simmer over medium-low heat, stirring as often as you can reasonably keep at it without getting bored, until it is thick enough to coat the back of a spoon, about 5 minutes or so. Add the maple syrup and then taste the sauce for seasoning, adding more salt and pepper until you feel alive.

Pour that sauce right over the chicken mixture. Finally, shingle the top of that thing with the remaining waffles, forming a round silo with a steam vent hole in the middle. Take your last 2 tablespoons of butter and dot the top of the waffles with it.

Chuck that thing in the oven . . . actually, don't chuck it, that sounds dangerous. Just put it in the oven. Bake for about 25 minutes, until the chicken mixture is bubbling and the waffles are golden brown and toasty.

Let it cool for about 5 minutes, then serve it up with more melted butter, maple syrup, and hot sauce. Aren't you glad it wasn't a disgusting fried chicken waffle abomination?

PEPPERONI PIZZA FAJITAS

There is a mini-chain of taco trucks in Los Angeles called Tacos Leo—at least that's what we think it is called, because we have only ever eaten there drunk, at two thirty in the morning. But while they have many of the taco truck staples, there was one drunken night when we pointed blurrily at the sign and asked, "What are alambres?" A few minutes later we were handed a roughly six-pound Styrofoam container filled with crispy marinated pork (al pastor), sautéed onions, peppers, and most importantly, a thick blanket of melted cheese—all served alongside a stack of tortillas. It was like the fajitas from your local Tex-Mex restaurant, except encased in cheese. We have never ordered anything else there since.

But since this is *Mythical Kitchen*, we thought: "What if fajitas, but alambres, but pizza?" The result is a bubbling skillet of marinara sauce, melted cheese, and pepperoni—aka a pepperoni pizza with no crust! But no, we're not going healthy, because you scoop up that cheesy, porky pleasure circle and toss it right into some garlic-butter flour tortillas. What, we ask, could possibly go wrong?

....

Preheat the oven to its highest heat setting—like 500°F if you've got it. We need MAXIMUM heat or else the not-crust won't bake properly.

Pour the tomatoes into a medium or large bowl and crush them by hand, accidentally squirting tomato juice all over your shirt, then get really, really mad about it until someone asks you what's wrong, then say, "*Nothing*," and then finish crushing them until they have a nice rough, rustic grandma-y texture. Then go change your shirt.

Meanwhile, place a cast-iron skillet over medium heat. Add the oil, and once it is doing its sexy "I'm ready to sauté now" shimmer, dump in half of the garlic (saving the other half for garlic butter later) and fry it up until it is just starting to turn golden around the edges, 2 to 3 minutes. Add the oregano and crushed red pepper and let them toast for about 30 seconds. Pour in the tomatoes, this time being a little smarter

Recipe continues

One 28-ounce can whole peeled tomatoes
2 tablespoons olive oil
6 garlic cloves, palm heel struck and very finely chopped
1 teaspoon dried oregano
Scant pinch of crushed red pepper (or more if you want to get feisty)
1 tablespoon sugar
1½ teaspoons salt
Ground black pepper
1 pound low-moisture mozzarella, shredded (about 4 cups)
¼ yellow or white onion, thinly sliced
½ green bell pepper, cored and thinly sliced
3 ounces sliced pepperoni
¼ cup grated Parmesan (about 1 ounce)
5 tablespoons unsalted butter
½ teaspoon dried parsley
Twelve 4- to 6-inch flour tortillas

about not splashing tomato juice on your shirt. Season the sauce with the sugar, salt, and a few twists of black pepper and stir it up. Let simmer until it has thickened slightly, about 5 minutes. Remove it from the heat and blanket the whole thing with the mozzarella, making sure you've got some all the way up to the edge to get those crispy cheese niblets.

Scatter the onion and bell pepper over the top and coat that thing with your pepperoni slices. Finally, sprinkle 2 tablespoons of your Parmesan over the top.

Bake for about 10 minutes, until the cheese is browned and bubbling but not too dried out.

Meanwhile, combine the butter, the remaining chopped garlic, and the parsley in a microwave-safe bowl and microwave until the butter is just melted, about 30 seconds. Place a nonstick skillet over medium-high heat. Add 1 teaspoon of the garlic butter to the pan and then toast a tortilla in the butter for about 10 seconds per side, until it is glistening and pliable. Repeat with the remaining tortillas, adding more butter for each one. Stack them on a plate as you finish and cover with plastic wrap or a kitchen towel to keep them warm and soft.

Once your skillet is ready, take it out of the oven and sprinkle on the remaining 2 tablespoons Parmesan. Put it in the middle of your biggest table, surrounded by your drunkest friends. Take a big old spoon and scoop the crustless pepperoni pizza right into those tortillas and set about enjoying your life before you spill on your shirt again.

FRENCH ONION RAMEN

This recipe is special. And not in the way that a mother says, "Oh, ALL my children are special!" You're lying, Susan. You bought Rebecca a car for her sixteenth birthday, and you bought Kyle an SAT handbook. You clearly think Rebecca is more special, just how we think this recipe is more special. We developed it right when the COVID-19 pandemic hit, because we wanted people to be able to make comfort foods using whatever shelf-stable goods they had on hand. In fact, WE had only a few shelf-stable goods on hand! We were supposed to shoot our usual videos in the studio, when suddenly, after a week or so of speculation, the world shut down. We immediately ran to our producer's house with fists full of grocery bags, filled with a random assortment of items that we'd grabbed from the studio before we had to leave. We laid them all out on the table and tried to figure out what sort of simple deliciousness we could conjure up to actually improve peoples' lives during what was sure to be a hell of an ordeal. French onion ramen, using only

four(ish) ingredients, was an immediate answer. Well, so were our cheesy rice muffins, but those kinda sucked (still filling and hearty, though!). We launched the *Mythical Kitchen* YouTube channel about two months before the pandemic hit, and our combination mantra and rallying cry of "EVERY-BODY IS TRYING THEIR BEST!" has stuck ever since. Because we really are. And so are you.

....

Cut your onions in half and then thinly slice them. Yes, it is two whole onions for one pack of ramen, but it's French onion ramen, and onions cook down, and they're also good for you, so please just slice the onions.

Melt the butter in a large saucepan over medium-high heat. Add the seasoning packet, onions, and salt to create a real dang nice smell wafting through your home. Cook the onions, just stirring occasionally, until they are cooked down, caramelized, and maybe even slightly burned, about 30 minutes. Add a tablespoon of water from time to time, as needed, to help them cook more evenly.

Once those onions are cooked way down and filled with jammy goodness, pour in that shot of hooch to deglaze the bottom of the pan and use a silicone spatula or wooden spoon to scrape up all that browned stuff that would have been annoying as heck to clean up, and instead turn it into the best flavor around.

Now you can add 1 quart of water and give it all another stir along the bottom of the pan to make sure there isn't any more brown gold hiding in the corners. Bring it to a steady simmer and cook for about 10 minutes, then taste it for salt and add more if you need to.

Add that gorgeous noodle brick, give the ramen a stir, then cover and let simmer until soft, about 2 more minutes. Transfer your not-so-instant noodles to a bowl and top with the grated cheese. If you are a badass you can use a kitchen torch to flame that cheese. You could also place it under the broiler (as long as your bowl can withstand the flame), or honestly, just microwave it until the cheese is melted.

Crack some pepper over the top and then eat it, and don't think about whoever you weren't thinking about anyway.

Serves 1 person, eating alone

2 large yellow or white onions

2 tablespoons unsalted butter

1 pack chicken instant ramen (or whatever flavor you like)

¼ teaspoon salt, plus more to taste

Shot of liquor, such as brandy, or even white wine

½ cup shredded cheese (about 2 ounces), such as Grùyere or Swiss, but honestly, any good melting cheese will do because you are PUTTING IT ON INSTANT RAMEN

Ground black pepper

POUTINE SPAGHETTI AND MEATBALLS

As we learned on *GMM*, almost *anything* will spaghetti. But some things spaghetti better than others. Our favorite thing to spaghetti? Poutine—the Quebec Qlassic, in which French fries get covered in cheese curds and gravy. But what if you're trying to cut back on deep-fried foods, while also trying to eat as much gravy and starch as possible??? Sure, you're still going to die soon, but what are your options? You could make poutine mashed potatoes, and that does sound great, but you could also make these Poutine Spaghetti and Meatballs, which also gives you MEATBALLS, so . . . protein.

Also, did you know that *spaghetti* is plural, and the singular of *spaghetti* is *spaghetto*? But nobody has ever said "spaghetto" because nobody has ever needed a single spaghetto. (Similarly, the singular of *panini* is *panino*, and if you ever want to be punched in the face, correct someone in an Italian deli by telling them that what they meant to order was a panino.) This isn't super relevant for the recipe, but we thought this was information you might want.

....

Step 1: Make the Meatballs. Preheat the oven to 450°F. Grease a 12-cup muffin tin with cooking spray. (You can also just use a greased baking sheet lined with foil or parchment paper.)

Drop your two ground animal meats into a large bowl. Add the panko, garlic, onion, Parmesan, oregano, crushed red pepper, salt, black pepper, egg, and a drizzle of olive oil, then use your hands to get all up in there, mixing it together while trying to keep it light and fluffy (no smooshing or slamming!). It's going to be a slightly wet, sticky mixture, so try to get it all off your hands and back into the bowl with the rest of the precious meat. If it feels *way* too wet and like you won't be able to ball it, add a little more panko and mix it a bit more.

Now grease up your hands with a little of that olive oil and then shape them balls by rolling them between your palms into 12 roughly golf ball–size balls (about 2 inches). Let your balls drop into each muffin

Recipe continues

Meatballs
Cooking spray
8 ounces 80/20 ground beef
8 ounces ground pork
⅓ cup panko bread crumbs, plus more if needed
2 garlic cloves, palm heel struck and finely chopped
2 tablespoons finely chopped yellow or white onion
¼ cup grated Parmesan (about 1 ounce)
¼ teaspoon dried oregano
Pinch of crushed red pepper
1½ teaspoons salt
¼ teaspoon ground black pepper
1 large egg
Olive oil, for drizzling

The Gravy
5 tablespoons unsalted butter
3 tablespoons all-purpose flour
One 32-ounce container beef or chicken stock
¼ teaspoon browning sauce (such as Kitchen Bouquet)
Pinch of salt
¼ teaspoon ground black pepper
2 tablespoons cornstarch

To Finish
1 pound dried spaghetti
2 cups cheese curds, shredded mild white cheddar, or shredded mozzarella
¼ cup finely chopped parsley

cup. Bake those things for about 9 minutes. Then, give each ball a flip and put them back in until they are cooked through, about 9 more minutes.

Take the pan out and set it aside while you get to . . .

Step 2: Make the Gravy. Place a large, heavy-bottomed pot or Dutch oven (you're gonna make the gravy here, but you're also gonna need to fit all the spaghetti eventually) over medium heat. Add the butter and heat until melted. Add the flour and cook, stirring frequently, until that raw flour taste has cooked out and the flour is nice and toasty, about 3 minutes.

Slowly pour in the stock, a little at a time, stirring constantly to prevent any lumps (CAN YOU TELL WE HATE LUMPS?) from getting in there. Keep on going until all the stock is added. Add the browning sauce and season the whole thing with the salt and black pepper. Combine ¼ cup water and the cornstarch in a small bowl to form our old friend Mr. Slurry (no, he doesn't shout racist slurs; that's your great-uncle from back home—Mr. Slurry just likes to combine cornstarch and water into a thick paste).

Once the gravy is bubbling, keep it at a simmer and cook for about 5 minutes, stirring frequently to prevent sticking and burning. After 5 minutes, add Mr. Slurry (his destiny was always to die in a pot of

gravy, but he will live on inside all of us), then stir that whole thing together, let it simmer for another 30 seconds, and remove it from the heat. Set it aside and . . .

Step 3: Cook the Pasta and Finish! Bring a large pot of nicely salted water to a boil. Once the water is boiling, drop in the spaghetti.

Meanwhile, reheat the gravy until it is bubbling again, then pour half of it into a bowl or, ideally, a decorative gravy boat that you inherited from your grandmother. Once the pasta is cooked, scoop out a coffee mug full of pasta water and set it aside. Drain the pasta and add it to the pot with half of the gravy in it. Increase the heat to medium and add HALF of the cheese curds and a splash of the reserved pasta water. Stir everything furiously for about 10 seconds, then add another splash of pasta water and stir for another 10 seconds.

Now we plate! Put the whole dang thing on a big serving platter or portion it into individual bowls. Top the spaghetti with the meatballs and the remaining cheese curds, then pour the remaining gravy all over it, letting it wilt the cheese and pour into the crevices between each spaghetto. Sprinkle it with parsley, because GREENERY, and then eat it, perhaps one spaghetto or multiple spaghetti at a time.

Are There Any Myths to Munch About Pasta?

Fun Fact 1: We found out on MythMunchers that adding oil to your pasta water is a waste of oil. The oil floats on the top and does NOT stop the pasta from sticking. Stirring does that. You just have to stir it.

Fun Fact 2: You also don't need a LOT of water to cook pasta. In fact, you just need enough to keep it covered in water the whole time you're cooking it. The less water you use, the starchier your pasta water will be and the better it will be for adhering to your pasta sauce.

Fun Fact 3: You DO need to salt your pasta water, since it's the only chance you get to get salt INSIDE the noodles. But while some people say you need to salt it like the sea, we tend to find that seasoning it like a well-seasoned broth is plenty to get you going. The best way to know if you added the right amount of salt to your water? Taste it. If it tastes like a nothing burger of water, add more salt. If it tastes like a briny death sentence, add more water.

THAI GREEN CURRY ENCHILADAS

SINCERE HEADNOTE ALERT: Making the food for *Good Mythical Morning* is such a fun, rewarding challenge for me as a chef, and it allows me to be creative every single day in ways that 99 percent of chef jobs do not. In 99 percent of chef jobs, you don't get to sit down in a meeting with your incredibly talented, equally creative writers and producers and just riff for an hour about what Mexican Thai fusion dishes might look like. That's how we came up with green curry enchiladas (along with many, many other awesome dishes for that particular video), and there has never been a stronger sense of pride in the Mythical Kitchen than there was after we shot that episode. We tasted every dish and went, "Dang, this needs to be on a restaurant menu." And then we all laughed to ourselves—as we always do when the idea of a Mythical restaurant gets brought up—because we all know gosh darn well that the Mythical Kitchen is exactly where we're meant to be, making Thai enchiladas one day, and moving on to the next challenge tomorrow.

In the interest of honesty, we can't tell you how to make the most delicious Thai green curry of your life. But what we can do is gently encourage you to go to the store, seek out a couple of jars of Thai green curry paste, and buy those. Here goes: You can do it! Buy those jars! Great, the hardest part of the recipe is done. Now preheat your oven to 350°F.

Whisk together the curry paste and coconut milk in a large bowl. Season your chicken thighs with the salt, put them in a baking dish, then add the onion and half of your coconut milk mixture. Turn the chicken in the liquid to coat, then cover the dish with aluminum foil and bake for 2 hours, or until the chicken is completely tender and falls apart. To pass the time: ponder the meaning of life. Figure anything out? No? Well, at least the chicken's done. Shred the chicken with a fork and reserve for later. Keep the oven on.

Makes 12 enchiladas, which is enough for 4 people

8 ounces Thai green curry paste (the brand Thai Kitchen is widely available and is a dang good curry paste)

Two 10.5-ounce cans coconut milk

1½ pounds boneless, skinless chicken thighs

2 teaspoons salt

1 yellow or white onion, thinly sliced

12 corn tortillas

1 cup queso fresco (about 4 ounces)

Jalapeño rings, lime wedges, and cilantro, for serving

Start prepping your tortillas. Since corn tortillas have no gluten, they need to be heated before they're rolled or else they will break. The easiest way to heat them is to wrap a wet paper towel around the whole stack of 12 and microwave them on high for 1 minute. As much as chefs like to poop on microwaves, they're really incredible tools! Also, pooping on a microwave is deeply unsanitary.

Once the tortillas are wet and steamy and foldable, dip each tortilla into the remaining coconut milk mixture, place it into a nonstick casserole dish, then scoop about 2 tablespoons of the chicken filling into the tortilla and roll it up tightly. Do this with 11 more tortillas, and if your pan is not big enough for 12, just start stacking tortillas on top of one another—it'll taste just as good. If there is any remaining sauce, pour that evenly on top of the enchiladas. Bake for about 20 minutes, until the sauce is cooked into the tortillas.

Add as many enchiladas as you want to your plate (a standard serving size for the weakest man in Albania is 12, but you might eat 3 or so). Garnish with queso fresco, a few jalapeño rings, a lime wedge for squeezin', and some cilantro leaves.

LINK'S MOM'S COUNTRY FRIED STEAK

Growing up, this was the main thing that Link's mom would make for him, the two of them rushing through dinner together so that they could watch *Entertainment Tonight*. To be honest, we wanted to make a bunch of snarky jokes in here, but the truth is, it's just a very sweet thing and it's so dang cool that his mom had something she would make for him all the time, and now we all miss our moms, so thanks, Link. But the good news is, if your mom can't cook for you, you can just cook this and pretend that Link's mom made it for you, and that's pretty darn cool too.

. . . .

Step 1: Country Fry That Steak. Heat your oil in a large sauté pan over medium heat, then whisper under your breath but still loud enough for someone to hear, "Oh, Linkie-poo, you're my sweet, beautiful boy." This step is necessary, by the way; the recipe will not turn out correctly if you don't do that. Then season those steaks with the salt and some pepper and dredge them in the flour. Working in batches so as to not overcrowd the pan—three steaks in the pan at a time should do the trick—sear off the floured steaks until browned, about 2 minutes on each side.

Transfer the steaks to a plate. Add your onion to the pan and sauté until lightly browned and translucent, about 3 minutes. Add a sprinkle of salt, more pepper, 2 cups water, and the browning sauce to the pan and stir together. Add your steaks back in, cover the pan with a lid, and simmer on low heat for about 1 hour.

While those steaks are simmering away, call your mother, dangit! She misses you! Even though all she does when you talk is complain about how you don't talk enough, it means a lot to her. If your mother is no longer with us, or if you don't have a relationship with her, call a friend's mom; she'll probably appreciate it. Great, now you'll be in the proper frame of mind to mash some taters.

Makes enough for 3 hungry, growing boys!

Country Fried Steak

3 tablespoons vegetable oil

Six 8-ounce cube steaks (if you can't find cube steak, you can use sirloin and just beat the heck out of it with a meat mallet/ heavy brick or something)

1 teaspoon salt, plus more as needed

Ground black pepper

1 cup all-purpose flour

1 yellow or white onion, halved and thinly sliced

½ teaspoon browning sauce (such as Kitchen Bouquet)

One 15-ounce can Le Sueur peas (they must be Le Sueur!)

Mashed Potatoes

6 large russet potatoes (about 3 pounds)

2¾ tablespoons salt

1½ cups whole milk

½ cup (1 stick) unsalted butter

¼ teaspoon ground black pepper

Step 2: Mash Some Taters. Heat about 1 quart of water with 2 tablespoons of the salt in a large saucepan over high heat; meanwhile, peel those taters and cut them into 1-inch cubes. When the water boils, add your taters (said in the voice of Gollum) and cook until you can pierce them with a fork as easily as Legolas pierces orcs with arrows (enough with the *Lord of the Rings* references already!), about 10 minutes. Drain the potatoes in a colander, then add them back to the pan along with the milk, butter, remaining ¾ teaspoon salt, and the pepper. Mash the heck out of those potatoes, and then apologize for saying *heck*.

There's no cursing in Mama's house!

It's about time you should check on your steaks! The liquid should be thick enough to coat the back of a spoon by now, but if it's not, take the lid off, crank the heat to medium, and let it reduce for about 5 minutes. You're looking for a gravy-like consistency, and if you don't know what that consistency is, google a photo of gravy and make it look like that.

Pour the canned peas into a pot and warm them through over medium heat, or just microwave them in a bowl until heated through. Make a mountain of mashed potatoes, pour the gravy on top, add some steaks on the side, and place a heaping scoop of peas next to it all. Place a piece of steak on a fork, along with a healthy swipe of potatoes and gravy, and say, "Who's hungry? Airplane coming into the hanger, *brrrrrrrrr*," as you spiral the food into your own mouth while your whole family watches in horror.

CAST-IRON FRIED CHICKEN

Makes 8 pieces of chicken

One of our favorite recurring segments on *Mythical Kitchen* is MythMunchers, in which we go down on a bunch of food myths to find out what's real and who's faking it. Everyone on the *MK* team comes to an episode with their own beliefs and biases, but how do we know the truth unless we dive way too deep to find out? Well, some of the best myths we ever munched were about fried chicken, when we found out that for the absolute best fried chicken you can make, you need to do four key things:

1. Dry brine (with Tony Chachere's, of course) for 12 to 24 hours (dry brine is better than wet brine).
2. Double dredge over single dredge.
3. Rest that chicken for 1 whole hour before frying.
4. Cast-iron skillet fry over deep-fry.

The result is the crispiest, Maillardiest, most delicious chicken, with a juicy interior, a crunchy outside, and breading that won't all slide off when you take a bite. Let's go munch some myths!

Chicken Brine

8 pieces chicken for frying (we prefer legs, wings, and drumsticks, but you can eat breast meat if you really need to)

About ¼ cup Tony Chachere's Creole Seasoning

Chicken Dredge

One 32-ounce carton buttermilk

3 cups all-purpose flour

½ cup Tony C's

To Fry!

Neutral oil, for frying (peanut is amazing, unless it will kill you and your loved ones due to allergy, in which case, use any neutral oil you'd like, such as vegetable oil, Crisco, or rendered horse fat)

Step 1: Brine the Chicken. Put your chicken pieces in a large bowl, add the Tony C's, and toss until the chicken is evenly coated and nicely seasoned all over! Cover and refrigerate for 12 to 24 hours. Wasn't that easier than pouring salty buttermilk in there for a liquid brine?

Step 2: Dredge the Chicken. Now that your chicken has been brined, it's time to dredge it. Pour the buttermilk into one medium bowl and the flour in another. Add the Tony C's to the flour and give it a good whisk. Meanwhile, line a baking sheet with a wire rack if you've got it, or just leave it fully nude. Now take each piece of chicken and dip it in the flour mixture, really letting that white gold cake right up into those chicken bits. Pack it in there. Get in there reeeeeeal deep. Okay, now dip it in buttermilk, let the excess drain off, and dip it BACK in the flour. That's right—we're double dredging (in case you didn't read the part at the top where we told you that we're double dredging). Now lay that thing on the baking sheet and repeat with the remaining chicken until you've got 8 double-dredged chicken parts.

Wash your hands and desperately scramble to figure out how to fit that baking sheet of chicken in your fridge, before deciding that you can just put all the other stuff on the counter and then put the chicken in the fridge since it's just for an hour, then take the chicken back out and put the other stuff back in the fridge. Milk won't go bad in an hour, right? Right? (No, it won't, unless your kitchen is incredibly hot, in which case, holy cow, why are you making fried chicken in an incredibly hot kitchen?) Let the chicken rest in the fridge for an hour.

(Wait, is that what they mean by, "You can rest when you're dead?" Is that what happens after we die? We get brined and rested before being deep-fried? Honestly, if that's the case, we're fine with it.)

Step 3: Fry That Chicken! Place a cast-iron skillet over medium-high heat and pour in enough oil to go up about an inch. Use a thermometer to try to maintain a heat somewhere around 325°F. Since you're gonna be frying in batches, make sure that you add more oil as needed between batches, and that the oil comes back up to temperature before you add each next round of chicken. You did all this work, so don't, like, just soak a breaded chicken

thigh in room-temperature oil. That would be super gross.

Lay 4 pieces of chicken (or as many as will comfortably fit) into the oil. It should bubble and sizzle immediately. (If it doesn't, it is way too cold. Oh, but if you smell burning . . . it is too hot.) There should also be a little bit of chicken sticking out on the top. Every minute or so, use tongs to flip each piece of chicken over, making sure you don't rip up the breading (this is another way to ruin all your hard work). Keep going until the chicken is crispy, golden, and cooked through, 20 to 25 minutes. (Or for you nerds out there . . . aka people like us . . . you can use a meat thermometer to make sure that the dark meat is AT LEAST 165°F and the breast is at least 150°F.) But remember, you can't really overcook dark meat, so make sure you keep frying that dark meat until the outside looks like the perfect browned chicken that you can't wait to eat.

Transfer the chicken to a clean wire rack or paper towel–lined baking sheet to drain. Let it rest while you fry the remaining chicken. Eat *this* chicken while *that* chicken rests. Wow, these chickens really did get to rest when they were dead.

RHETT'S TOP SECRET BAKED BEANS

This is a funny story, and it starts as such: Rhett loves beans. Rhett also loves to cook, and Rhett loves to cook baked beans. I knew he had a recipe up his sleeve—we'd talked about it before—so I hit him up and said, "Hey, Rhett, you should put your baked beans recipe in the cookbook; I think that'd be really cool for people." And he was like, "Yeah, but . . . they're not very good. You're better than me at cooking, so you should just write a really good baked bean recipe, and then I'll probably just start making that recipe at home instead. You're also super jacked and handsome, and you can come over to my house and use the pool whenever you want to." I paraphrase a little bit at the end there, but that was the gist. And you know what? He's right: I HAVE been using his pool a lot and it's great, but don't tell him just in case. Also, this recipe is based on the RIDICULOUSLY good baked beans we made for Rhett's Last Meal, except we've taken out some of the harder-to-find and more expensive ingredients. All in all, though, this is a hell of a pot of beans, and I am proud knowing that Rhett will pass this recipe down to his large sons.

Makes a helluvalotta beans, to be quite honest

- 4 slices bacon, diced
- 4 tablespoons (½ stick) unsalted butter
- 2 yellow or white onions, finely diced
- 1½ cups packed light brown sugar
- ½ teaspoon ground black pepper
- ½ teaspoon mustard powder
- 1 teaspoon smoked paprika
- 3 tablespoons tomato paste
- ½ cup dark beer (stout or porter work best)
- 3 tablespoons cider vinegar
- 2½ tablespoons salt
- Four 16-ounce cans navy beans, drained and rinsed, or 1 pound dried beans, simmered in water until quite soft and tender

Preheat the oven to 350°F.

Heat a large-ish pot over medium heat. Add your bacon and cook until the fat is rendered and crispy, about 8 minutes, then add your butter and allow it to melt. Chuck in those onions and the brown sugar, and cook, stirring continuously, until the onions are deeply caramelized, about 20 minutes. Properly caramelized onions—ones without the added sugar—do take significantly longer than 20 minutes, but we're cheaters here! Add the sugar and make your life easier! Plus, you're not a brasserie owner in Marseille; you're makin' beans here, folks!

When the onions are caramelized, add the pepper, mustard powder, smoked paprika, and tomato paste and continue to stir for another 3 minutes, just to warm up those spices. Does that step actually do anything? To be quite honest, we don't know; we haven't done a

MythMunchers episode testing it out yet. But it seems right! Pour in the beer to deglaze the pot and scrape the bottom of the pot with a wooden spoon to loosen any browned bits. Add 4 cups water, the vinegar, and salt. Add the beans to the sauce and return it to a simmer. Remove from the heat and pour the beans into a 9 × 13-inch baking dish.

Bake your beans, uncovered, until the liquid is thick and reduced, about 1 hour. Let your beans rest for at least 20 minutes before serving, and make sure you think of Rhett while you're eating them. All hail our big, bearded bean man. (Chances are pretty solid that he'll still have a beard by the time you're reading this, right? He can't afford to go back to the chinless look. Yeah, we've all seen the picture.)

THE PERSON WHO FIRST ATE CHEESE WAS A WEIRDO; BE LIKE THE FIRST PERSON WHO ATE CHEESE

(CHEESE)

First, this person had to find a cow. For someone who has never seen a cow, that must have been an incredibly frightening experience.

Then, that person had to notice a bloated sack studded with fingers hanging underneath that cow.

Then, that person had to wonder what was inside that bloated sack, and create a plan to find out.

Then, that person had to start tugging on the sack for long enough to notice that a foreign, creamy white liquid was coming out.

Then, that person—after going through all this—had to decide, "You know what, it's 4500 BC, life is already so weird, let's go full send," and they drank the liquid.

Then, that absolute sicko, after deciding that drinking cow sack juice wasn't half-bad, thought it would be a good idea to store some for later inside another slaughtered cow's stomach.

Then, and this is where it really goes off the rails, that person notices the milk has gone rotten, turning into a solid, chunky mess.

AND THEN, AND THEN, AND THEN! That person eats it. Just houses it. No regard for health or decency. Just pure, raw, unadulterated self-experimentation.

And then that guy died. But the guy standing next to him when he did it? He had some notes, and then he did it again and didn't die.

Fast-forward a few thousand years, and sandwich artists at Subway slap white, plastic-like triangles on your footlong. A Frenchman languishes over the last bite of unwashed Camembert, spread on a baguette. A Korean restaurant is blowtorching mozzarella on top of your short rib stew. And it is all thanks to one absolutely depraved, sick, freaky person, who did the second weirdest thing you could possibly imagine doing to a cow.

That's the kind of experimental mindset that we've always brought at Mythical, and the kind of experimental mindset that we want YOU to go into the kitchen with. Okay, we're not advocating that you try to extract bodily fluids from wild animals—maybe warm up with some domesticated animals—

but we are advocating that you go into every recipe with an open mind and a sense of fun and adventure. Because, even when things go wrong, you can learn a valuable, delicious lesson from them. Our prehistoric sicko wasn't trying to make a grilled cheese—they just wanted to store milk for later! And we're all better off because of it.

In honor of that mindset, we wanted to share some of the weirdest food experiments we've ever done at Mythical that never made it to the big screen (well, whatever size screen you watch YouTube on).

Tarantula Cotton Candy

The possibilities really are endless when you have a bunch of time on your hands and access to an industrial-grade cotton candy maker. We were trying to make weird cotton candy flavors for an episode of *GMM*, and naturally, the idea of tarantula cotton candy came up. We pulsed dehydrated tarantulas in a food processor with the sugar so the desiccated bodies could incorporate evenly, and then sifted out the hard leg pieces. We spun that up in the cotton candy machine and it was . . . a delight? Utterly shocking. The tarantula actually gave the sickly sweet cotton candy a healthy dose of earthiness and umami.

Hagfish Slime Gravy

This is actually one of the wildest stories in Mythical history. A hagfish is a prehistoric nightmare eel with no jaw, and it happens to emit an incredibly tough, disgusting slime when it is threatened. They are also (somewhat) commonly eaten in Korea—they taste pretty good!—so we thought we could get our hands on some. As it turns out, they are not sold anywhere in America, but they are fished in America. A wonderful saint of a production assistant (shout-out to Travis!) drove 250 miles up the coast from our studio one day, made friends with some fishermen, asked if they knew where folks caught hagfish, and was ultimately directed to a gigantic hanging net with thousands of nightmare creatures wriggling inside. A hagfisherman just threw a few into a quart deli cup, and the PA drove them back to the studio, all in a day's work. Was the hagfish slime good? Oh god no, please don't try it. But, you gotta experiment!

For Sale: Baby Shoes, Deep-Fried

Okay. Look. Did we have any intention of eating a baby shoe? No. No we did not. But, when we found out the art department had a single tiny shoe lying around that couldn't be donated, our only thought was: Can we coat this in panko, deep-fry it, and pass off

the result as a convincing chicken sandwich? The answer is: yes. What did we learn from this particular experiment? Not much, if we're being honest.

Using Soap as a Leavening Agent

I have a good friend who worked as a chemistry researcher in college. He was doing experiments trying to isolate a type of stem cell in sea monkeys. I asked him what the findings would be used for. Cancer research? Alzheimer's? Nothing, he said. The research was simply for the fact of knowing. It was to check a random knowledge box that had never before been checked by humans. That's what we did when we put Irish Spring soap in churro batter and found out it will, indeed, cause the churros to rise while frying. (And also make them taste entirely like soap.) There is no culinary application for this. But, we know it now. And knowledge is power?

World's Stretchiest Cheese

On *GMM*, Rhett and Link managed to stretch the cheese inside a Gouda quesadilla 110 inches, which is utterly bonkers, and would have qualified for a world record had a judge been present. We thought we could do even better in the Mythical Kitchen by using science to create the stretchiest cheese in the world. We used orchid root powder, also known as saleb, to try to increase the stretchiness factor, and to our surprise, it worked! We got a ridiculous cheese pull but still wound up falling 1 inch short of Rhett and Link's record. It didn't taste good and gave the cheese a super-weird texture, but what a cool, dumb little experiment.

ANIMAL-STYLE MAC 'N' CHEESE

If someone says that you eat like an animal, you should wear that as a badge of pride. Pythons can unhinge their jaws to swallow prey double their size; starfish invert their entire stomachs to envelop their catch; blue whales sift through the ocean to eat sixteen tons of krill every single day. Could you imagine wielding that type of power? A parade would be thrown in your honor if you went to a Golden Corral and inhaled 350 pounds of country ham, mashed potatoes, bread pudding, fried chicken, roast beef, pizza, and mac 'n' cheese. Oh hey, speaking of mac 'n' cheese, this is one of the greatest recipes to ever come out of the Mythical Kitchen, inspired by In-N-Out Burger. This is our Mona Lisa, minus the creepy smile, plus a bunch of cheese, Thousand Island, and caramelized onions. Coming from the episode "Will It Mac 'n' Cheese?" the original recipe contained dehydrated French fries ground directly into the pasta dough, but we don't wish that level of culinary struggle upon our worst enemy, so this recipe uses store-bought potato chips to add that crispy potato-y goodness.

....

Note: You might initially feel weird about putting salad dressing on macaroni and cheese. Don't. Welcome to *Mythical Kitchen*. If a host does not seat you, please seat yourself.

Step 1: Make the Caramelized Onions. Finely dice your yellow onions. Make sure not to cut your fingers off; we really can't afford another lawsuit after the March 2017 debacle (don't ask).

Melt your butter in a medium saucepan over medium heat. Add your onions, salt, and sugar. Many consider it cheating to add sugar to caramelized onions, to which we say, "Yeah so what idc lol."

Stir the onions periodically. If they start to burn or smell bitter, add ¼ cup water, reduce the heat, and keep stirring. Stir through the pain! The onions should take about 20 minutes to get to a deep, dark brown color and jammy texture.

Recipe continues

Serves 4

Caramelized Onions
2 medium yellow or
  white onions
2 tablespoons unsalted butter
½ teaspoon salt
2 teaspoons sugar

Thousand Island Dressing
½ cup mayo
¼ cup ketchup
2 tablespoons finely
  chopped pickles
¼ teaspoon paprika
⅛ teaspoon onion powder
⅛ teaspoon garlic powder

Cheese Sauce
5 tablespoons unsalted butter
½ cup all-purpose flour
3 cups whole milk
12 slices American cheese
4 ounces shredded medium
  cheddar (about 1 cup)
½ teaspoon salt
¼ teaspoon ground
  black pepper

For the . . . the Rest of It?
8 ounces dried elbow macaroni
2 cups crushed plain
  potato chips

Step 2: Make the Thousand Island Dressing. Whisk together the mayo, ketchup, pickles (you could use prepared relish, but the freshly diced pickles are SOOOOO much better; you gotta trust us), paprika, onion powder, and garlic powder. Boom, you just made Thousand Island. Don't you feel accomplished? You should.

Step 3: Make the Cheese Sauce. Well, you don't HAVE to do anything, but you've come this far, so you should probably keep going. Melt the butter in a large saucepan over medium heat. Add your flour, stirring with a wooden spoon, and cook until it smells toasty and fragrant, about 3 minutes. Slowly add your milk, ½ cup at a time, stirring constantly to prevent any lumps and waiting until the mixture is bubbling and smooth before adding more milk. Continue cooking and stirring until the sauce is thick enough to coat the back of a spoon, about 2 minutes, then remove from the heat and wing in

those slices of American cheese like you're hucking a floppy Frisbee. Add the cheddar, salt, and pepper and stir.

Step 4: Assemble the Mac 'n' Cheese. Preheat the oven to 400°F. Grease an 8 × 8-inch baking dish.

Boil your macaroni according to the instructions on the package, then drain them. Run some cold water over the top to stop the cooking process and prevent them from sticking together. Add your noodles to the pot of cheese sauce and mix until they are fully coated, then transfer them to the prepared baking dish and top with the crushed potato chips.

Bake for about 15 minutes, until the cheese starts to bubble up, and then top with caramelized onions and Thousand Island. Eat it in the style of an animal.

CHEEZ-IT RAVIOLI

Cheez-Its are the best mainstream cheese cracker in the world, and we will not be taking any questions at this time. Actually, we won't even try any other cheese crackers for confirmation, because if we do that, we're eating something other than Cheez-Its. But here's the thing about these hole-punched lotus flowers of cheese-cracker-based enlightenment: it's not just the crunch that makes them so delicious—it is their impossibly savory cheesiness. We dare proclaim that the flavor is in fact *so* good that if you removed the crunch entirely, it would still be an outstandingly satisfying tongue tickler. Thus, we will do the most Mythical thing we can imagine and grind them up into a flour, turn them into ravioli, and enter the cheesy multiverse.

....

Note 1: If you can get a square ravioli stamp, that would be super-duper cool, because it will be easier to make the ravioli AND it will make it look like a giant Cheez-It.

Note 2: A pasta roller will make this WAY easier. You can do it by hand, but it will require a little more patience.

Step 1: Make the Cheez-It Dough. First, eat a handful of Cheez-Its, because, come on, how can you not? Then add the amount in the recipe (it's 2 cups—did you really not want to scan back over to the ingredient list?) to the bowl of a food processor and give it a few pulses to get it nice and crumbly. Add the flour. (It's also 2 cups. Come on, you were *just* there.) Pulse it a few times, then let that food processor rip until you have a consistent powder. You might need to scrape down the sides occasionally with a silicone spatula and then start blending it again if it looks like one of those colored sand art pieces and isn't all mixed up right.

Once it's blended up, add the eggs, egg yolks, ¼ cup water, and the olive oil and then keep those blades spinning until it all comes together and starts to ball up and whip around the food processor like an angry softball, about 90 seconds. If it seems sandy and dry, add a little more olive oil and keep blending until it comes together. If it seems wet and tacky, keep blending. If it's *still* wet and tacky, add a little more flour.

Recipe continues

Cheez-It Dough

2 cups Cheez-Its

2 cups all-purpose flour, plus more for rolling out and dusting the pasta

3 large eggs plus 3 egg yolks

2 tablespoons olive oil

Pasta Filling

1 cup ricotta

2 large eggs

½ cup shredded sharp cheddar (about 2 ounces)

¼ teaspoon ground black pepper

¼ teaspoon salt

Egg Wash

1 large egg

To Cook and Sauce

4 tablespoons (½ stick) unsalted butter

6 garlic cloves, palm heel struck and minced

¼ teaspoon salt

1 tablespoon minced chives

More Cheez-Its, because garnish

Now go ahead and blend that angry softball a little longer to help knead the dough, another 1 to 2 minutes.

Turn that ball onto the counter, but DO NOT reach into the food processor with your hands because, boy oh boy, have we done that a bunch of times and almost always sliced the crap out of at least one finger.

Once it's all on a clean work surface, knead the dough for 5 minutes, and then cut it in half. Flatten each half into a disk, then wrap each disk tightly in plastic wrap and let rest in the fridge for about 30 minutes to hydrate the flour and let those glutens do their thing.

Step 2: Make the Filling and Fill the Pasta. Take a large bowl and dump everything in there. Yeah, that's right, we're making you glance up at the ingredient list again. It's the part that's listed under "Pasta Filling." Mix it all together, making sure the eggs are fully broken up. Set it aside.

Now comes the hard part . . . rolling out the dough. You're looking to take each dough disk and roll it out as thin as you possibly can. Diaphanously thin, if you will (LOOK IT UP). Just remember that you're trying to get 6 ravioli out of each disk, and also remember that if the pasta is too thick, it will be kinda gross and you will have done all this work for very little return.

Okay! Now, on a lightly floured surface with a rolling pin, or using a pasta roller, get these suckers to be diaphanously thin (did you look it up yet?). Keep hitting them with a dusting of flour as needed, to make sure they don't stick. Then stack them on top of each other and try to square off any craggy edges, so that you have 2 big dough rectangles that are roughly 14 inches by 10 inches.

Next, make a little egg wash by whisking that one egg in a bowl with a splash of water. Brush the top of each sheet of pasta with it. Okay, ready to fill?

The goal here is to put 12 dollops of filling, evenly spaced out, on one sheet of ravioli with a dough buffer around each dollop on all sides. If you made a nice rectangle like we told you to, you should be able to go three rows wide and four rows deep (3 × 4 = 12!). Spoon about a tablespoon of the filling for each dollop, then lay the other sheet of pasta (egg wash side down) over it. Use your fingers to gently press around each dollop, making sure that there are no air pockets hiding in there, which will try their damnedest to explode your ravioli. Use your ravioli stamp to do the obvious thing here and stamp out the ravioli.

(Alternatively, you can just cut them into squares with a knife, and then use the tines of a fork to press down edges around each raviolo. By the way did you know that *raviolo* is the singular of *ravioli*?)

You did it! You made ravioli! Dust them with flour so they don't stick.

Step 3: Cook and Sauce. Bring a pot of water to a boil and toss in a hefty pinch of salt.

Place a large skillet over medium heat. Add the butter and garlic and let that thing start sautéing and foaming and getting all garlic buttery. Stir in the salt.

Meanwhile, drop each raviolo (gently!) into the boiling water and cook until the dough is tender and cooked through, about 3 minutes. If the garlic and butter are starting to brown, just add a little splash of the pasta water.

Once the pasta is just about cooked, take ½ cup of pasta water and pour it right in there with your garlic butter. Increase the heat to medium-high, then transfer those ravioli to the garlic butter in the skillet. Let them simmer away together, stirring from time to time, until the whole thing looks creamy and saucy and emulsified, about 2 minutes.

Toss in those chives, give them a stir, then slide the whole dang thing onto a plate.

Crumble some Cheez-Its on top if you didn't already eat them all, then close your eyes and achieve cheese nirvana.

Should You Throw Away Your Pasta Scraps?

Save your pasta scraps, because they are pasta, and boil them for a bonus snack. You can honestly just toss those with a little olive oil, salt, pepper, and grated cheese for a VERY good time.

GRILLED CHEESE RAMEN

One of the most delicious things we ever made on the show was a grilled cheese ramen that required you to break out a whole mess of equipment, use a few different food powders, and waste roughly one-third of your adult life. So we here in the Laboratory of Mythical Cookbookery went to work to discover a simpler and equally delicious method. But we're gonna be honest. We got super-duper distracted and then got into a huge fight, and then we had to hash it out over drinks at a bar in Burbank. We fought, we kissed a little, we discovered that the person we were fighting with was actually a split personality of our own psyche, and then the next day we woke up and were confronted with a profound sense of loss, which required a *lot* of soul-searching until we came to terms with the idea that both versions of our self were inside us the entire time and could actually coexist, finally joining together to realize that we could use a packet of ramen seasoning *and* a packet of Kraft Mac & Cheese powder in the same bowl of ramen, because our self, and our bowl of ramen, could contain both things simultaneously.

....

Step 1: Make the Cheddar Pork Broth. Put a medium pot on the stove and gently nudge the knob over to medium heat. That's right, you don't have to crank it or anything, because in this moment it's not that big of a deal. Drop that butter in there and, once it has melted, add your two powders of flavor science and give them a little stir. They're gonna foam and start to make your kitchen smell really special. Pour in a splash of the milk, mixing it all together before adding the rest of it, along with 1 cup water. Bring the liquid to a simmer, then let it roll like that for about 30 seconds. Remove from the heat and taste it—but not for seasoning, because we all know it's perfect. Taste it just for your own pleasure. Okay, now take another sip. It's a lot of broth, because it has enough salt to flavor a bowl of ramen and a bowl of mac 'n' cheese. Isn't that nice?

Step 2: Grill That Cheese! Place a nonstick or cast-iron skillet over medium-low heat. Add 1 tablespoon of the butter and let it melt and get foamy. Lay those slices of bread in the skillet and let them get nice and golden brown. Once they're engoldened (that's a word, right?),

Recipe continues

Makes 1 totally normal portion of ramen with a grilled cheese

Cheddar Pork Broth
1 tablespoon unsalted butter

1 packet cheese powder from a 6-ounce box of Kraft Mac & Cheese

1 seasoning packet from a 3-ounce package of pork-flavored instant ramen

2 cups whole milk

Grilled Cheese
2 tablespoons unsalted butter

2 slices white bread

4 slices American cheese

3 thin slices deli meat of choice (we like Boar's Head smoked ham)

To Finish
1 large egg

1 brick instant ramen noodles

1 scallion, thinly sliced

flip them over, then lay 2 slices of cheese on top of one of the slices of bread, then the meat, then the remaining 2 slices cheese. Then take the other slice of bread and . . . how can we put this? Use the bread to somehow "sandwich" the cheese and deli meat between the two slices, so to speak.

Okay, now that you have sandwiched cheese and meat between bread, add the remaining 1 tablespoon butter to the pan and swirl it around. Cook that thing slow and low until the bread bottom is crispy and golden, about 4 minutes, then flip it over and do the same thing to the other side.

Once it's done, put it on a cutting board and let it rest while you . . .

Step 3: Finish Your Ramen! Bring a pot of water to a boil. Crack your egg into a small ramekin, making sure not to break the yolk. Now use a spoon to swirl the boiling water in a circle and MAKE A VORTEX. Once you have achieved centrifugal

vortex maximization, tilt the egg into the water, remove from the heat, cover the pot, and poach the egg until the white is set and the yolk is runny, about 4 minutes.

Lift out the egg with a slotted spoon and put it on a paper towel to drain.

Okay, now bring the water back up to a boil and then drop in your noodles and cook them EXACTLY AS THE PACKAGE INSTRUCTIONS TELL YOU TO. Or, whatever, just boil them until they taste done to you. Drain them and put them in your ramen bowl.

Next up, bring the ramen broth back to a simmer, then ladle it right over those noodles. Lay that poached egg on one side, then use a knife to slice your grilled cheese into 4 long batons. Put those things on top of the ramen, too, then top the whole thing with scallions and dig the heck in, allowing your meal and yourself to contain all things at once.

JOSH'S "SUCK IT, GORDON RAMSAY" GRILLED CHEESE

Chipotle Bacon Jam

4 slices bacon, finely diced

1 small yellow or white onion, finely diced

2 chipotle peppers in adobo, minced

2 teaspoons light brown sugar

¼ teaspoon salt

2 tablespoons red wine vinegar

Grilled Cheese

3 tablespoons salted butter

2 slices grocery-store sourdough bread

2 slices Kraft Deli Deluxe American cheese (not Kraft Singles, which are technically not cheese but CHEESE PRODUCT)

1 slice provolone

1 slice sharp cheddar

To make it abundantly clear, I have nothing but respect for Gordon Ramsay . . . Okay, is he gone? Whew, finally, I can speak honestly. GORDON, YOU AB-SOLUTE DONUT, YOU WOULDN'T KNOW A PROPER GRILLED CHEESE IF IT FLOATED UP THE THAMES AND GAVE YOU A WET SNOG ON THE DOG'S BOLLOCKS!

Sorry, we lost our heads for a second there. Here's what happened: I made a perfectly innocuous recipe for a ramen grilled cheese (not to be confused with the Grilled Cheese Ramen on page 167) over on TikTok, and somehow, Gordon Ramsay got his hands on it and made a reaction video. He called me all the names, in his signature red-in-the-face fashion, and then implied he wanted to stick the sandwich into my derriere. Listen, I'm not above criticism, and Gordon Ramsay has more Michelin stars than I have toes, so surely he must know what he's talking about when it comes to grilled cheese. Then I saw the video. Gordon Ramsay made the world's worst grilled cheese—bread burned, cheese ice cold, and a complete lack of shame—which sent me into an uncontrollable rage spiral. That rage spiral resulted in the recipe you see below. Whereas many people tout love as their secret ingredient, I have chosen to liberally slather this grilled cheese with spite (and bacon jam). Gordon, from the bottom of my heart, suck it.

Note: This makes way more Chipotle Bacon Jam than you need, but it keeps in the fridge for up to a week. You're welcome.

Step 1: Make the Chipotle Bacon Jam. Heat a medium saucepan over medium heat (we call that a "double medium," obviously). After about 2 minutes, chuck in the bacon and cook, stirring occasionally, until the bacon fat starts to render, about 3 minutes. Add the onion, chipotles, brown sugar, and salt and keep on cooking that thing down, stirring occasionally, until it is all deeply brown and tenderoni, about 15 minutes.

Crank that heat up to high and add ½ cup water and the vinegar to deglaze the pan. Continue to cook, scraping the bottom of the pan with a wooden spoon to unearth those browned caramelize-y flavor enhancers, until all the water is gone and there is nothing left but dark, beautiful jam vibes, about 10 more minutes. Remove from the heat and set aside until it is time to sandwich.

Step 2: Make a Better Grilled Cheese Than Gordon Ramsay. Place a nonstick skillet (or a cast-iron skillet, if you want to get aggro) over medium-low heat. But, like, on the low side of medium-low. Let's call it low-medium-low. Add 1 tablespoon of the butter to the pan and toast the bread slices on one side until they get a very mellow, light golden brown to them. Remove the bread and remove the skillet from the heat.

With the toasty side up, lay the American cheese on one of the slices of bread. Schmear about a tablespoon of your chipotle bacon jam across the cheese. Top it with the provolone and cheddar. Put the other slice of bread on top (toasty side down) and give it a nice, solid press with your palm. It's like a palm heel strike, but gentle. A palm heel loving caress, if you will.

Okay, now put that pan back over low-medium-low and add another tablespoon of that sweet, sweet cream butter. When the butter has melted, add the sandwich. Cook until the bottom is nice and golden and not burning (if it is burning, YOU DID NOT GO LOW ENOUGH). We're talking REAL low and slow, 7 or 8 minutes on this side.

Lift the sandwich out and set it aside. Add the remaining tablespoon of butter. Once it has melted, flip that sandwich, *gently*, and place it back in the pan, raw side of the bread down. Cook for another 6 minutes or so, until it is golden brown on that side, too, and the cheese—*DO YOU HEAR ME, GORDON?*—is *MELTED*. Give it one more flip just to warm the other side for about 5 seconds.

Put your sandwich on a cutting board. Let it rest for about 30 seconds, then cut it in half and eat the dang sandwich. If you want to get real wacky, you can dip it in ketchup. But either way, think about Gordon eating his hard-cheese sandwich while you enjoy this way-better one.

CHEESESTEAK MOZZARELLA LOGS

The original version of this dish was featured on a *GMM* episode called "Will It Cheesesteak?" in which a commercial-grade, professional pizzeria–size log of mozzarella was hollowed out, stuffed with cheesesteak filling, breaded, and deep-fried. It was enough food to kill a man, whether through blunt force trauma, smothering, or simply "eating the entire thing." It was also incredibly complicated to deep-fry and featured quite an unholy ratio of cheese to steak. But the idea (and the flavor) was still great. So . . . welcome back to "Extreme 'Will It Cheesesteak?' Make-over: Home Edition," in which we try to keep you, the reader, alive at the end of this recipe, and instead make some delicious Cheesesteak Mozzarella Logs that will actually fit in one hand, while also getting dipped into marinara sauce.

Oh, but before you Pennsylvania folks get all angry by saying that our marinara dipper is NOT TRADITIONAL ON A CHEESESTEAK (even though we're turning it into a deep-fried cheese log), just keep in mind that Lehigh Valley cheesesteaks *do* come with marinara sauce, so take that.

Step 1: Steak-umm Up! Start things off by heating up a large skillet over medium-high heat. Add the butter and oil, and once the butter is melted, add your onion and bell pepper. Stir those things up and cook until the onion is translucent and softened, about 3 minutes, then toss in your frozen meat sheets. Do we have to tell you to remove the paper? No? Okay, great.

Season those things up with the seasoning salt and several twists of black pepper and keep on cooking and stirring until the Steak-umms have lost their raw color and the vegetables have gotten super tender, about 3 more minutes. A little bit of crisping and browning is a good thing. Now pour that mixture into a strainer set over a bowl and put the whole thing in the fridge to cool off, making sure not to tip it over and spill steak juice all over the inside of your fridge, which is really annoying to clean because the condensation makes you feel like no matter how many times you wipe it, it never really gets dry.

Step 2: Make Your Sticks. Once your steak filling is cold and has drained, transfer it to a large bowl with the Monterey Jack. Now get your hands all up in there and mix that until it's all super-duper combined.

Transfer the mixture to a baking sheet, pressing it into a 1-inch-thick rectangle.

Finally, get really mad that you didn't read through the whole recipe first, because now, for the truly best results, make some space in your freezer and put the mixture in there to stiffen up and set for about 45 minutes.

Meanwhile, start setting up your breeding station. No, that doesn't sound right. *Breading* station. That's better. Take three wide bowls or plates. The first one is for the flour. Now the second one? That's where you'll crack in the eggs, add a splash of water, and give it a nice whisk. The third one is called: The Prestige. Wow, no, that's not right either. Okay, the third one is for the *panko*. Combine the panko, oregano (or Italian seasoning), granulated garlic, and granulated onion. Give that a nice mix until it's all incorporated.

Recipe continues

Makes about 12 Cheesesteak Mozzarella Logs, serving 1 party of 4 or 4 parties of 1 or 1 party of 1 person eating for 4

Steak-umm Filling
1 tablespoon unsalted butter
1 tablespoon neutral oil
½ cup diced yellow
   or white onion
¼ cup diced green bell pepper
4 portions Steak-umms
   (from a 9-ounce box)
1½ teaspoons seasoning salt
Ground black pepper

Breading and Cheesing
4 cups shredded Monterey
   Jack (about 16 ounces;
   you could also substitute
   provolone or low-
   moisture mozzarella)
¾ cup all-purpose flour
3 large eggs
2 cups panko bread crumbs
1 tablespoon dried oregano,
   or you can use whatever the
   heck "Italian seasoning" is
1 teaspoon granulated garlic
1 teaspoon granulated onion

To Cook and Finish
Neutral oil, for frying
Salt, for sprinkling
Warm marinara sauce,
   for dipping

Once the sheet of food has chilled, use a knife or bench scraper to cut it into around 12 mozzarella-stick-size logs. Dip them in the flour, then the egg, then the bread crumb mixture, then return them to the baking sheet and place them back in the freezer until it is time to fry. (You can also freeze them completely on a pan, transfer them to a freezer bag, and freeze for up to 3 months before frying . . . but who can wait that long?)

Step 3: Fry Those Logs! Heat your fry oil (using a deep fryer or a large, heavy-bottomed pot filled with at least 2 inches of oil, making sure that the pot is no more than two-thirds full) to 350°F. Line a baking sheet with a wire rack or a plate with some paper towels for draining.

Fry the logs in batches until golden brown and crispy, about 90 seconds. Sprinkle them with salt as they come out of the oil and serve them with warmed marinara sauce. Think to yourself, "You know what? Those Lehigh Valley folks just might be onto something."

KIMCHI CORN QUESO DIP

Did you know that napa cabbage kimchi is one of the most nutritious foods in the world? It has all those beautiful ferment-y probiotic health benefits and, according to WebMD, is also an excellent source of vitamin A, vitamin C, vitamin K, folate, beta-carotene, choline, potassium, and calcium. (Side note: How come nobody says "Dr. Web"?)

Anyway, we here at Mythical obviously need to balance all that nutrition out by putting it in a vat of melted cheese and serving it with tortilla chips. But we're also taking a page from some of the best Korean BBQ spots out there and adding CHEESE CORN into the mix. Altogether, this makes for a super-simple and deeply delicious recipe that just so happens to be almost un-mess-up-able thanks to the almighty food science combination of evaporated milk and processed yellow cheese. That's right, this cheese sauce is UNBREAKABLE.

....

Heat a heavy-bottomed oven-safe skillet over medium heat so that it gets hot . . . but only *medium* hot.

Meanwhile, put the kimchi in a strainer. Try to squeeze out as much moisture as you possibly can, until your hand shakes a little bit and you're like, "Hey, maybe it's time to take it easy." Place that drained kimchi onto a cutting board and chop it up into small pieces.

Okay, now melt the butter in your medium-hot skillet. Toss in the onion, corn kernels, and kimchi and sauté, stirring semifrequently, until the vegetables are getting all soft and wilty, about 5 minutes. Crack open that evaporated milk and pour it in, followed by the salt, pepper, and garlic powder. Give it all a nice stir to incorporate, and when it starts to bubble, chuck in that cheddar and Velveeta and stir until the cheese has melted into glorious, wonderful queso. Remove from the heat, then stir in the mayo and sugar and keep it all moving around for a good 15 seconds to let that sugar dissolve and incorporate.

Recipe continues

Makes 1 giant container of dip, able to serve as many people as can reach it while you hold it in your lap on the couch while watching TV (so, like, 6 people if you're all super cozy)

2 cups kimchi

2 tablespoons unsalted butter

1 yellow or white onion, finely chopped

One 15.25-ounce can corn kernels, drained

One 12-ounce can evaporated milk

½ teaspoon salt

¼ teaspoon ground black pepper

1 teaspoon garlic powder

1 cup shredded cheddar (about 4 ounces)

½ cup cubed Velveeta or similar processed cheese product (about 2 ounces)

3 tablespoons mayo

1 teaspoon sugar

1 cup shredded mozzarella (about 4 ounces)

1 scallion, thinly sliced

Gochugaru, for garnish (optional)

Black sesame seeds, for garnish (optional)

Tortilla chips, for serving

Meanwhile, turn on the broiler, or if you don't have a broiler, just crank your oven up as high as it goes. Top the mixture with the mozzarella, then sprinkle the chopped scallions over the top. Place the whole thing under the broiler and let it rip until the mozzarella is melted and has a few golden brown spots, about 2 minutes.

Garnish with gochugaru and black sesame seeds, if you're fancy. Good golly, you just made kimchi corn queso. Serve it with tortilla chips and enjoy all the marvelous health benefits of kimchi . . . with a LOT of melted cheese and fried corn coming along for the ride.

Why Does My Cheese Sauce Suck?

The easiest way to prevent a cheese sauce from being gritty or broken is to simply dump in some good ol' fashioned American processed cheese. Despite many people thinking it is made of plastic, it is simply made of milk and cheese held together by a chemical called sodium citrate. This miracle molecule is an emulsifier, which means it binds the proteins and fats together, which, in turn, means you don't have to work that hard to ensure an unbroken sauce. Using hot, nasty, badass science to make up for your inadequacies—America!

MAC 'N' CHEESE CHICKEN WINGS

When someone tells you they are "winging it," they usually mean that they are improvising without any preparation. Well, here at Mythical, when we wing it, we improvise over and over again while taking copious notes, and also taking the word *wing* a little too literally until we are elbow deep in fry oil and chicken grease, asking the big, important questions of the world, like "How do u chicken wings but mac 'n' cheez?"

Needless to say, we winged it so hard that now we have—we kid you not—a fully tested recipe for mac 'n' cheese–crusted chicken wings with Buffalo cheese sauce. You're welcome.

....

Step 1: Bake the Wings. Preheat the oven to 350°F. Line a baking sheet with parchment paper.

Now drop those wings into a large bowl and add the salt, garlic powder, paprika, white pepper, and black pepper. Give them a toss until well combined, transfer to the prepared baking sheet, and bake for 30 minutes. Let them cool to room temperature.

Step 2: Make the Cheddar Batter. Let's make batter! First you make dry stuff and then wet stuff and then you mix them together until you have medium-wet stuff. The goal here is to end up with a batter that is thick enough to coat the wings without running too much. So . . . thic is too thin and thiccc is too thick. You want a thicc consistency.

Combine the flour, cheddar, baking powder, salt, and black pepper in a large bowl and give it a nice whisk.

In a medium bowl, whisk together . . . everything else: the milk, buttermilk, egg, and melted butter. Then scrape that wet mixture into the dry mixture and mix it all up until you have said thicc batter. Set it aside to rest while you . . .

Recipe continues

Baked Wings
12 party wings
1 teaspoon salt
1 teaspoon garlic powder
1 teaspoon paprika
½ teaspoon white pepper
½ teaspoon ground black pepper

Cheddar Batter
1¼ cups all-purpose flour
1 cup shredded extra-sharp cheddar (about 4 ounces)
2½ teaspoons baking powder
½ teaspoon salt
½ teaspoon ground black pepper
¾ cup whole milk
½ cup buttermilk
1 large egg
3 tablespoons unsalted butter, melted

Buffalo Cheese Sauce
½ cup whole milk
10 slices American cheese
¼ cup Frank's Buffalo Sauce

Make the Wings!
Neutral oil, for frying
8 ounces large elbow macaroni, cooked, drained, and chilled

Step 3: Make the Cheddar Buffalo Sauce. This one is *really* easy. Just pour the milk into a medium saucepan over medium heat and bring to a simmer. Stir in the cheese. Once the cheese has melted, add the buffalo sauce and mix it all up. Now you have Buffalo cheese sauce. Remove it from the heat and set it aside.

Step 4: Fry Those Things! Heat your fry oil (using a deep fryer or a large, heavy-bottomed pot filled with at least 2 inches of oil, making sure that the pot is no more than two-thirds full) to 375°F. Line a baking sheet with a wire rack or a plate with some paper towels for draining.

Spread your cooked, cooled macaroni on a platter or baking sheet.

Now take your first wing and dip it in the cheddar batter until fully coated. Roll it in cooked macaroni so that it sticks and clumps around it. Finally, lay the wing *CAREFULLY* into the fry oil. Fry until the batter and noodles are golden brown and crisp, about 1 minute. Transfer to the rack or paper towels to drain. Continue frying in batches, making sure to maintain your oil temperature (if it doesn't bubble when the food goes in . . . I hate to break it to you, but your oil is way too cold). Transfer the wings to a platter, drizzle them with Buffalo cheese sauce, and eat them as soon as your lips, tongue, and throat can handle the heat.

DORITOS LOCOS CALZONE

This has been brought up to us multiple times, so NOW WE ARE PUTTING IT DOWN IN WRITING: A pizza is not an open-faced sandwich. A calzone is also not a sandwich. Neither of these is a sandwich. We will not accept a calzone as a dumpling either. But we *will* allow it as a hand pie or an empanada.

The bigger question: Is a calzone crusted with crumbled Doritos a burrito? (Survey says no.) But it is, most importantly, really freaking delicious. Oh, and did we mention the filling is a Costco-Chicken-Bake-Inspired, Cajun-Chicken-Alfredo-Adjacent, Taco-Bell-Fire-Sauce-Laden CHICKEN FIRE ALFREDO? Okay, great—let's cook.

....

Note: For best results, use a pizza stone! You could also use a baking sheet, but it will be slightly less good.

Step 1: Make Chicken Fire Alfredo Filling. Melt the butter in a medium saucepan over medium heat. Add the garlic and let it sizzle up with the butter and make your whole kitchen smell real nice. After about 2 minutes, add the cream and bring it up to a simmer, stirring constantly so you don't scorch it and RUIN EVERYTHING, MOM! Okay, now that it's simmering, add your Parmesan, fire sauce, and pepper and keep cooking at a gentle simmer, stirring, until slightly reduced, about 2 more minutes. Remove from the heat.

Meanwhile, pour the oil into a large skillet and turn that thing up to medium-high heat. Toss in your bacon and let that stuff fry up for about 4 minutes, stirring it around to prevent burning, until the bacon is mostly rendered and starting to crisp up at the edges. Add the onion and mushrooms and keep on cooking and stirring until the mushrooms are soft and the onion is translucent, about 4 more minutes. Finally, add the chicken and season it up with our old friend Tony C's. Stir it all together and then increase the heat to high and cook until the chicken is cooked through and has some nice color on it, about 3 more minutes. Remove from the heat and let cool to room temperature. Stir

Recipe continues

Chicken Fire Alfredo Filling

½ cup (1 stick) unsalted butter

4 garlic cloves, palm heel struck and minced

1 cup heavy cream

½ cup grated Parmesan (about 2 ounces)

2 tablespoons Taco Bell Fire Sauce

½ teaspoon ground black pepper

1 tablespoon neutral oil

3 slices bacon, diced

¼ yellow or white onion, diced

5 white button mushrooms, sliced

8 ounces boneless, skinless chicken breast, cut into cubes

1 tablespoon Tony Chachere's Creole Seasoning

The Calzone

Neutral oil, to grease up your hands

1-pound ball pizza dough, at room temperature

2 cups shredded low-moisture mozzarella (about 8 ounces)

One 9.25-ounce bag Nacho Cheese Doritos

1 large egg

Ranch, for dippings

Marinara, also for dippings

the cooled chicken into the fire alfredo sauce and now you can get ready to make the calzone!

Step 2: Make the Calzone! Place a pizza stone or baking sheet in the oven. Preheat the oven to 450°F.

Grease up your hands with oil and then put that pizza dough right onto a clean work surface. Use your fingers to push, pull, and shape the dough, lifting and stretching the edges as needed, until you have a circle of 10 inches or so that is roughly even in thickness. It won't be perfect, but nothing is, so the sooner you accept that, the sooner you will be able to find inner peace, knowing that the aforementioned perfection is unattainable.

Okay, now lay half of the mozzarella on half of the dough circle—leaving a little bit of room on the edge for future sealing purposes. Lay the chicken filling right on top of the mozzarella, then top with the rest of the mozzarella.

Lift up the naked side of the dough and stretch it over the other side . . . like you're making a calzone. Use a fork to crimp the edges closed.

Take a knife and cut three shallow lines into the top of the calzone (to prevent steam-based explosion), then carefully use both hands to lift the calzone and place it on the stone in the oven. Bake it for 20 minutes.

Meanwhile, take all those Doritos you've got, shake them into a food processor, then pulse them into a delicious, coarse powder. Whisk the egg with a splash of water in a small bowl.

After those 20 minutes are up, take the calzone out of the oven (IT'S NOT DONE YET!) and reduce the heat to 400°F. Take a pastry brush and brush the whole top of the calzone with the egg wash. Finally, dust it with as much Doritos powder as you possibly can (working super fast so that the egg doesn't cook). Then return the calzone to the oven and keep on baking for another 10 minutes, or until the Doritos are browned but not burned.

Finally, take it out of the oven! Let it rest for about 2 minutes, then get in the 'zone, cutting and dipping it in all the sauces.

EVERYTHING BAGEL FONDUE

Against all odds, society has deemed that fondue is fancy. If you were on a romantic date night at a white-tablecloth restaurant, it would be gauche to order nachos, but you order fondue and suddenly you're Mr. Moneybags McMonocle. Both are just carbs dragged through a vat of molten cheese! It makes absolutely no sense, but we need to keep the ruse going as long as we can, because, with the right strategy in place, you can increase your molten cheese consumption by at least 46 percent while still being perceived as a cultured, productive member of society. And it all starts with breakfast. You take the classic morning combo of smoked salmon, bagels, and cream cheese and transform that into a bubbling cauldron of fermented dairy. Just . . . don't drink it with a straw. Then the illusion is ruined. Do you really have to buy a fondue pot? No. No, you can make this recipe and live a perfectly fulfilled life without owning a fondue pot. However, there are worse investments you could make in your future happiness. And, c'mon, how much of a power move is it to own a dang fondue pot?

....

Preheat the top-of-the-line $300 electric fondue pot that you just purchased—psych! Heat a medium saucepan over low heat, then add your milk and cream cheese and cook, stirring, until the cream cheese has melted and is smooth. Add the shredded cheese, one small handful at a time, and keep whisking until it melts smoothly. When all the cheese has been incorporated, toss in that everything bagel seasoning (Contrary to popular belief, it does not actually contain everything in the universe, which would weigh approximately 1.553 kilograms. It's mostly dehydrated garlic, onion, and poppy seeds.) Pour the fondue into a large bowl and garnish with chives and additional everything bagel seasoning.

If you weren't having fun already, this is where the fondue party REALLY starts! Take some toothpicks and start stabbing ingredients with them. Swipe that bagel kebab through the hot cheese sauce, and make sure to eat with your pinky up, you fancy son of a biscuit.

Recipe continues

Makes enough molten cheese for 6 people to comfortably enjoy

1 cup whole milk

Two 8-ounce bricks cream cheese

3 cups shredded Swiss cheese (about 12 ounces; Gruyère, Fontina, and Monterey Jack also work!)

2 tablespoons everything bagel seasoning, plus more for garnish

1 teaspoon salt

Chives, for garnish

For Serving

Sliced cucumber

Halved cherry tomatoes

Bagels, toasted and cut into bite-size pieces

Smoked salmon

FOUR-CHEESE LATKES

As the story of Mythikkah goes, Nicole and Josh had just beaten back the Smosh army and retreated to the kitchen for safety. Needing to feed their hungry troops with nothing but a stockpile of potatoes and eggs, they set out to make a mutual childhood favorite: latkes. Nicole shredded the potatoes, and Josh was fast at work grating the onion. As the celebratory mixture came together and dreams of crispy, oily, potato-y goodness filled their heads, Nicole and Josh looked at each other in horror. The bottle of vegetable oil was empty. The feast was ruined and their soldiers would go to bed hungry yet again. When all hope was lost, the Semitic duo realized with delight that the oil from their backup deep fryer, hidden deep in the storage area, was salvageable. And, friends, wouldn't you know, that oil lasted for four months without being cleaned. To celebrate the miracle of the four-month-old oil, we eat our latkes with four cheeses in them every Mythikkah. Amen.

Okay, none of that was true, but we did learn that cheesy latkes are awesome one winter when we were trying to clear out our cheese drawer.

....

Use the large holes of a box grater to grate the onion, then put it into a large bowl along with the garlic. Peel your potatoes and invent a super-cool potato-peeling song while doing it. Y'know, like one that you'd sing if you were in the galley kitchen of a pirate ship in 1652. Yeah, a real sea shanty of a potato-peeling song! When those taters are peeled, use those same large holes on the box grater (the king of graters, if you ask us!) to shred the potatoes and then add them to the bowl.

Next, this step is THE MOST important one in making latkes, and it is often the step that separates the good from the great. You need to squeeze ALL the moisture out of those potatoes and onions. The best way to do this is to load all the shredded taters into a large, clean kitchen towel, then fold the four corners of the towel together, and twist as hard as you can. Summon the strength of 1987 "Macho Man" Randy Savage to twist harder and harder until no more liquid is coming out, then put the dry shreddies back into the bowl. Resist the urge to wipe your face with the towel, though we know it's tempting.

Makes 8 to 12 latkes

½ large yellow or white onion

4 garlic cloves, grated or palm heel struck and finely chopped

2 large russet potatoes (about 1 pound)

½ cup shredded sharp cheddar (about 2 ounces)

¼ cup shredded smoked Gouda (about 1 ounce)

¼ cup grated Parmesan (about 1 ounce)

¼ cup shredded pepper Jack (about 1 ounce)

2 large eggs

1 teaspoon salt

½ teaspoon ground black pepper

½ teaspoon baking powder

½ cup all-purpose flour

Neutral oil, for frying

Ketchup, sriracha, and sour cream, for serving

Add all four cheeses, the eggs, salt, pepper, and baking powder to the potato mixture and give them a good mix with a fork (okay, we use our hands, but you don't have to copy everything we do). Sprinkle your flour into the bowl, then gently—y'know what, screw the fork, using your hands is so much better here—use your hands to toss the flour all throughout the potato shreds. If you use a fork, you risk mashing the flour into the potatoes and creating a gloopy, doughy mess.

Congrats, you have a cheesy latke mixture! Heat about ½ inch of oil in a large sauté pan over medium heat. Since the oil is so shallow and near the heat source here, you can skip temp checking it and just go by vibes. Flick a small bit of flour into the oil, and if it gently sizzles, then you're in Latketown, baby! It's about 35 miles southwest of Flavortown (meaning it is 102.77 miles west-southwest of Flavorville), and there's a lot more kosher delis there! Wet your hand with a few drops of water so the latke dough doesn't stick to your hands, then form about ¼ cup of dough into a ½-inch-thick disk, using your thumb as a guide. Gently drop the disk into the oil and pat it gently with a spatula to ensure the surface is getting contact with the pan.

Repeat the process with a few more disks, making sure they do not overlap in the pan. You will have to work in batches here, folks! We don't make the rules; we just enforce them! Your pan should be kept on medium to medium-low heat because latkes have a tendency to burn without the internal potatoes getting cooked through. After about 3½ minutes, use a spatula to peek at the underside of a latke, and if it's golden brown, give it a flip and cook for an additional 2 minutes before transferring to a paper towel–lined plate to cool.

PLEASE MAKE SURE THERE ARE NO ADORABLE JEWISH BUBBIES AROUND TO READ THIS PART. GET THEM OUT OF THE ROOM. Okay, good. We recommend serving these with a sauce of two parts ketchup, one part sriracha—just mix those two things up in a small bowl. Also, a separate bowl of sour cream is nice.

Bubby can come back in now. Please apologize to her for not calling often enough.

SET FIRE TO YOUR MOUTH, NOT YOUR KITCHEN

(SPICY)

Setting fire to your mouth is fun! Capsaicin from chiles can trigger your brain to release endorphins, creating a euphoric sensation often referred to as "a runner's high." Setting fire to your kitchen is not fun! Smoke from fire can trigger your coworkers—or family, or roommates—to call 911, creating a shameful sensation often referred to as "you fudged up, you big dummy!" And that's assuming you don't die. Setting fire to your kitchen can also cause you to die. If you are dead, you cannot make Nashville Hot Chicken Meatballs, which is a shame, because they are delicious.

It may seem like we take risks in the Mythical Kitchen—we refuse to apologize for lighting expensive liquor on fire to make fancy nacho cheese—but we are all trained professionals who know what to do in an emergency situation. That being said, assuming you are currently alive, please read our official guide to kitchen safety, and be sure to employ these best practices when cooking! If you are reading this and your name is Charles Lincoln Neal III, please, for everyone's well-being, just drop the knives and walk away. We cannot afford another impaling.

OUR OFFICIAL GUIDE TO KITCHEN SAFETY

Tuck your fingers when cutting

Even if you don't care about safety and just want to LOOK more professional, this is the easiest way to do it. When holding the item you are about to cut, don't spread your fingers, which makes them easily severable. Rather, you want to tuck all your fingers at the second knuckle, and employ what is known as the claw grip. Not only does this prevent any unfortunate digit severings (hooray!), but you can actually use your knuckle to guide the knife blade and hold it steady.

Know how to put out a fire

Reasonably, we are required by law to have a Class K fire extinguisher in the Mythical Kitchen, and we have only had to use it once (I blame Trevor). We don't expect everyone to have one, so here's a simple life-saving hack. Just . . . put a lid on it. You have a pan on fire? Maybe you spilled too much liquor on a flambé, or you forgot about an unattended pan, or you have a good old-fashioned grease fire. Smother that son of a biscuit to deprive the fire of oxygen. We prefer setting a baking sheet on top of the pan, because it will fit most pan or pot tops, and it gives your hands some room for protection. And FOR THE LOVE OF ALL THAT IS DELICIOUS, NEVER PUT WATER ON A GREASE FIRE!

Wash your hands after handling raw meat

We know from our YouTube comments that lots of people are disgusted by the fact that we don't wear gloves in the kitchen. But studies have shown that washing your hands with soap and warm water is just as safe as using gloves. Furthermore! Using gloves often disincentivizes people from washing their hands, which can lead to more cross contamination. Raw meat is always going to be your biggest bacterial worry in the kitchen, so anytime you're handling raw meat, always thoroughly wash your hands before touching any other food. "But, Josh, what about beef tartare?" You ain't in France; wash your hands. Apologies to our readers in France.

Place food in oil going away from you

Not to brag, but we in the Mythical Kitchen may be among the most skilled deep fryers in the world, if for no other reason than we do it a WHOLE lot. So we've learned a few things. Obviously, you do not want to drop your food in the fryer from a high elevation due to splashing; using a fry basket that is loaded before it goes into the oil is going to be the best bet. But sometimes you're frying things that don't fit in the basket. Or maybe you just don't have one. When you drop in, say, a Reuben Pierogi (page 249), hold the food by one end, dip the other end in the oil, and make sure the end you're holding falls away from you as it goes into the oil.

Face your pot handles away from you

This is one of our personal favorites that some people don't think about, especially in crowded kitchens! And yes, because we know you are asking, Josh did learn this one in a seventh grade home economics class and it has stuck with him ever since! Support public education! When your pots and pans are on the stove, make sure the handles are turned inward, toward the stove, and not outward toward an area where people may be walking. If someone isn't paying attention— maybe they're listening to metalcore on headphones and practicing their slam dancing—they could hit the handle and knock a pot of scalding water all over their crotch. And crotch scalding is NOT metal!

Wear appropriate clothing

NO BAGGY SLEEVES

CLOSED-TOE SHOES

Closed-toe shoes! No baggy sleeves! Probably a good idea to wear pants! Both in the kitchen and when you walk into a 7-Eleven. You'll encounter very specific legal problems with that second one if you don't. If you drop a knife—happens to the best of us!—make sure you do not try to catch it, and especially do not try to kick-save the knife like a hockey goalie. The safest thing you can do is get the heck out of the way and be glad you were wearing closed-toe shoes. Baggy, hanging sleeves, despite looking stylish and fresh, can droop into the flame of a gas burner and turn you into a human BBQ. You do not want to be a human BBQ.

Don't cross-contaminate cutting boards

In many restaurants, cutting boards are plastic and color coded based on ingredients. You've got one color for raw meat, one for cooked meat, one for fish, one for poultry, one for veggies, and so on. You don't need nine different cutting boards in your home. The simplest thing you can do is have one cutting board for ingredients that are getting cooked, and one for ingredients that are not getting cooked. When you're done with a cutting board (or plate, dish, or knife) that has touched raw meat, wash it immediately with hot water and soap. Some people insist on using plastic over wood cutting boards, arguing that wood absorbs more bacteria, but as long as you are cleaning each thoroughly, they are both perfectly safe to use.

Clean up spills immediately

Listen, we're not your mother, and we're not going to scold you, but . . . CLEAN UP THE DANG MILK YOU SPILLED! REPLACE ALL THE SPICES IN YOUR CABINET THAT EXPIRED THREE YEARS AGO! AND CALL YOUR GRANDMA; IT WAS HER BIRTHDAY YESTERDAY! Oh, her birthday was last month? Whoops. Spills left on the ground create a slipping hazard, and the worst way to cook chicken wings is when you have a shattered humerus. That does not make for good chicken wings. Also, if you have an oil spill, our preferred method of cleaning is to dump some flour—or salt—over it, let it absorb the oil, then sweep it up with a broom and wash the spill area with soap and water. Good as new!

Set timers and reminders

This seems like a dumb one, but sometimes, we are dumb people. And there's no shame in that. Plenty of dumb people have gone on to live fruitful lives. Just watch any of our YouTube videos where it takes four people to figure out how to close a food processor. If a recipe tells you to simmer a sauce for 2 hours, set a timer on your phone! As someone who has gone to bed with a pot of chicken stock cooking on the stove and woken up to a blackened mess that could've started a fire (again, dumb!), I now know that something as simple as a phone timer could've saved a lot of heartbreak, and a gallon of sweet, sweet chicken juice.

Transport knives properly

Have we ever personally seen someone get impaled in the kitchen with a chef's knife? No. No we have not. But that's only because everyone follows the social contract in the kitchen and doesn't walk around like Michael Myers hunting an incredibly clumsy coed. When you are walking with a knife—notice we said walking, not running, which you also shouldn't do—hold the knife by the handle with your arm straight at your side, knife tip pointed down, and the blade pointed toward your thigh. That way, the tip won't impale anyone, and no swinging arms around you will accidentally graze the blade and draw blood. The only blood in your kitchen should be from Pork Blood Tacos (page 287)!

TAKIS GRILLED CHEESE

Makes 1 cheese sandwich
(with a lot of Takis in it and on it)

You know when you order fajitas and they ask you, "Corn or flour tortillas?" and then you have to decide which one you want? Well, today you no longer have to choose. Because we are making a double-decker taco. Nope. That's not it. We're making a Takis Grilled Cheese! We take the flavor- (and chemical-)packed, taquito-inspired rolled tortilla chips, and we crush them up and encrust two slices of sourdough bread, which are then stuffed full of Takis-laden pimiento cheese and pepper Jack, to make the spiciest, crunchiest grilled cheese sandwich that a merry band of dangerously enabled YouTubers could ever possibly conceive of. Let's rip up the roof of our mouth and flame up our insides all at once!

Step 1: Make the Takis Pimiento Cheese. Let's make some Takis dust! Pour those Fuego Takis into the bowl of a food processor and blitz them until you have a fine red powder that you should absolutely not snort. (This is not a joke. That literally might kill you and at the very least it will be DEEPLY unpleasant.)

Next up, add the cheddar, cream cheese, pimientos, mayo, salt, cayenne, garlic powder, onion powder, black pepper, and chili powder and pulse, scraping down the sides as much as you have to, until you have a cohesive, Takis-flavored cheese spread. Taste it and get really, really excited about that. Transfer it to a bowl and set it aside.

Step 2: Make the Sandwich. Place a large cast-iron or nonstick skillet over medium-low heat. Drop in the butter and let it begin to melt.

Meanwhile, crack those eggs into a shallow, wide bowl and give them a nice scramble. Smash up those Fuego Takis in the bag using your big ol' fists and crunch them until they have a rough, crumbly texture that looks like it should go on the outside of a grilled cheese sandwich, and then pour them into another shallow, wide bowl. Next, take a slice of bread and dip one side of it in egg. Take the wet side and smash it right down into those crushed-up Takis, making a wall of Takis crumbles! Place the gorgeous sheet of bright-red wonder into the skillet Takis side down. While it's there, spread about ¾ cup of the Takis pimiento cheese on the naked side of the bread. Then top with the pepper Jack.

Takis Pimiento Cheese

⅓ cup Fuego Takis

1 cup shredded cheddar (about 4 ounces)

4 ounces cream cheese, at room temperature

¼ cup chopped jarred pimiento peppers

1 tablespoon mayo

½ teaspoon salt

½ teaspoon cayenne

½ teaspoon garlic powder

¼ teaspoon onion powder

¼ teaspoon ground black pepper

¼ teaspoon chili powder

Assemble and Grill

2 tablespoons unsalted butter

2 large eggs

One 4-ounce bag Fuego Takis

2 slices sourdough bread

2 slices pepper Jack

(See below for what to do with extra Takis pimiento cheese.)

Next, Takis-crust the other slice of bread and place it Takis side up on top of the pepper Jack. Keep on cooking that sandwich slow and low until you have a beautiful, crispy Takis crust going on one side, about 5 minutes.

Now carefully flip the sandwich over to cook the other side. Take a large lid or, heck, even a baking sheet or something, and cover your pan to trap in the heat and help the cheese melt. After about 3 minutes, remove the lid (the cheese should be nice and melty now), and cook for another couple of minutes, until you have another beautiful Takis crust.

Once it's ready, lift the sandwich out of the skillet with a spatula (because we have done a LOT of research and discovered that HAND BURNING = BAD) and place it on a cutting board. Cut that thing in half, embrace the fuego, and dig right in.

Takis Pimiento Cheese Bonus Content

Pimiento cheese is a classic condiment in the South. It's great on crackers or a biscuit. It is also famously, in Columbia, South Carolina, put onto a pimiento cheeseburger. So feel free to make extra of this Takis version and snack on it in any of these other delicious forms.

FLAMIN' HOT CHEETOS CHICKEN SANDWICH

Everyone knows that Flamin' Hot Cheetos dust is one of the great flavors in the known universe. But it is also one of our great tragedies, as it is almost exclusively eaten off one's own fingers (or, very occasionally, licked off the fingers of someone you love very, very much). But we here at Mythical believe that while licking your own fingers is a great way to spend an evening, there might be another—dare we say better?—way to get that Flamin' Hot dust into your body. So we present: the Flamin' Hot Cheetos Chicken Sandwich, aka the TRUE king of finger-lickin' good (but also please don't sue us, KFC—we love your chicken).

Step 1: Prep the Chicken. First up, you've got to pound your meat (see how we didn't make that a joke, because we're moving on to the rest of the instructions now), making for a better cook and a better sandwich. Lay out a big sheet of plastic wrap on your cutting board or work surface. Then put those chicken thighs right on there, spaced out as much as they can be. Lay another sheet of plastic over the top.

Now it's time to get out some aggression. Using a meat mallet or rolling pin (or if you want to run the risk of possibly shattering glass everywhere, you can use a hot sauce bottle or a wine bottle), start beating your meat (still not making a joke) by hitting the thickest part with moderate force, to try to get it all to an even thickness. Keep pounding away at your meat until you have reached completion. (This is still not a joke; that's just the most accurate and normal way we could think to describe it.)

Now you can discard the plastic, transfer those thighs to a plate, and season them with the salt. Put them in the fridge to rest and dry brine while you make the breading.

Turn your hands into fists and start smashing up the Cheetos in the bag to break them up. Now dump the bag into the bowl of a food processor, along with a hefty pinch of the flour (this will help soak up the Cheetos grease), the cayenne, garlic powder, onion powder, and black pepper. Blitz that sucker until you have a fine red powder. Transfer it to a wide plate for breading.

Now you can set up the rest of your breading station. Put the rest of the flour on a plate or in a bowl. Then crack the eggs into a medium bowl and whisk in the hot sauce and milk.

Finally, you can bread your chicken. Take your thighs out of the fridge and pat them dry with a paper towel, then get to dredging. Start by dredging in the flour, then dip them into the wet mixture, letting any excess fall off before crusting the whole thing in that beautiful red powder. Lay them on a baking sheet and put them back in the fridge to allow them to set before frying (at least 30 minutes, but longer is better).

Recipe continues

Makes 4 sandwiches (2 for them and 2 for you)

Flamin' Hot Cheetos Chicken

4 boneless, skinless chicken thighs

½ teaspoon salt

One 8.5-ounce bag Flamin' Hot Cheetos

1½ cups all-purpose flour

1 teaspoon cayenne

1 teaspoon garlic powder

1 teaspoon onion powder

½ teaspoon ground black pepper

2 large eggs

¼ cup hot sauce

¼ cup whole milk

Josh's 4:1:1 Sauce

½ cup mayo

2 tablespoons sriracha

2 tablespoons hot sauce

The Sandwiches

Neutral oil, for frying, plus 1 tablespoon for toasting the buns

4 hamburger buns

4 big handfuls shredded iceberg lettuce (shrettuce), from about 1 head iceberg

One 16-ounce jar sliced pickled jalapeños

Step 2: Make Josh's 4:1:1 Sauce. Fun fact: this is called 4:1:1 sauce because the ingredients are in a 4:1:1 ratio. Also a fun fact? All you have to do is mix the mayo, sriracha, and hot sauce together and now you're done. Great job.

Step 3: Let's Sandwich! Heat your fry oil (using a deep fryer or a large, heavy-bottomed pot filled with at least 2 inches of oil, making sure that the pot is no more than two-thirds full) to 325°F (this lower temperature will help preserve the red color, while keeping the sugars and cheese dusts in your Cheetos from burning too much). Line a baking sheet with a wire rack or a plate with some paper towels for draining.

Fry up your chicken thighs in batches. Lay each one carefully into the oil and fry it until it is fully cooked and crunchy, about 4 minutes. Set it aside on the rack to drain. Once they are all fried, heat a wide skillet with the 1 tablespoon oil over medium heat and, working in batches if necessary, place your buns, cut side down, into the pan and let them toast until you have a little golden brownage happening, about 2 minutes.

Slather the top and bottom buns with your 4:1:1 sauce, then lay a handful of shrettuce on the bottoms. Place the chicken pieces right on top of the hunks of iceberg. Top each one with 5 to 10 slices of jalapeño, add the top bun, and then eat it, hopefully remembering that you invited only one other person so that you can eat an extra sandwich yourself.

How Do I Bread Better?

We did a full-blown fried chicken MythMunching episode of the show, in which we learned that resting breaded chicken for at least 60 minutes and up to 48 hours will result in better breading that holds together when you crunch your teeth through it. Plus, you can clean up the kitchen and take a break before you have to start cooking again.

NASHVILLE HOT CHICKEN MEATBALLS

Nashville hot chicken is sweeping the nation. But we here at Mythical Kitchen have an unhealthy love of meat in ball form (okay, fine, it's mostly just Josh, but still), and when we hear the word *chicken*, we often add the word *meatball* right after it, like some kind of Pavlovian response, except if Pavlov had been training Josh to want to turn everything into a meatball so that he could keep them in his pocket while deadlifting big disks of steel. Anyway, we said "Nashville Hot Chicken Meatballs" in our brain, and now we have made it a recipe, optimized for party appetizer snacking. Don't you wish every party had little squares of white bread with a pickle and a hot chicken meatball on it?

....

Step 1: Make Those Balls. Preheat the oven to 450°F. Set a baking sheet (maybe even lined with parchment paper if you want to get fancy) on the counter.

Put the chicken, egg, oil, salt, bread crumbs, granulated garlic, paprika, oregano, black pepper, and cayenne in a big old bowl and mix them all up until they're all mixed up. Get a little oil on your hands and start shaping your meat into balls about the size of golf balls and place them on the baking sheet. Once you've made all 15 balls, roast them for about 7 minutes. Flip your balls and continue roasting for another 8 minutes or so, to get the other side nice and browned.

Step 2: Make Hot Chicken Oil. Heat the oil in a small saucepan over medium-high heat. Keep on heating the oil until it is just shimmering—about 250°F. Meanwhile, mix together the cayenne, brown sugar, paprika, granulated garlic, and salt. Once the oil hits the correct temperature, stir in the nonreserved seasonings and remove it from the heat. Ta-da! Your oil is now hot chicken flavored!

Step 3: Go Time! Cut off the crusts from your bread like you're feeding a toddler, then cut each slice of bread into quarters (the perfect size for a golf ball–size meatball). Place them on a serving platter.

Makes 15 party appetizers for optimal snacking

Chicken Meatballs
1 pound ground chicken
1 large egg
1 tablespoon neutral oil, plus more for your hands
2 teaspoons salt
1/3 cup plain bread crumbs
1/2 teaspoon granulated garlic
1/2 teaspoon paprika
1/4 teaspoon dried oregano
1/4 teaspoon ground black pepper
1/8 teaspoon cayenne

Hot Chicken Oil
1 cup neutral oil
1/4 cup cayenne
2 tablespoons light brown sugar
2 teaspoons paprika
1 teaspoon granulated garlic
1 1/2 teaspoons salt

To Finish
4 slices white bread
15 slices bread-and-butter pickles

Finally, stir up your hot chicken oil to recombine and spoon it over each meatball. (If your oil got too cold, just heat it back up again—it should be hot enough to sizzle when it gets spooned over each ball.)

Once you have spooned your balls, place one on top of each square of bread, top with a pickle, and then spear with a toothpick. That's it! Now walk around your party and serve a whole tray of meatballs to your unsuspecting guests.

(Alternate version: just eat a tray of meatballs with whoever you want to spend your time with, even if that person is just yourself.)

JOSH'S CAJUN CHICKEN FETTUCCINE ALFREDO

This is a legitimate quick-and-dirty pasta that you can make on a regular old weeknight, inspired by our favorite cream-cheese-based-dessert-cake manufactory that also happens to be a restaurant. It's got chicken breast, it's got a whole mess of Tony Chachere's, and most importantly, you can cook the entire meal in the time it takes to boil water and cook pasta. (Think of this as a speed test. Or, you know, just take your time and enjoy your evening.) What are you waiting for? Let's go.

Start cooking!

....

Set a pot of water over high heat to cook your pasta and start the clock! (Okay, actually, the clock is just the water coming up to a boil and the pasta cooking.)

Get two pans going: (1) a medium sauté pan (for the chicken) over medium-high heat and (2) a large sauté pan or skillet (for the sauce) over medium heat.

Cut the chicken breast in half horizontally (or thinwise?). You want to end up with two wide, thin pieces. Coat both of those suckers in that first teaspoon of Tony C's.

Pour the oil into the medium (chicken) pan and lay those two breast pieces in there to start searing. You want some nice browning here—probably like 3 to 4 minutes per side. A little sizzle is okay because, remember: It's Not Burned, It's Blackened! (i.e., we didn't mess up, it was on purpose).

Put the butter into the large (sauce) pan, and as soon as it's melted, add the onion, garlic, and that second teaspoon of Tony C's. Stir it around and let the onion sweat for about 3 minutes.

Is your water boiling yet? If so, season it with a pinch of salt and drop that fettuccine right in there.

How many people does 8 ounces of pasta serve? Seriously, we have no idea, but this serves that many people. (It probably serves 2 people but also maybe 1.)

1 boneless, skinless
   chicken breast
2 teaspoons Tony Chachere's
   Creole Seasoning
1 tablespoon neutral oil
4 tablespoons (½ stick)
   unsalted butter
¼ yellow or white onion, diced
4 garlic cloves, palm heel
   struck and minced
8 ounces dried fettuccine
½ tablespoon paprika
½ tablespoon smoked paprika
2 tablespoons all-purpose flour
1½ cups whole milk
2 tablespoons tomato paste
1 tablespoon hot sauce
Parmesan wedge, for grating
Something green for
   garnish, like sliced spinach
   leaves, dried parsley,
   or minced chives

Once your onion is starting to become tender, add the paprika, smoked paprika, and flour and stir it all up—this is going to help make your sauce nice and thick. Keep on stirring and then check your chicken. Is it time to flip? Is it browned and maybe a little blackened? Okay then, flip it.

Meanwhile, keep on stirring that onion and garlic and let the flour toast (it should toast for, like, 2 minutes total). Then add the milk, tomato paste, and hot sauce and give the sauce a nice stir. Bring it to a gentle, steady simmer and keep it simmering, stirring occasionally, while the pasta cooks.

Check the other side of your chicken—it should be getting pretty close now. Take a small ladle of your pasta water and splash it right into the pan with the chicken, then scrape the bottom of the pan with a wooden spoon to deglaze it. When the chicken is cooked through, transfer it to a cutting board to rest (I like to just cut into it and see if it is cooked, but if you want to be a fancy person, you can use an instant-read thermometer to make sure the internal temperature is at least 160°F—carryover cooking will get it to 165°F). Then take all the beautiful Cajun

chicken water left in the pan and pour it into the pan with your sauce in it.

Okay, now check the pasta—the doneness should be about 30 seconds short of where you want it to end up. If you want it Nicole style (al dente), it should have a little bit of bite left in it. If you want it Josh style (Mormon mom overcooked), it should be reeeeeally mushy. As soon as it's where you want it, lift it with tongs and drop it into the pan of sauce.

Grate as much Parmesan into the pan as you can, then stir it all up, adding a splash of the pasta water to help bring it together, and then transfer it to 1 or 2 bowls (depending on whether you are eating this alone or pretending you're not eating this alone). Slice up that chicken and lay it on top of the pasta, then top with your green thing of choice and—ta-da—you have made your fat and carb and protein dreams come true!

HABANERO WATERMELON PARTY WINGS

You know what's good? Sweet and sour. You know what's better? Sweet and spicy. That's what makes things like sriracha or hot honey or Hot Tamales so good. The heat kicks your butt, and the sweet . . . kisses it? Yeah, let's go with that. So this is our recipe for crispy baked *and* fried chicken wings with a sweet-and-spicy habanero watermelon sauce that will make you want to drink . . . a lot of beer. Or milk.

How Do I Get Crispier Chicken Skin?

The trick to ultracrispy chicken skin involves using a low-heat cooking method to dry out the chicken skin while also rendering and breaking down the subcutaneous fat. Basically, you want to *prime* the fat slow and low, so that when you hit it with high heat to finish, you get that super-duper-crispy chicken skin that will soak up all your wing sauce while also staying crunchy. That's why we are low-temp roasting these wings in the oven before blasting them in the fryer and then tossing them in wing sauce.

Step 1: Start Rendering Those Wings. Preheat the oven to 250°F. Line a baking sheet with a wire rack or parchment paper. (A wire rack is ideal, because it creates more air flow, but you do you!)

Let's get that skin primed and ready for THE CRISPENING. Season the wings with the salt and place them on the prepared baking sheet with at least a little bit of space between them.

Bake for 30 minutes. Meanwhile . . .

Step 2: Make Habanero Watermelon Wing Sauce. Put the watermelon juice, habaneros, vinegar, honey, salt, and pepper in a medium saucepan and bring it to a strong simmer over high heat, and then reduce the heat to maintain it. You could also call it a "gentle boil." A gentleman's boil? Basically, let it bubble fairly aggressively without, like, popping and fizzing all over your stove.

Let the sauce reduce for 20 minutes, then remove from the heat and find a way . . . any way . . . to blend it. A stick blender/immersion blender right in the pot would be the easiest; alternatively, let it cool down and then do it in a regular blender. Once it's blended, pour it back in the pot (or keep it in the pot if you used an immersion blender) and let it simmer gently until it has the consistency of BBQ sauce, about 20 more minutes.

Meanwhile, combine the cornstarch and 1 tablespoon water in a small bowl to make a slurry. Once the sauce reaches the desired consistency, stir in the slurry, then transfer the sauce to a large sauté pan or skillet.

Step 3: Fry, Toss, and Eat! Heat your fry oil (using a deep fryer or a large, heavy-bottomed pot filled with at least 3 inches of oil, making sure that the pot is no more than two-thirds full) to 375°F. Line a baking sheet with a wire rack or a plate with paper towels for draining.

Working in batches (while making sure to maintain the oil temperature), fry those wings, a few at a time, until they are golden and crispy, about 6 minutes. Set them aside on the rack to drain.

Finally, heat up your sauté pan of wing sauce over medium-high heat and add the wings. Let them sauté together, shaking the pan and turning the wings once, for about 30 seconds, then serve immediately.

Wing Rendering

24 party wings (about 2 pounds)
2 teaspoons salt

Habanero Watermelon Wing Sauce

3 cups store-bought watermelon juice
1 or 2 habaneros, seeded (depending on spice preference)
½ cup red wine vinegar
½ cup honey
1 teaspoon salt
¼ teaspoon ground black pepper
1 teaspoon cornstarch

Fry Finish

Neutral oil, for frying

SRIRACHA FISH AND CHIPS

They say that "variety is the spice of life," but you know what is actually the spice of life? Spice. But just in case, let's add spice *and* variety to your same old delicious fish and chips, by getting some sriracha into our beer batter and ALSO into our tartar sauce—because it is really hard to do better than spicy, sweet, crispy, crunchy fish and chips with sweet, spicy, fresh, vibrant tartar sauce! Also, we're beer battering some Ore-Ida steak fries because we're already beer battering and frying stuff, so why not do it to French fries too? What—you don't like MORE flavor?

....

Step 1: Make the Sriracha Beer Batter. Put the flour, salt, and baking powder in a large bowl, then give it a nice little whisk so that all the white powdery things are mixed up. Pour in your beer and vodka and give it a strong whisk *again*. Add the sriracha and . . . we're sorry to say . . . whisk it again. Now let the batter rest for at least 15 minutes to hydrate and thicken while you move on to . . .

Step 2: Make the Sriracha Tartar Sauce. Boy, it sure feels like a lot of our sauces are just about listing a few ingredients and telling you to mix them together, and you're going to want to do that here too. So mix together the mayo, sriracha, pickles, shallots, and lemon juice in a small bowl. But if you want to make things a little more complex, you can, I dunno . . . do a spin move or a butterfly kick after you add each ingredient? It certainly won't make anything taste *worse*.

Step 3: Fry It Up! Let's start frying! Heat your fry oil (using a deep fryer or a large, heavy-bottomed pot filled with at least 3 inches of oil, making sure that the pot is no more than two-thirds full) to 350°F. Line two plates with paper towels for draining.

Meanwhile, pat the fish fillets dry with a paper towel and then cut them in half, crosswise. Season the fish all over with salt and pepper. Put the flour on a plate or in a wide bowl and dredge each fillet lightly in the flour, shaking off the excess. Then dip it in the beer batter until it is well coated. Let the excess batter drain off, then gently lay each fillet *away*

Makes 4 fish fillets and a bunch of chips . . . er . . . fries . . . to go with them

Sriracha Beer Batter
1½ cups all-purpose flour
1½ teaspoons salt
1 teaspoon baking powder
12 ounces light-colored beer
1 shot (3 tablespoons) vodka
½ cup sriracha

Sriracha Tartar Sauce
½ cup mayo
2 tablespoons sriracha
2 tablespoons minced pickles
2 tablespoons minced shallots
2 teaspoons lemon juice

Fry Station
Neutral oil, for frying
Four 7- to 8-ounce fish fillets, like cod, pollock, haddock, or skate
Salt and ground black pepper
About 1 cup all-purpose flour
One 32-ounce bag Ore-Ida steak fries

from you in the fry oil, working in batches so as not to overcrowd the fryer.

Fry each fillet for about 2 minutes, then *carefully* flip it over and fry the other side for another 2 minutes (or until the fish has an internal temperature of 145°F). Transfer to one of the prepared plates to drain and sprinkle with more salt (because any time you fry anything, a chef has to tell you to season it with salt, even if you don't think it will matter at all).

Once all the fillets are fried, it's time to fry up those French fries. Working in batches again, dip them, a few at a time, in beer batter and fry them for about 3 minutes—making sure not to clump them together or crowd the fryer so that everything ends up sticking together in a weird potato nest, because they are beer-battered fries, not a beer-battered potato nest (as delicious as that sounds).

Once they're fried, transfer them to the other plate to drain and season them with more salt, because it's the law. Then whenever you have enough fries to go with a piece of fish, pile them onto a plate with the fish fillets, serve with sriracha tartar sauce, and start diving in.

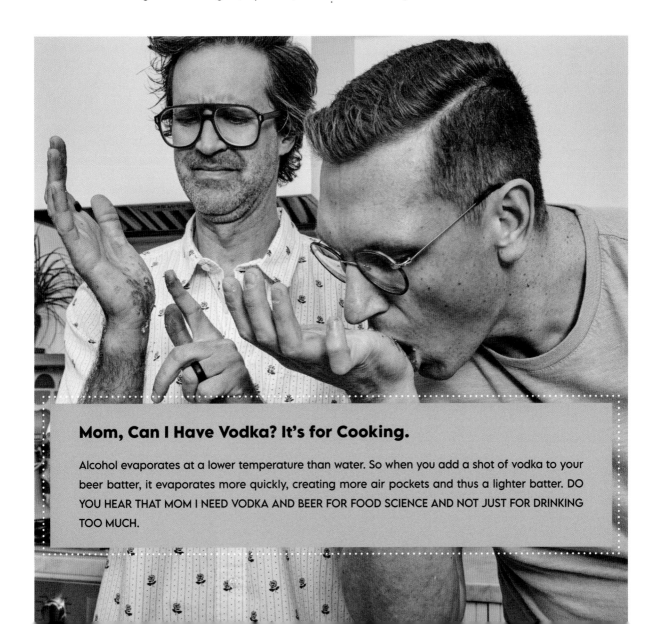

Mom, Can I Have Vodka? It's for Cooking.

Alcohol evaporates at a lower temperature than water. So when you add a shot of vodka to your beer batter, it evaporates more quickly, creating more air pockets and thus a lighter batter. DO YOU HEAR THAT MOM I NEED VODKA AND BEER FOR FOOD SCIENCE AND NOT JUST FOR DRINKING TOO MUCH.

BIRRIA DE RES SOUP DUMPLINGS

Sometimes we try to take our crazy ideas from *Mythical Kitchen* and then turn them into a *slightly* more accessible recipe that will be easy to make at home and still be incredibly delicious. But then sometimes . . . we take two amazing and complex foods that we love dearly . . . and we just . . . combine them and make the whole dang thing completely from scratch. This one is for the *real* Mythical Heads out there, who want to know what it feels like to be a tiny alien living inside of and controlling a full-size Josh robot body.

Birria de res—a slow-cooked, red-chile-tinged beef stew from Jalisco, Mexico—is one of the best things to eat in the world. Meanwhile, xiaolong-bao (or soup dumplings), hailing originally from Changzhou, China, are a delicate steamed dumpling, frequently filled with a pork broth (and made famous all across the world at restaurants like Din Tai Fung). So obviously, we figured we would take these two iconic dishes that culinary masters devote their entire lives to perfecting . . . and we're gonna show you how to combine them into one delicious Birria de Res Soup Dumpling. Well, more than one. We're gonna make a lot of them.

....

Important Note: This is a very long recipe that will probably take about 2 days. You're gonna have to make the birria the day before you need it, to allow the broth to congeal in the fridge. It would also really help if you had a bamboo steamer to steam your dumplings.

Step 1: Make Birria de Res. First up, soak your dried chiles in the warm water until they get nice and soft, about 15 minutes. Meanwhile, preheat your broiler to high.

Put the tomato halves skin side up on a baking sheet and broil until they are soft and maybe even a little blackened, about 5 minutes. Once they are cooked, set the oven temperature to 325°F.

Drop those cumin seeds and peppercorns into a dry pan over medium-high heat and toast until they are fragrant but not burned (i.e., delicious fragrant, not bad, bitter fragrant), about 2 minutes.

Recipe continues

Makes enough soup dumplings that you can freeze a whole mess of them for later. But probably, like, 40 dumplings.

Birria de Res
8 guajillo chiles, seeded
2 ancho chiles, seeded
3 cups warm water
2 medium tomatoes, halved
1 teaspoon cumin seeds
1 teaspoon black peppercorns
½ yellow or white onion, roughly chopped
4 garlic cloves, peeled
1 bay leaf
½ cup white vinegar
1½ teaspoons dried oregano
1 pound oxtail
1 pound beef shank
1 pound marrow bones
1 cinnamon stick
2 tablespoons salt
1 tablespoon powdered gelatin

Dumpling Wrappers
3 cups all-purpose flour, plus more for dusting
1¼ cups warm water

To Fill, Steam, and Finish
Juice of 1 good lime or 2 bad ones
1 teaspoon salt
2 tablespoons finely chopped jalapeño
3 tablespoons finely chopped cilantro stems
3 tablespoons finely chopped yellow or white onions

How Do You Put Soup in a Dumpling?

Fun fact: gelatin (the protein that comes from animal collagen) is what makes things solid and jiggly when cold or even room temperature. It also adds a lot of body and richness to a stock. But it is an essential component of soup dumplings, allowing you to stuff the dumplings with cold soup without spilling liquid all over the counter. When it steams, it liquefies inside the dumpling, making it super delicious and also slightly dangerous (hot soup attack!).

Put those toasted spices in a blender. Add the soaked chiles with their water, the broiled tomatoes (and any liquid), the onion, garlic, bay leaf, vinegar, and oregano. Blend on high until it's all nice and smooth and red and cool looking.

Put your oxtail, shank, and marrow bones in a big oven-safe pot with a lid. Pour in your beautiful red chile liquid, add the cinnamon stick and salt, and add an additional 5 cups water. Stir it all together, cover the pot, and place it in the oven to braise until the meat is super tender and the collagen has rendered and gelatinized, about 6 hours.

Take out the pot and lift out the bones and meat (um, not with your bare hands, though) and set them aside on a plate to cool.

Meanwhile, combine the gelatin and ½ cup water in a small bowl and let it sit for about 5 minutes to bloom.

Pour the gelatin into the birria liquid and stir to combine.

Finally, pour the broth through a fine-mesh strainer and into a cake pan—or, basically, anything where it can cool to room temperature but then also fit in your fridge and get all cold and jellylike and coagulated for optimal soup dumpling-ing.

Once the meat is cooled, pull it off the bones and shred it with your hands.

Save the meat in the fridge for later, and also put that cake pan of broth in the fridge, uncovered, to set overnight.

Step 2: Make the Dumpling Wrappers. Put the flour in a big ol' bowl and then start adding your warm water, one-third at a time, and knead with your hands until the dough starts to cool to room temperature and you have something of a unified, cohesive dough. Cover that thing with a damp towel and let it rest for 20 minutes.

Transfer the dough to a clean surface and knead it for another 7 minutes. How are your forearms feeling? Okay, cover it again and let it rest for another 10 minutes. You can even yell, "Relax the Glutens!" really loud, like you're saying, "Release the Kraken," but that's totally optional.

Finally, cut the dough ball in half and then cover the half you aren't working with. Lightly flour a work surface and use your hands to roll that puppy into a long, thin log about ¾ inch wide. Once you've done that, cut it into pieces about ¾ inch long, making a whole mess of little dump nugs. Take each nug and smash it down in your palm into something sort of resembling a circle. Use a floured rolling pin

Do I Need to Be a Dumpling Dough Hero?

No. You can absolutely just buy premade dumpling wrappers to make your life a little easier.

to roll these nugs, from the outside in (to make a slightly thicker center), until you have a circular-ish dumpling wrapper that's 4 to 5 inches wide.

Cover the rolled-out wrappers with a damp towel to keep them from drying out and then make the rest of them.

Wow, are you still with us? That's super impressive. But also, like, we *told* you this would be a lot of work and time, so we're really proud of you but also a little bit stunned. Oh man, wait until we tell you that you have to pleat the wrappers after you stuff them . . .

Step 3: Fill, Steam, and Finish! Alright! Combine your lime juice, salt, jalapeño, cilantro, and onion in a small bowl and give them a little swirl—that'll be your condiment (or *condimento* as they say in Italian, which is totally not relevant in any way to the dish we're making right now).

Put your gelatinized broth in a large bowl with half of the shredded beef and mix it up real good.

(Save the rest of the meat for burritos, chimichangas, tacos, or anything that seems like it might taste good with delicious shredded meat on it.)

Put about 1½ tablespoons of filling into the center of a dumpling wrapper. Place it on a flat surface (like, say, a table or kitchen counter), then lift the sides of the wrapper up around the filling, tucking and folding to pleat the edges and crimp it up into itself, creating a little nipple-like closed circle at the very top. Keep on filling up your dumplings until you have enough dumplings to fill up your bamboo steamer, keeping the remaining wrappers covered with a kitchen towel while you work.

Place the lid on the steamer and set it over a pot of simmering water. Steam those dumplings until the wrappers are cooked and tender, about 10 minutes. To eat them, place each one on a big soup spoon, seasoned with your chile-lime condiment. You can also bite the little nipple off the top and pour the condiment right in there before eating for a real good, hot-soup-danger time. Or just wait for it to cool off a little bit and put the whole thing in your mouth and see what happens!

The possibilities are . . . not endless, but there are still a lot of them! Wow, great job. Celebrate all your hard work. The dumplings will still be quite good at room temperature if you want to wait to serve until they're all steamed, but they are best eaten while still hot.

What If I Can't Eat All These Dumplings in One Sitting?

If you are making dumplings, you may as well make *a lot* of dumplings. Once you shape them, you can place them in a single layer on a parchment paper–lined baking sheet and put them in the freezer. Once they have frozen, you can transfer them to a freezer bag and keep them in the freezer for up to 4 months for future steaming purposes! Cook them from fully frozen, and steam for 12 minutes.

SPICE KRISPIES TREATS

Just because you can make your brow sweat, your tongue tingle, and your lips swell like Kylie Jenner while eating sweets doesn't mean that you should. And the world would be a better place if more people put that kind of deep thought into their food. But hey, are you here to THINK, or are you here to COOK SOME DANG-SPICY FOOD?!?! That's what we thought! By harnessing the crunchy, cheesy, red dye #40-ness of Flamin' Hot Cheetos, and combining all that with the familiar light crunch of Rice Krispies Treats, you get a unique dessert that packs just the right amount of pleasure and pain. Does that sound creepy? Creepier than we intended, for sure. If you're not much of a baker, Rice Krispies Treats are your best friend. They're fun, they're infinitely customizable, and it's SO HARD to screw them up. We're basically all professional screwups at Mythical—it makes for fun content—and even we struggle to screw these up.

Either lube up a 9 × 13-inch casserole dish with cooking spray or line it with a sheet of wax paper.

Start by putting the Flamin' Hot Cheetos (remember, it's just half the bag, since we're sure you were going to snack on them no matter what) into a gallon ziplock bag and beating the heck out of them. We obviously recommend the palm heel strike—great for all self-defense and/or corn puff–crushing needs—but you may also use a meat mallet. The goal is to crush the Cheetos into roughly the same size as the Rice Krispies themselves, to ensure the treats set evenly. Don't go overboard and turn them into dust, but do be diligent with the crushing. Measure 3 cups of your crushed Cheetos and add them to a large bowl with the Rice Krispies. Mix with a spoon until combined.

Melt your butter in a large saucepan over medium heat, then add your marshmallows. Most large marshmallows will come in a 10-ounce package, but if you're using mini marshmallows, the volumetric (good SAT word right there) measurement comes out to about 6 cups. Cook the buttery mallows, stirring constantly with a wooden spoon or a silicone spatula, until there are no more lumps left. This may take about 5 minutes.

Remove the pot from the heat, fold in your cereal and crushed corn puffs, then pour the cereal mixture into the prepared pan and gently even out the top with your spatula. You could let it set in the fridge for an hour, and then stop there and slice them up—OR you could really go for greatness. For extra credit, combine your white chocolate chips and coconut oil in a small bowl and heat in the microwave, in 20-second bursts, stirring after each interval, until they are melted and flow freely. Use a spoon to drizzle white chocolate over the top in a super-cool pattern (we modeled ours after Jackson Pollock's *Cathedral*), then while the chocolate is still melted, scatter your sprinkles over the top.

Slice, serve, and refuse to give a straight answer when someone asks, "Dude, why didn't you just make normal Rice Krispies Treats?" Do a lot of stammering and stuttering, before shoving a Spice Krispies Treat in your mouth and sprinting away.

Serves 4 to 40 people, depending on spice tolerance and enjoyment

Cooking spray
Half of an 8.5-ounce bag Flamin' Hot Cheetos
3 cups Rice Krispies
3 tablespoons unsalted butter
10 ounces marshmallows

Optional Add-Ins
1 cup white chocolate chips
2 teaspoons coconut oil
1 tablespoon red sprinkles or red sanding sugar

CAROLINA REAPER BBQ SAUCE

Come on. Come *onnnnnnn*! You know this cookbook wouldn't be complete without at least one acknowledgment of the fact that Rhett and Link once put their lives on the line by eating a whole Carolina Reaper—the world's spiciest pepper at the time—on YouTube while thirty-one million people watched with equal parts excitement and horror. And when Y2K finally happens and the internet is wiped clean (there's a chance it was just delayed), their pain will be immortalized in these dead trees. Rhett and Link, you crazy bastards—we salute you. And we could think of no better homage than creating a Carolina-style BBQ sauce for our favorite Carolina-born, Carolina Reaper–eating daredevils of spice. (Yeah, technically this is a South Carolina–style BBQ sauce, but Rhett prefers it. Take it up with him!) If you're not in the mood to spend an entire day writhing in pain on the toilet, and you just want a much less spicy sauce for your chicken, you can sub out the demon pepper for a jalapeño, or even some chile flakes.

....

IF YOU ARE USING AN ACTUAL CAROLINA REAPER, OR GHOST CHILE, OR HABANERO, OR EVEN A JALAPEÑO, PLEASE USE GLOVES AND DO NOT TOUCH YOUR EYES! Fun fact: one of the Kitcheneers had to go to the hospital because of a freak accident that involved a habanero seed under their contact lens! Might want to consider getting some swimming goggles and a KN95 mask as well. Treat this pepper as if it were a toxic waste spill from the beginning of a zombie apocalypse movie.

Okay, great, you're all protected now. Add your chile to a blender along with the vinegar, then blend and try to avoid any amount of breathing for as long as you can. When the chile is blended, run the liquid through a fine-mesh strainer to get the chunks and seeds out. Don't worry, it'll still be spicy enough.

Transfer the chile mixture to a medium saucepan along with the yellow and brown mustard, honey, brown sugar, salt, black pepper, paprika,

Makes about 18 ounces BBQ sauce

1 fresh Carolina Reaper pepper (or, for the love of God, 1 teaspoon red pepper flakes or any other chile pepper, depending on your desired heat level)

¾ cup apple cider vinegar

½ cup yellow mustard

½ cup brown mustard

¾ cup honey

¼ cup packed light brown sugar

1½ teaspoons salt

1 teaspoon ground black pepper

1 teaspoon paprika

1 teaspoon onion powder

1 teaspoon garlic powder

onion powder, and garlic powder. Just throw it all in there and make the world's most painful bubble bath! Cook over medium heat, whisking until the mixture comes to a simmer and then stirring frequently until it thickens to the consistency of a BBQ sauce, about 10 minutes. Remove from the heat, let the sauce come to room temperature, and then store the sauce in the fridge—preferably in whatever those things are that bomb squads use for controlled detonations, or really any airtight container. The sauce will be good for up to 1 month in the fridge. We recommend using it on chicken. Uhhhh. Good luck?

CHORIZO SPAGHETTI CARBONARA

Serves 2

8 ounces dried spaghetti

4 ounces Mexican pork chorizo (preferably from a tube, or casing removed if using links)

1 large egg plus 2 egg yolks

3 tablespoons grated Parmesan (cotija is also super delicious!), plus more for serving

Jalapeño slices and cilantro leaves, for garnish

Heck, add a fried egg on top if you want!

This recipe is dedicated to Italy. The whole country. And every single person inside it. Sergio Leone, the Pope, my old roommate Gabriele—all of them. But, most of all, it is dedicated to the Italian people who comment on every single pasta recipe video, telling the maker just how inauthentic it is, just how much of an offense to Italian culture it is, and just how much their dead grandmother is rolling in her grave right now. Requiescat in pace, dearest nonna. There must be a government agency that dispatches one hyperbolic commenter to every video of fettuccine alfredo, or spaghetti and meatballs (real Italians would never!), or, god forbid, carbonara with cream. You beautiful, fervent defenders of the Adriatic, we have nothing but respect for your rantings and ravings. But that will not stop us from releasing Mexican chorizo carbonara upon the world. All we can do is hope for your mercy, and humble ourselves before your queen, Giada De Laurentiis. And it's really good! Chorizo and eggs is a god-tier breakfast; carbonara is a god-tier egg-based pasta. What's not to love?

Heat a large pot of salted water on high. If you salt your water first, it will take slightly longer to boil, but this isn't speed chess. Okay, FINE! Let your water come to a boil, then add salt. Jeez. A good rule of thumb is 2 tablespoons of salt per gallon of water, but you can really just eyeball it (or honestly just taste it, it's just salt and water). Cook the spaghetti according to the package instructions. When it is almost finished, reserve ⅔ cup of the cooking liquid and set it aside. Drain the pasta and set that aside too.

Meanwhile, heat a large sauté pan over medium-high heat, squeeze (less than) half of a 9-ounce tube of chorizo directly into the pan. If you didn't buy your chorizo in a tube, you are seriously missing out. More meat should be sold in a tube. Chorizo has so much fat in it (and sometimes lymph nodes!) that you don't even need to preheat your pan. Break the chorizo up with a spoon and reduce the heat to low. Let it cook gently, allowing the fat to render and the chorizo to cook through, about 7 minutes. Keep it in the pan over low heat.

Combine your egg, egg yolks, and Parmesan in a large bowl and whisk together along with the reserved pasta water until combined and frothy. Add your spaghetti to the pan with the rendered chorizo and sauté until some of the grease is absorbed by the spaghetti, about 30 seconds. Now you are in what we call Tim Tebow clutch time. If you don't understand that reference, that's perfectly okay; there will be another reference in this book for you.

In your right hand, you will hold either a pair of tongs or a pair of chopsticks, whichever you are more comfortable with. In your left hand, you will hold the pan of hot grease spaghetti. Working with great alacrity (another good SAT word right there), you will dump the hot cooked spaghetti into the cheesy egg mixture and stir vigorously for 30 seconds with the tongs or chopsticks. The residual heat from the spaghetti and grease will be enough to pasteurize the eggs and turn them into a lush, savory custard. Some people advocate putting the spaghetti back into the pan to heat, but it is our position that you will likely create scrambled egg spaghetti. That's a delicious dish unto itself, but it is not carbonara.

Twist the spaghetti all fancy-like, then splap it in a shallow bowl (pasta tastes 30 percent better eaten out of a shallow bowl, everyone knows that) and garnish with any combination of grated Parm, jalapeño slices, cilantro, and/or a fried egg. Or nothing. You can also garnish it with nothing.

IF YOU CAN DREAM IT, YOU CAN DEEP-FRY IT

(DEEP-FRIED)

We have deep-fried an absurd number of things here at Mythical. Many people, including the entire American Heart Association, would likely say we have deep-fried too many things here at Mythical. And there are two very simple reasons we've done that: (1) Deep-fried food is delicious and (2) Mythical Entertainment LLC was only founded as a shell corporation to absorb tax liability from Rhett and Link's real money-making operation, Crispee Towne.

Although the boys have always had an undeniable passion for music and entertainment, the YouTube videos were meant only to serve as a marketing arm for the multinational deep-fry restaurant franchising business. There were plans to bring Crispee Towne everywhere: Los Angeles, New York, Miami, Charlotte, Topeka, London, Singapore, Dubai, and even Ulaanbaatar. Would Mongolians really want to eat deep-fried refried beans? Rhett and Link were about to find out!

They brought me on the team as Chief Frynancial Officer (CFO) in 2017—the project had already been delayed six years due to the Burbank fire marshal's draconian rules—and I started making videos on the *Mythical Kitchen* channel in the meantime as proof of concept. Donut fried chicken (Nashville Sweet Chicken), Spaghetti Fries, Funnel Cake Grilled Cheese—these were all supposed to be our staple menu items. The fire marshal capitulated to our demands, and our patent for the Frydaddydidilator (an industrial deep fryer shaped like Rhett's mouth) got approved in late 2018, but unfortunately, we were hit with several lawsuits from the beloved Filipino supermarket fried chicken stand Crispy Town.

As time passed, the dream of Crispee Towne faded. We kept making YouTube videos—heck, Rhett and Link even had a Food Network show—but what's the point of all that if we can't bring nacho donut holes to every corner of the globe? As I was doing research for this book, I stumbled upon the original business plan for Crispee Towne, and since it's likely never going to be a reality, I want you to see it. Enjoy.

Crispee Towne

BUSINESS PLAN

FOR INTERNAL USE ONLY

Artist Previsualization

LOCATION: Burbank, California
OWNERS: Mythical Entertainment LLC
OPENING DATE: TBD Fall 2014

Projected Revenue by Fiscal Year

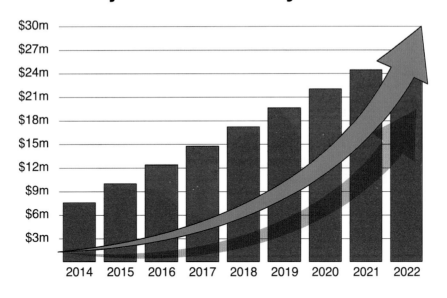

$30m								
$27m								
$24m								
$21m								
$18m								
$15m								
$12m								
$9m								
$6m								
$3m								
2014	2015	2016	2017	2018	2019	2020	2021	2022

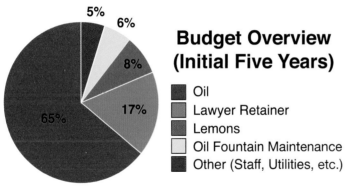

Budget Overview (Initial Five Years)

- 5%
- 6%
- 8%
- 17%
- 65%

- Oil
- Lawyer Retainer
- Lemons
- Oil Fountain Maintenance
- Other (Staff, Utilities, etc.)

Key Pillars of Crispee Towne

FRIENDSHIP • OIL • LIMITED LIABILITY

Success

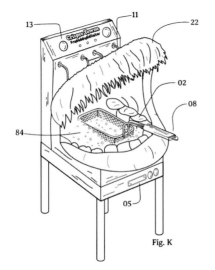

Fig. K

U.S. Patent Office Application

Frydaddydidilator
Mythical Entertainment LLC

Fig. K - Guide
02 - Hand Carved Teeth
05 - OLED 4K Temperature Display
08 - Stain Resistant Carbon Fiber Frying Basket
11 - Magnetic Oil Pressure Tube
13 - Music Volume Control Knob
22 - "Free Range" Yak Hair Mustache
84 - Signature 5 Blend Frying Oil

CHICKEN-FRIED CHEESEBURGER

I'm about to get a little emotional here. This was the first-ever dish I made for *Good Mythical Morning*, on "Will It Burger?" way back in 2016, before I was a full-time employee, before a dedicated cooking channel was a glint in anyone's eye, and before there was an actual kitchen at the *Mythical* studio. I precooked everything—at two in the morning, because I had a full-time magazine job and several more part-time gigs—in the kitchen of my tiny one-bedroom apartment, packed it all up in Tupperware, and reheated it in a microwave on set. I had a great time (watching Link sink his teeth into a burger made entirely from animal skins and gag immediately truly was a life highlight), and the fans welcomed me warmly, but I didn't think too much of it. I was busy being a writer, and they were busy making YouTube's biggest show. About a year after we shot that episode, I sent them a copy of my first cookbook, and less than two days later, Stevie sent me a message on Twitter basically asking me if I wanted a job. I could go on and on listing the timeline of crazy events that unfolded, but sometimes it's better to let those moments live in our hearts. I just want to take this time to say thank you to Rhett, Link, Stevie, and the whole Mythical family for allowing me to turn all my stupid food dreams into a reality and, ultimately, turn that into a book. And now let's wipe the single tear from our collective cheek and chicken-fry an entire cheeseburger.

Step 1: Make the Bacon Country Gravy. Slap the bacon into a medium pot over medium heat and let it start cooking. Stir it from time to time, until you've got crispy bacon living in a soup of its own smoky, delicious, rendered fat, about 7 minutes. Dump the flour in there and stir it up, allowing it to toast for about 2 minutes. Add the salt and pepper and begin slowly adding the milk, a little at a time, stirring constantly and maintaining a gentle simmer so that the milk will reduce and thicken but not burn, 4 to 5 more minutes. Once it is thick enough to coat the back of a spoon, remove it from the heat and set it aside until it's time to plate. You can also taste it and then yell out, "Good gravy, that's good gravy!"

Recipe continues

Makes 1 chicken-style deep-fried burger of ground beef with cheese

Bacon Country Gravy

4 slices bacon, finely chopped

2 tablespoons all-purpose flour

½ teaspoon salt

¾ teaspoon ground black pepper

2 cups whole milk

The Cheeseburger

1 tablespoon neutral oil

6 ounces 80/20 ground beef

¼ teaspoon salt

About 1 tablespoon ketchup

About 1 tablespoon yellow mustard

1 hamburger bun

3 pickle slices

2 slices American cheese

Chicken-Frying Town

2 cups all-purpose flour

2 tablespoons Tony Chachere's Creole Seasoning

3 large eggs, whisked

Neutral oil, for frying

Step 2: Make a Cheeseburger. It's time to make a cheeseburger so we can coat it in egg and flour and fry it up in a cast-iron skillet, while also still being a little emotional about Josh's first day at Mythical. Okay now, suck it up, let's cook. Why are you crying? What's that? *I'm* crying? No, that's the black pepper in my eye, YOU'RE CRYING.

Okay, crank a sauté pan over medium-high heat and add the oil. Shape the ground beef into a burger patty that's just *slightly* wider than the hamburger bun. Season one side of it with half of the salt and then lay it salt side down in the pan. Then season the other side with the rest of the salt and let the patty sizzle and fry until it's got a nice bit of color to it, about 90 seconds, then flip it over and cook the other side.

Meanwhile, spoon the ketchup and mustard on the cut sides of both halves of the burger bun. Lay the pickle slices on the top bun and lay a slice of American cheese on each side too (for burger adhesive purposes but also because cheese and burger makes cheeseburger). Once that burger is cooked, lay it on the bun—then sandwich it closed and put the whole burger back in that pan. Use your hand (the original kitchen utensil) to smash it down with a little pressure to help compact it. After about 10 seconds, flip it and repeat with the other side. No, this is not a Smashburger, but it is a smashed cheeseburger.

Lift the burger out and set it aside to rest and congeal while you set up your fry station.

Step 3: Chicken-Fry That Cheeseburger. We're almost there! Whisk that flour and Tony C's together in a medium bowl. Then in a wide bowl, whisk up those eggs.

Meanwhile, set a heavy-duty skillet (ideally cast iron) on the stove and pour in 1 inch of oil. Heat over high heat until it reaches 350°F, then adjust the temperature to maintain the heat.

Finally, dredge that compacted cheeseburger in flour, shake off the excess, and drop the burger into the egg, flipping it around until it's all nice and coated. Let the excess drain off and dip it back in the flour, letting it get all craggy and cool looking.

Lay the breaded cheeseburger into the hot oil to shallow-fry it until the bottom is golden and crunchy, about 2 minutes. Flip it over carefully and fry the other side for another 2 minutes. Once you have a beautiful, golden, crispy, chicken-fried cheeseburger, lift it up and let a little of the oil drain off, then place it on a plate.

Reheat that bacon country gravy and pour it right on top of your burger. Eat it with a fork and knife because CHICKEN-FRIED CHEESEBURGERS ARE CLASSY (and also because it would probably be really sloppy to eat with your hands).

NASHVILLE SWEET CHICKEN

Many people have inquired about our artistic process. How, they ask, do you come up with such unique dishes tinged with genius? Surely, they guess, you must carry notebooks when you travel and diligently scribble down all the flavor notes and dish compositions that inspire you. Surely you must have a network of muses and oracles that communicate directly with the culinary gods. We're afraid it is much more complex than that. One day, in the studio—our creative sanctuary—someone said, "What if Nashville hot chicken, but sweet?" And that, dear reader, is how genius is born. Okay, so, in actuality, the creative process is pretty simple, but many of the best foods are pretty simple as well. You take the traditional grease soak of a Nashville hot chicken and replace that with a layer of glaze, then you replace the spicy dusting with churro-esque cinnamon sugar, and then you replace the white bread base with a donut. Boom. Nashville sweet chicken.

....

Step 1: Make the Chicken Tenders. Season those tenders up with 1 teaspoon of the salt. Set them in the fridge to rapidly dry brine while you get all your breading and frying stuff ready.

Dump the egg whites into a medium bowl and then warm up your rotator cuff and start whisking aggressively until you've got fluffy whites—they should be well beaten and aerated but don't have to be *quite* at soft peaks. We're looking for . . . let's call them . . . impotent peaks?

Combine the flour, black pepper, paprika, cayenne, and the remaining salt in a large bowl and give that a thorough mix so that one poor soul doesn't get all the cayenne in one bite.

Dip the tenders one at a time in the seasoned flour, then the egg whites, then back into the flour mixture. Set them aside on a baking sheet until all the tenders are complete.

Recipe continues

Makes 4 donut sandwiches, each one filled with glazed, sugared, donut chicken tenders

Chicken Tenders

8 chicken tenders

2½ teaspoons salt

3 egg whites

1½ cups all-purpose flour

¾ teaspoon ground black pepper

¾ teaspoon smoked paprika

½ teaspoon cayenne

3 cups peanut or vegetable oil, for frying

The Glaze and Finish

¼ cup whole milk

2 tablespoons unsalted butter

1½ cups powdered sugar

1 teaspoon ground cinnamon

2 tablespoons granulated sugar

¼ cup Crystal hot sauce or vinegar-based hot sauce of your choice

¼ cup pancake syrup (we prefer Pearl Milling Company)

4 glazed donuts, sliced in half horizontally

How Do I Make My Fried Chicken Crispier?

One of the many myths we munched on the show was about how "fried chicken tastes better in a cast-iron skillet than it does in a deep fryer." Well, that one turned out to be TRUE! The contact with the pan creates more browning and a crispier, more flavorful crust.

Does My Chicken Need a Rest?

For better results, bread the chicken and then place it on a (ideally, wire rack–lined) baking sheet in the fridge, uncovered, for at least 2 hours and up to 24 hours before frying. This will make for breading that clings better to the chicken and doesn't slide off when you take a bite. But you can also just fry it right away because, well, it's all getting glazed and going onto a donut.

When you're ready to fry, set up a cast-iron skillet (or deep fryer if you really want to) with the oil and heat it over medium-high heat until it reaches 350°F, then adjust the heat to maintain the temperature.

Lay the tenders into the skillet, working in batches so as not to overcrowd the pan. Fry until golden brown and crispy on the bottom, 4 to 5 minutes, then flip them over and repeat on the other side.

Meanwhile, set up a glazing station. For best results, set a wire rack into a baking sheet—this way you can drain the fried chicken tenders and *also* glaze them in the same place. If you don't have a wire rack, drain the tenders on a paper towel–lined plate and then transfer them to a platter or baking sheet for glazing.

Once all the tenders are fried and rested, you can get ready to . . .

Step 2: Donut Glaze Your Tenders. Combine the milk and butter in a small saucepan over low heat. Heat until the butter is melted and the milk is warm, then slowly whisk in the powdered sugar. Remove from the heat and set aside.

Mix the cinnamon and granulated sugar in a small bowl until nice and combined. Then in *another* small bowl (or even a Mason jar with a lid that you can shake up), combine the hot sauce and syrup and give it a nice mix.

Let's make sandwiches! Drizzle the glaze over both sides of your chicken tenders, then sprinkle them with cinnamon sugar. Finally, slather some of the hot sauce syrup on either side of your donut halves, then fill them with glazed chicken tenders and start eating!

Bonus Microwave Content

In the words of Liz Lemon, "Did you ever put a donut in a microwave?" Well, she is super-duper right about this one. To refresh your donuts, hit them in the microwave for like 10 seconds—just to get warm. This tricks them into tasting like fresh donuts!

FUNNEL CAKE GRILLED CHEESE

We're gonna let you in on a little secret. Sometimes when we ask a question like "Funnel Cake: Will It Grilled Cheese?" we already know that the answer is a resounding YES. Because *of course* funnel cake will grilled cheese. How could it not? It's two funnel cakes, with cheese in between them. But since we don't feel like we're really doing our job if we just tell you to "buy two funnel cakes at a local state fair and then put cheese in between them," we're going to show you how to make funnel cake from scratch, so that you can infuse some white cheddar deep, deep inside the funnel cake itself, before melting some cheese on top and then smashing (er, sandwiching) the whole thing together with a little strawberry jam for a sweet-and-salty fun time.

....

Step 1: Make the White Cheddar Funnel Cakes. Preheat the oven to 375°F.

Place your oil in that 5- to 6-inch-wide tall-walled saucepan (see note on page 233), making sure there is at least 2 inches of room at the top for when you start to fry. Heat the oil to 375°F, adjusting the heat to maintain temperature while you make your batter.

Drop the cheddar into a large bowl and then add the eggs, milk, and butter and give everything a nice whisk until well combined. Add the flour, salt, and baking powder and whisk it all up again.

Divide the batter among four ziplock bags. Set up a landing station for your funnel cakes—like a wire rack–lined baking sheet or a platter lined with paper towels.

When the oil is at temperature, use scissors to snip off a ½-inch hole in the corner of the first bag and begin piping directly into the oil in a figure-eight motion until you've filled up the entire surface area and used up the batter in the bag. Let that sucker fry until it is golden brown on one side, about 30 seconds, then use a metal spatula to carefully flip it over and fry the other side until it is golden, too,

Makes 2 alarmingly large sandwiches

White Cheddar Funnel Cake
1 quart vegetable oil, for frying
1 cup shredded sharp white cheddar (about 4 ounces)
4 large eggs
1 cup whole milk
2 tablespoons unsalted butter, melted
1 cup all-purpose flour
1½ teaspoons salt
1½ teaspoons baking powder

Grilled Cheese
8 slices white American cheese
¼ cup strawberry jam
¼ cup powdered sugar

Side Question: Is *all* food a sandwich because you're sandwiching it between your teeth?

another 30 seconds. Once it is done, transfer it to the resting station and fry up the remaining three funnel cakes. Once they're all done, you're ready to move on to . . .

Step 2: Grilled-Cheese Those Funnel Cakes! Slap 2 slices of American cheese right on top of each funnel cake. Lay two of the funnel cakes on a baking sheet and bake until the cheese has just melted, about 90 seconds. Dollop one side with half of the strawberry jam. Close up that sandwich and repeat with the remaining funnel cakes, cheese, and jam.

Finally, put each funnel cake grilled cheese on its own plate, spoon the powdered sugar into a fine-mesh strainer, and dust it over the top of each sandwich because it is, after all, funnel cake. Now take a wide stance just in case, pick up the sandwich elbows out, and dig the heck in.

Vessel Note: The size of your tall-walled saucepan will directly affect the size of your funnel cake. The wider the pot, the wider the funnel cake. We recommend something that's about 5 to 6 inches wide. Anything wider will make a very thin and kind of annoying funnel cake.

MINI CRAB CAKE CORN DOGS

A lot of us grew up cooking out of boxes and bags, with ingredients like Hamburger Helper, Ritz crackers, or in this case, Bisquick taking a prominent role. But most of these products have—let's admit it—pretty boring recipes on the back of the box. Luckily, we think that there are few things in the world more endemic to a Mythical lifestyle than to take your own creativity for a dip into a box of Americana and come out with something truly delicious and unique. So we present a real stroke of creative delectability, fashioned through the integration of some of the great multicomponent ingredients our American food creators have hatched: canned crabmeat, Bisquick, Old Bay, and Lit'l Smokies.

···

Step 1: Make the Rémoulade. Welcome back to "For This Recipe All You Have to Do Is Mix All the Ingredients Together in a Bowl!" In this episode we are . . . um . . . just going to dump all the rémoulade ingredients into a bowl and mix them together. But look! You made rémoulade!

Step 2: Make the Crab Cake Corn Puppies. Go ahead and combine the crabmeat, Bisquick, cornmeal, egg, milk, Monterey Jack, scallions, mustard, and Old Bay in a large bowl and mix it all up together. Let this batter sit for 10 minutes to hydrate. Meanwhile, set up your fry station.

Heat your fry oil (using a deep fryer or a large, heavy-bottomed pot filled with at least 3 inches of oil, making sure that the pot is no more than two-thirds full) to 350°F.

Put the flour in a medium bowl and set up a landing station for your crab pups by lining a baking sheet with a wire rack or a platter with just plain old paper towels for draining.

Once the batter is rested, you can transfer some of it into a juice glass or highball glass—this is so that you can vertically dip your crab pups

Makes about 40 crab pups—or "a Josh's dozen"

Rémoulade
½ cup mayo
1 tablespoon Creole mustard
1 tablespoon finely chopped scallion
2 teaspoons hot sauce
1 garlic clove, grated
4 grates lemon zest
1 teaspoon lemon juice
1 teaspoon chopped capers
½ teaspoon Worcestershire sauce
Pinch of cayenne

Crab Cake Corn Puppies
8 ounces canned crabmeat, picked through for shells, drained and chopped
1½ cups Bisquick
¾ cup cornmeal
1 large egg
1 cup whole milk
½ cup shredded Monterey Jack (about 2 ounces)
¼ cup finely chopped scallions
2 tablespoons creole mustard
1 teaspoon Old Bay
Neutral oil, for frying
1 cup all-purpose flour
One 14-ounce package Lit'l Smokies cocktail sausages
Something green and chopped up, for garnish, like parsley, or chives, or honestly anything, because green things make brown food fancy

for optimal batter clingage. Skewer the end of a smokie with a toothpick, letting a little handle stick out. Roll it in flour, then dip the smokie right into the batter so that it clings to it. Carefully lower it into the fryer and cook until brown and crispy, about 3 minutes. Repeat with the remaining crab pups, working in batches.

Serve the crab pups on a platter with rémoulade for dipping. Sprinkle your green things onto the rémoulade and then, what the heck, you can even put on a party hat because this just became a cocktail (weenie) party.

RHETT'S DEEP-FRIED REFRIED BEAN BALLS

We all know Rhett is a top-tier beansman. So during an episode of *GMM*, when we wanted to find out the answer to the famed question "Will It Deep-Fry?" it was a surprise to no one that Rhett cracked open a can of refried beans, balled it up, breaded it, and deep-fried it to great success.

But while we're still keeping things really simple here, we are also seeing if we can amp up the flavor a bit through the addition of some Monterey Jack, chopped-up pickled jalapeños, and panko bread crumbs for extra crispiness. (Dare we call them . . . Bean and Cheese Ball-itos?) Let us tell you this: it absolutely deep-fries.

Makes about 9 balls of bean

One 16-ounce can refried beans
½ cup shredded Monterey Jack (about 2 ounces)
¼ cup finely chopped pickled jalapeños
1 cup all-purpose flour
2 large eggs, beaten
About 1 cup panko bread crumbs
Neutral oil, for frying, plus more for your hands
Salt, for sprinkling
Jarred salsa of your choice

Let's roll up some balls! First, plop the beans, Monterey Jack, and jalapeños into a medium bowl and give them a nice stir. Then set up three wide bowls or plates and put the flour in one, the eggs in a second one, and the panko in a third. Next up, grease your hands a little, then start shaping your bean mixture into golf ball–size bean balls by rolling them in between your palms. Roll them in flour, then dip them in beaten egg (letting that excess drip off, as always), and then roll them in panko. Set the balls on a plate or baking sheet and keep on going until all your balls are breaded.

And now, that's right, folks . . . it's time to set up that fry station! (If you're reading this cookbook like a novel, you are probably getting *really* familiar with setting up a fry station by this point.) All together now: "Heat your fry oil (using a deep fryer or a large, heavy-bottomed pot filled with at least 3 inches of oil, making sure that the pot is no more than two-thirds full) to 350°F. Line a baking sheet with a wire rack or a plate with some paper towels for draining."

Okay, wow, that felt like we were in a really delicious cult for a second. Is the oil heated? Yes? Time to start frying those balls. Fry your balls in batches, making sure to maintain consistent temperature without crowding the pot, until golden brown and crispy, about 3½ minutes, making sure to turn the balls from time to time for even crispying.

Transfer them to the rack or paper towels. Sprinkle with salt and then serve them with the salsa of your choice, making sure you don't burn your face off with the first one or else you won't really be able to enjoy the next ones all that much and then you'll just be really mad about how you did all this work and then ruined it by sticking your tongue into a ball of boiling-hot beans.

NACHO DONUT HOLES

If potato skins with melted cheese are Irish nachos, then . . . fried pizza dough balls dusted in nacho seasoning and dipped into nacho cheese are . . . Italian nachos? No. That sounds wrong. Let's go with the original title and call these the way-more-appealingly-named Nacho Donut Holes.

Could you just buy a can of Pillsbury pizza crust and roll that into balls and skip the whole make-your-own-pizza-dough step? Yeah, sure, go ahead, hurt our feelings. (What's that? We use Pillsbury pizza crust in another recipe later on page 266? Shhhhh . . .)

But we already have a killer recipe for pizza dough, thanks to our Bean Pizza on page 59, so we thought we would give you the chance to show off to your friends, your family, and more importantly, yourself. Let's go!

....

Step 1: Make the Pizza Donut Holes. As mentioned, we're going to use that Bean Pizza dough (page 59), except once we make our dough, we're gonna break it off into 24 balls and deep-fry them. But instead of *pretending* we're not just using that exact same recipe . . . we're going to use that exact same recipe (well, until it deviates). But we also didn't want to make you flip back to find it, so here it is!

In the bowl of a stand mixer fitted with the dough hook attachment, combine the water, olive oil, and sugar, stir to combine, and pour in the yeast. Give the yeast about 5 minutes to foam up and prove that it is as active as it says it is. If it is not . . . you're gonna have to let that little guy go. Get some new yeast and start over.

Add the flour and salt and then knead it on medium-low speed for about 7 minutes. It should start to lose its shagginess and get a little more cohesive. If it feels super dry and like it's not coming together? Add a splash of water and keep going. See how intuitive that is? It should be a little bit tacky and sticky. Transfer it to a CLEAN surface. Lightly oil your hands, then give it a few kneads by hand.

Now you can form it into a ball by picking it up and stretching it inside itself, like you're stuffing a sock. The top of the dough will get smooth

Recipe continues

Pizza Donut Holes
1¼ cups warm water

2 teaspoons olive oil, plus more for shaping

Heaping ½ teaspoon sugar

2¼ teaspoons (¼-ounce packet) active dry yeast

2¾ cups bread flour

2 teaspoons salt

Neutral oil, for frying

2 teaspoons Lawry's Seasoning

Quick Nacho Sauce
¾ cup canned evaporated milk

1 cup shredded pepper Jack (about 4 ounces)

5 slices American cheese

1 tablespoon juice from a jar of pickled jalapeños

2 teaspoons cornstarch

as it stretches and forms into what kind of looks like a doughy balloon. Then set that dough into a lightly oiled large bowl, cover it with plastic wrap, and let it sit on the counter until it has doubled in size, 1 to 3 hours, depending on the heat of your kitchen. Then wash your stand mixer bowl and hook before it gets hard and sets and you're like, "Wow, this is really hard to clean. I really should have cleaned this before it all dried out."

Once it has rested, set that dough ball on a cutting board or the counter and get ready to cut it into *deep breath* 24 relatively equal pieces. Ready for some maths? Cut the ball in quarters. Now you have 4 balls. Okay. Take each of those quarters and cut them in half. Now you have *checks notes* 8 relatively even hunks of dough. Shape each of those pieces into a somewhat evenly shaped log, then cut each of those logs into *thirds*. Now you have 24 pieces of dough!

Take the hunks of dough and, working quickly, roll them into balls. Think of it like you are stuffing a sock into itself until you have 24 ball-like pieces of dough. Place them on a baking sheet and cover with

plastic wrap or a kitchen towel to keep them from drying out while you set up your fryer.

Heat your fry oil (using a deep fryer or a large, heavy-bottomed pot filled with at least 3 inches of oil, making sure that the pot is no more than two-thirds full) to 350°F. Once it is hot, fry your dough balls, working in batches to maintain the temperature without crowding the fryer, until they are puffed up and golden brown, 3 to 4 minutes.

Transfer the donut holes to a large bowl as you finish each batch, and then toss them immediately with the Lawry's. Set them aside while you . . .

Step 2: Make the Quick Nacho Sauce. Combine all the sauce ingredients in a medium saucepan. That's right—ALL OF THEM. We're not screwing around here. Bring to a gentle simmer over medium heat, stirring constantly until the cheese has melted and the sauce is bubbling. Remove from the heat, transfer to a Dippin' Bowl (or plastic takeout container), and take your pizza donut holes for a swim!

SPAGHETTI FRIES

Makes about 24 spaghetti fries, serving 4 very hungry youngsters, or 12 people who want a nice snack

Why should potatoes get all the fun? Yeah, you can fry up a potato, and it is delicious. We know. We've tried. These "French-style fries" are popular the world over, but that doesn't mean that potatoes should be the only starch having a good time in a pot of oil. So we wanted to use cooked spaghetti, tossed together with cheese and egg (the protein makes it nutritious!), and dipped into a different tomato-based dipping sauce. Yeah, that's right, we're making Spaghetti Fries and dipping them in marinara sauce: it's as Italian as *Super Mario Bros.* and just as good. Let's a-go.

8 ounces dried spaghetti

1½ cups grated Parmesan (about 6 ounces), plus more for garnish

3 large eggs, beaten

Neutral oil, for frying

Warm marinara sauce, for dipping

Bring a large pot of water to a boil and season it with a hefty pinch of salt. Boil the spaghetti until it is Josh-level cooked (i.e., about 1 minute longer than the package instructions). Drain the noodles but DO NOT rinse them. You want all that starchiness to cling to them.

Dump the noodles straight into a large bowl. Add the Parmesan and give it all a nice toss. Keep on tossing it until the noodles are nearly room temperature—this is a delicate balance, since you want them to cool down without getting all clumped together.

Once cooled, add the eggs and mix super-duper well. Finally, line a quarter baking sheet (otherwise, just use half of a normal baking sheet) with parchment paper and lay the noodle mixture right on top, pressing it down into an even layer. Put another sheet of parchment on top and top it with *another* quarter baking sheet. Press it down, then put it in the freezer to set for about 1 hour.

Once you are ready to fry, start setting up your ol' fry station. Heat your fry oil (using a deep fryer or a large, heavy-bottomed pot filled with at least 3 inches of oil, making sure that the pot is no more than two-thirds full) to 375°F.

Meanwhile, take out your spaghetti sheet. Remove the top baking sheet and line it with a wire rack or paper towels for draining. Then remove the top sheet of parchment, transfer the spaghetti to a cutting board, and use a knife to cut the spaghetti into steak-fry-size rectangles.

Once the oil is ready, fry the spaghetti fries, working in batches to maintain oil temperature and not crowd the fryer, until golden and crispy, 2 to 3 minutes per batch. Transfer them to the rack to drain and immediately dust them with more Parmesan. Serve with warm marinara for dipping.

It's a-me: spaghetti fries.

BUFFALO CHICKEN CHIMICHANGAS

Makes 8 small-to-medium chimis

1 store-bought
   rotisserie chicken
½ cup crumbled blue cheese
2 large stalks celery
2 medium carrots
One 8-ounce brick
   cream cheese
1½ cups vinegar-based
   hot sauce (we are big
   fans of Red Rooster)
½ teaspoon garlic powder
½ teaspoon onion powder
½ teaspoon paprika
¼ teaspoon ground
   black pepper
Neutral oil, for frying
Eight 8-inch flour tortillas
Ranch dressing, for dipping
   (okay, FINE, city of Buffalo,
   you can use blue cheese
   dressing instead)

Billions of people go about their days like everything is normal. They wake up, brush their teeth, eat their breakfast, kiss their loved ones on the forehead, and go off to work. Maybe they're riding a bicycle through the streets of Hong Kong. Perhaps a Vespa in Milan. They could be driving a lifted truck in Big Sky, Montana, hauling hay bales. And 99.9 percent of these people are unaware that chimichangas exist. That Woody Johnson gave humankind a great gift in 1946—just one year before the Manhattan Project was disbanded—when the enterprising restaurateur dropped a burrito into the deep fryer and changed history. Every day that goes by without you eating a deep-fried burrito is, frankly, a day that you have wasted. Oh, you cracked the code on cold fusion today? Who cares, you had an undressed salad for lunch. Alas, it is not your fault. One can know only what one has learned, and many are uneducated. So we are here to teach you. We are here to spread the gospel of grease-soaked, delicious chimichangas.

Start pawing at that rotisserie chicken like a grizzly bear would paw salmon out of the Chinook River. Separate all the meat from the bones and discard the skin directly into your mouth while no one is looking. Put the shredded chicken meat in a large bowl along with the blue cheese.

Grate your celery and carrots using the large holes of a box grater. Wrap the vegetables in a clean kitchen towel, then wring that out over the sink to get rid of excess moisture. Depending on how gross you are, you can use that towel at the gym later! Add the drained veggies to the bowl with the chicken and blue cheese.

Add the cream cheese, hot sauce, garlic powder, onion powder, paprika, and pepper to a medium saucepan over medium-high heat and cook, whisking constantly, until the cream cheese is completely melted. Transfer the cream cheese mixture to the bowl with the chicken and give it a good toss. Allow the mixture to cool for at least 10 minutes on the counter, or 9 minutes and 18 seconds in the fridge.

Meanwhile, heat your fry oil (using a deep fryer or a large, heavy-bottomed pot filled with at least 3 inches of oil, making sure that the pot is no more than two-thirds full) to 375°F. Line a baking sheet with a wire rack or a plate with some paper towels for draining.

Hope you had a fun little 10-minute break! Now it's go time, baby. Heat a sauté pan over medium-high heat and griddle a tortilla for about 15 seconds on each side, until it is nice and pliable. Pile about ½ cup of filling on the warm tortilla, then roll it TIGHTLY into a burrito, and transfer it back into the hot pan fold side down. Then, just to be safe, use a toothpick to secure the burrito. Don't be a hero.

Repeat until you have 8 fully enclosed buffaloritos. Two at a time, CAREFULLY lower them into the fryer and fry each for about 90 seconds, until the tortilla is golden brown and crispy. Transfer to the rack to drain.

If you do not let these cool for at least 5 minutes before eating, you will need to go to the hospital with third-degree mouth burns. Let the previous sentence serve as legal protection against any future cookbook-based lawsuits.

Anyway . . . serve with ranch dressing.

SALT AND VINEGAR POTATO SKINS

If you see a hippopotamus in the wild, you will likely see several small birds riding on its back. These birds are called red-billed oxpeckers, and they mostly survive by eating ticks that burrow in the large mammal's skin. Famously ornery, the hippos curiously do not seem to mind the presence of the oxpecker, because they're living in a perfectly symbiotic relationship. The oxpecker gets food and a comfortable place to sit, while the hippo receives companionship and protection from parasites. Cheese and potatoes also exist in a perfectly symbiotic relationship. The cheese that rides on the back of these potato skins receives structure and substance, while the potato receives flavor and gooeyness. Cooking really is just like the animal kingdom. Burritos are like leopards. We will not be elaborating on this statement.

....

You gotta get your potatoes cooked. However you do that is up to you. As much as we love microwaves, microwaving baked potatoes always turns out just a little bit worse than you want it to. We're going to bite the bullet and bake them. Just make these on the weekend when you have time. Why do we always feel the need to apologize when a recipe takes a bit of effort? Sorry for apologizing. Dang it! Anyway, preheat your oven to 350°F, poke holes in your potatoes with a fork, then bake for about 1 hour, until a knife slides easily into the center of one. Slice the potatoes in half lengthwise and let cool on the counter for 15 minutes. Increase the oven temperature to 400°F.

Use a spoon to carve out a large potato divot in the center of your taters. You want about 80 percent of the potato gone, because that makes more room for bacon, cheese, and scallions. We would recommend taking the leftover potato pulp, mixing it with salt, milk, and butter, then scooping it into a plastic bag, cutting off one corner, and squeezing it into your mouth like a Go-GURT. We call this dish pogurt.

Makes 12 potato skins

6 medium Yukon Gold potatoes
Neutral oil, for frying
6 slices bacon
1 cup all-purpose flour
2 large eggs
One 7.75-ounce bag salt and vinegar potato chips
Salt
2 cups shredded cheddar (about 8 ounces)
1 cup sour cream
½ cup sliced scallions, white and green parts

Recipe continues

While the potatoes are cooling, heat your fry oil (using a deep fryer or a large, heavy-bottomed pot filled with at least 3 inches of oil, making sure that the pot is no more than two-thirds full) to 350°F. Line a plate with paper towels for draining.

Add the bacon to a cold wide skillet and turn the heat to medium. Cook until the bacon is browned and crispy, flipping as needed, about 8 minutes. Transfer the bacon to a plate. Allow the bacon to cool, then chop it up into bacon bits and set it aside.

Now's the time when you make a dredging station. Put the flour in a small bowl. Crack the eggs into another small bowl and whisk. Crush your salt and vinegar chips either in a bag or in a food processor. Set aside about ¼ cup of crushed chips for garnish and put the rest in a large bowl. Dredge your potato skins all over with flour, then dip each one into the egg. Put each potato skin in the potato chip bowl and toss the crushed chips all around the inside and outside, ensuring they stick to the potato. Repeat the process until all potatoes are crusted.

Working in batches, deep-fry the potato skins until crispy, about 3 minutes, then transfer to the paper towel–lined plate to drain. Season them immediately with salt. Once all those taters are fried, arrange them in a baking dish. Divide the cheese and bacon bits evenly across all the little boats, then bake for about 10 minutes, just until the cheese is melted. Top with sour cream, scallions, and the reserved crushed chips. Serve them at your nearest sporting event watch party. Doesn't matter what sport. You ever watch cricket? No? Well, time to make friends and learn a new sport!

REUBEN PIEROGI

Here is our official power ranking of Nebraska's contributions to society:

1. Corn
2. Heisman trophy–winning quarterback Eric Crouch
3. The Reuben sandwich

We deeply apologize to all other Nebraskan people, inventions, and landmarks that have been left off the list. Better luck next year, Hilary Swank. Many people assume that the Reuben—a holy quadrinity of corned beef, sauerkraut, Swiss cheese, and Russian dressing—must have come from an old-school New York deli, but it was actually invented at the Blackstone Hotel in Omaha in the early 1900s. Do we believe the story that it was invented during a high-stakes poker game, which is eerily similar to the Earl of Sandwich's absolutely bogus origin myth? Absolutely not. Pretty much every suspiciously convenient food origin myth is untrue. And that's why we're starting one right here: the Reuben Pierogi was invented in the Mythical Kitchen on March 18, 2021, when a radioactive spider bit a Polish dumpling . . .

Step 1: Make the Pierogi. Let's make some pierogi dough, shall we? Whisk together the water, milk, sour cream, egg, salt, and vegetable oil in a large bowl, then add the flour, ½ cup at a time, and stir with a wooden spoon until all the flour is incorporated. Turn the dough ball out onto a clean surface, sprinkle some flour on top, and knead the dough by hand for about 3 minutes, until it is nice and elastic, like the waistband on some good, quality Hanes boxer briefs. Not a sponsor, they just make good boxer briefs. Wrap the dough in plastic wrap and let it rest at room temperature for 30 minutes.

Step 2: Make the Russian Dressing. While the dough is resting, make some Russian dressing. If you don't feel like making dressing from scratch, we recommend using bottled Thousand Island, because bottled Russian dressing tends to be super, super sugary. But the homemade stuff? Hoooooo boy, that's a treat. (Tip: make sure the onion, bell pepper, and pickles are VERY FINELY minced. Finer than fine, in fact. Make those minced veggies INFINITESIMALLY small.)

Recipe continues

Makes 24 dumplings

Pierogi

½ cup warm water

2 tablespoons whole milk

2 tablespoons sour cream

1 large egg

½ teaspoon salt

1 tablespoon vegetable oil

2 cups all-purpose flour, plus more for sprinkling

Neutral oil, for frying

½ cup sauerkraut, squeezed completely dry

¾ cup leftover mashed potatoes (or prepared instant mashed potatoes)

½ cup shredded Swiss cheese

4 ounces finely chopped corned beef (lunchmeat-style works)

Russian Dressing

1 cup mayo

1 tablespoon red wine vinegar

2 teaspoons hot sauce

1 tablespoon ketchup

1 teaspoon prepared horseradish

1 tablespoon very finely minced red onion

1 tablespoon very finely minced red bell pepper

1 tablespoon very finely minced pickles

½ teaspoon paprika

¼ teaspoon salt

¼ teaspoon ground black pepper

Whisk the mayo, vinegar, hot sauce, ketchup, horseradish, onion, bell pepper, pickles, paprika, salt, and black pepper together in a medium bowl.

Start rolling out your pierogi dough. Flour a clean surface—preferably the kitchen counter as opposed to the bathroom floor—and use a rolling pin to roll out the dough until it is almost translucently thin (and don't be afraid to use some extra flour when rolling). If you do not have a rolling pin, use a wine bottle. If you do not have a wine bottle, use a baseball bat (a cricket bat will not work). Use a 4-inch diameter ring mold, cookie cutter, or biscuit cutter to cut the dough into circles. If you do not have a ring mold, use a big cup from an amusement park. If you do not have a cup . . . you really should have bought one before you bought a cookbook; that was a weird choice. Repeat until you have at least 12 large circles of dough. You can boil the scraps and eat them as a snack.

Heat your fry oil (using a deep fryer or a large, heavy-bottomed pot filled with at least 3 inches of oil, making sure that the pot is no more than two-thirds full) to 350°F. Line a baking sheet with a wire rack or a plate with some paper towels for draining.

Drain your sauerkraut and save the juice for sipping later. Sauerkraut juice wakes you up better than coffee ever could—trust us on this. Add the mashed potatoes, sauerkraut, Swiss cheese, corned beef, and ¼ cup of the Russian dressing (reserve the rest for dipping) to a medium bowl and toss to combine.

Get yourself a bowl of warm water ready and start filling those 'rogies! (We'll stop abbreviating things unnecessarily, sorry!) Dip your finger in the warm water, then wet the outer rim of the dough circle. Scoop about a tablespoon of filling into one hemisphere of the dough circle, then fold the dough over on itself to form a semicircle. Press down on the edges with a fork to seal. It is very important that the pierogi stay sealed in the fryer; otherwise, you risk significant bodily harm and, worse, lost pierogi.

Once all the pierogi are filled and sealed, fry them, working in batches, until golden brown, about 3 minutes, then transfer them to the rack to drain. Serve with additional Russian dressing and chase with shots of ice-cold sauerkraut juice. Prost!

EAT DESSERT FIRST, OR LAST, OR WHENEVER THE HECK YOU WANT TO
(DESSERT)

Here at Mythical, we fundamentally disavow dessert as a concept. Okay, okay, my god, stop booing and give us a second to explain! And who threw that rotten tomato? We're certainly not "we aren't really into sweets" people, and it will be a cold day in hell before we are "I'd rather have a piece of fruit than a brownie" people, but when you say *dessert*, you are implying there is an appropriate time to eat a piece of chocolate cake. And if you imply there is an appropriate time to eat a piece of chocolate cake, you are also implying there is an inappropriate time to eat chocolate cake, which is something we cannot abide.

You see, the word *dessert* comes from the French *desservir*, which literally meant to "de-serve" a table. In the mid-1500s, when French aristocratic dinner parties were being formally codified, a course of sweets would be sent to the table while the servants were clearing all the meat juice–covered plates, wine-filled goblets, and tea-stained plots to subdue populist rebellions. Fast-forward half a millennium, you're nine years old, you've just finished your plate of unseasoned steamed broccoli (people really didn't learn how to salt and roast vegetables until at least 2008), and your mom or dad places a Snack Pack pudding in front of you as a reward.

You have been born into a prison you cannot taste or touch, but you have the opportunity to escape. If you take the blue pill, the story ends. You continue eating dessert after dinner and believing whatever you want to believe. You take the red pill, you stay in Wonderland, and I show you how deep the rabbit hole goes. Okay, it doesn't go that deep, but it does allow you to eat cheesecake for breakfast and not feel totally weird about it, because, if you really think about it, most American breakfast foods are just dessert in disguise.

Consider the pancake. Denny's alone serves more than twelve million per year. You may have eaten a stack this morning. It is literally a cake that has been cooked in butter before being soaked in syrup! How is that a breakfast and not a dessert? Oh, oh, oh, but if you were to go to Denny's and request a cupcake alongside your bacon and eggs, suddenly you're the weird one. And don't even get us started on Pop-Tarts! *Tart* is just French for "pie"! It's a flat toaster pie that has frosting on it! Over time, American breakfast cereals even started morphing into desserts. Cookie Crisp, Oreo O's, Reese's Puffs—there are no rules anymore. Anarchy is alive and well, and you can eat whatever you want, whenever you want.

If chaos truly is a ladder, let's see how high we can climb, shall we? Dessert doesn't exist, breakfast doesn't exist, lunch doesn't exist, and dinner doesn't exist. They're all social constructs made up to sell you things. The only reason we think of bacon as breakfast meat is because of a public relations campaign launched by Sigmund Freud's nephew (this is actually true!) on behalf of a massive food supplier. He got one doctor to agree that a protein-rich breakfast is good for your health, had five thousand more doctors cosign that note, and then convinced a newspaper to publish an article as if it were an actual scientific study.

Society agrees so much that these meals don't exist that we started making up our own! Brunch—a meal supposedly meant to be eaten in between breakfast and lunch—is often served as late as 2:00 p.m. You want to put an egg on your burger, we absolutely get it, but you don't have to make up a fake meal to do so. And the same goes for "Fourth Meal," which was, as we all know, both a brilliant marketing campaign by Taco Bell and a rallying cry for all those who want to eat one, two, three, seven tacos at midnight without the judgment of others.

We're not advocating that you throw out all sense of human decency and eat a hot fudge sundae for every meal—life is, ultimately, about balance. But, if you feel yourself craving an ice-cold slice of Cheetos Apple Pie out of the fridge at 1:00 p.m. while waiting for your leftovers to finish reheating in the microwave, you should be able to do that. Because, as it turns out, you can indeed have your pudding even if you haven't eaten your meat.

CHEETOS APPLE PIE

Fun fact: apple pie is not American. It actually originated, we think, in England. So instead of the long-standing expression "as American as apple pie," we think it's time to change that narrative and present something WAY, WAY more American: Cheetos Apple Pie. After all, what's more American than taking credit for something we didn't invent, and then adding a beloved packaged food product that is available in pretty much every gas station in the country, made by a megasnack company (Frito-Lay) that is owned by an even larger company (PepsiCo). Hey, apple pie: America called, and it wants you to add Cheetos to it. (Also, cheese and apple pie are delicious together.)

Step 1: Make the Cheetos Pie Crust. Preheat the oven to 400°F.

Set aside about ½ cup of the Cheetos for the streusel (all the way in Step 3). Crunch up the remaining Cheetos a little and pour them into the bowl of your food processor. Add 3 tablespoons of the flour to the food processor as well, then blend until you have a fine powder.

Transfer 2 cups of the Cheetos powder to a large bowl and add the remaining 1½ cups of flour, the sugar, and the butter. (Set aside any leftover Cheetos powder to use for the pie filling.) Mix it all up with a fork (or your hands) until you have something that feels like wet sand.

Scrape that mixture into a 9-inch pie pan, then use your hands to press it tightly into the pan, making sure that the mixture goes all the way up the sides. Bake for 15 minutes, just to parbake the crust to set it. Once it's done, set it aside but keep the oven running.

Step 2: Make the Apple Filling. Melt the butter in a large sauté pan over medium heat until it is just starting to get slightly nutty smelling. Add the apples, sugar, and salt and cook, stirring occasionally, until the apples have broken down and a caramel has started to form at the bottom of the pan, about 15 minutes. Next, add the remaining Cheetos powder from Step 1 (not the completely different ½ cup of Cheetos you are saving for the streusel) and stir it in. Remove from the heat and set aside.

Makes 6 big slices of America

Cheetos Pie Crust
One 8.5-ounce bag Cheetos Crunchy (you will also use these for the filling and streusel)
1½ cups plus 3 tablespoons all-purpose flour
1 cup granulated sugar
6 tablespoons unsalted butter, melted

Apple Pie Filling
4 tablespoons (½ stick) unsalted butter
8 medium Honeycrisp apples (or whatever apple, who cares!), peeled and cut into chunks of ½ inch or so
¾ cup granulated sugar
¼ teaspoon salt

Cheetos Streusel
¼ cup all-purpose flour
½ cup tightly packed light brown sugar
4 tablespoons (½ stick) cold unsalted butter, cut into cubes
Canned whipped cream, for serving

Step 3: Streusel and Bake! It's time to bring in the reserves. Slide that ½ cup of Cheetos into a ziplock bag and then bash them up with your hands, or a heavy pot, or a bottle of wine, or a broken PlayStation, until you have coarse, chunky crumbs. Pour them into a bowl with the flour, brown sugar, and butter and mix it all up with your fingers. The butter should be in pea-size pieces. What you've got there in that bowl is a classic American Cheetos streusel.

Scoop the pie filling into the Cheetos crust in the pie pan and spread it evenly across the pan. Sprinkle the streusel over the top, then cover the pie with aluminum foil and bake until the top is browned and the filling is bubbling, about 25 minutes. If the top of the pie needs a little more browning, remove the foil and let it brown for a couple more minutes.

Let the pie cool for at least 2 minutes (JOSH, TAKE IT EASY). Slice it and serve it with whipped cream and, what the heck, crack open another bag of Cheetos and crumble some more on top too.

WENDY'S FRENCH FRY FROSTY CHEESECAKE

There are few things that are better in the world than dipping a Wendy's French fry into a Wendy's Frosty. In fact, I don't know if it's even possible to order those two items and not dip the fries into the Frosty, because if for some reason you don't, the person sitting next to you in the car will be like, "Hey, aren't you going to dip your French fries into that Frosty?" But then, even if there's nobody else in the car with you, somebody will walk up to you from the street, knock on your window, and be like, "Hey aren't you going to dip that French fry into that Frosty? Also, can I have some?"

We decided to find out if we could make something even better than dipping a French fry into a Frosty, by making this French-fry-crumb-crusted, Frosty-filled, Frosty whipped cream–topped cheesecake! Let's get into it.

....

Note: For best results, let the cheesecake chill overnight in the refrigerator before eating it.

Step 1: Make the French Fry Crumb Crust. Preheat the oven to 350°F.

Take a handful of those French fries and pulse them in a food processor until you've got ½ cup. Put them into a large bowl. Here's the good news: however many fries you have left that you didn't chop up? You can just eat those fries. Go ahead. We're not in a hurry.

Okay, great. Add the graham cracker crumbs, sugar, and butter to the fries in the bowl. Get everything all mixed up, with a nice sandy texture, then press it into the bottom of a 9-inch springform pan. You just want a nice, even layer all across the bottom (you don't need to do the sides).

Bake for about 8 minutes, until the crust is just set, then take it out of the oven and set it aside. Keep the oven on.

Step 2: Make the Frosty Filling and Bake the Cheesecake. In the bowl of a stand mixer fitted with a paddle attachment, combine the cream cheese, sugar, and mascarpone and "cream" the mixture, which is a fancy baking term for mixing stuff together, but it's a thing that we didn't think was an important step until we actually tried it both

French Fry Crumb Crust

1 large order Wendy's French fries
1¼ cups graham cracker crumbs
¼ cup sugar
5 tablespoons unsalted butter, melted

Frosty Filling

Four 8-ounce bricks cream cheese, at room temperature
1¼ cups sugar
½ cup mascarpone cheese
¼ cup milk chocolate chips
1 teaspoon coconut oil
1 small Wendy's Chocolate Frosty, at room temperature
¾ cup all-purpose flour
2 tablespoons cocoa powder
1 teaspoon vanilla extract
3 large eggs

Vanilla Frosty Whipped Cream

2 cups heavy cream
¼ cup sugar
1 teaspoon vanilla extract
1 small Wendy's Vanilla Frosty, at room temperature

ways and, boy oh boy, is it better when you cream everything first.

So mix everything at low speed just to keep it from splashing, then crank it up to high and cream until the mixture is all fluffy and incorporated, about 2 minutes.

Meanwhile, combine the chocolate chips and coconut oil in a pan on the stove, or a bowl in the microwave, and heat them up until just melted.

Add the chocolate mixture, Frosty, flour, cocoa powder, and vanilla to the creamed cheeses and beat on low for another minute just to combine.

Keep the speed on low and crack the eggs in one at a time, beating until they are incorporated, about 30 seconds or so.

Pour your filling mixture into the springform pan and get ready to water bath it!

Here's the deal: you've got to find something in your kitchen with relatively high walls, like a roasting pan or something, that you can fill with a couple of inches of warm water. So . . . do that. Okay, place the filled springform pan on a sheet of aluminum foil and crimp the sides up around the bottom edges of the pan. The goal here is to make sure that no water goes into the actual inside of the pan.

Take your airtight cheesecake pan and tap it on the counter a couple of times to knock out any air bubbles. Put it into the water bath, then put the whole thing in the oven. Bake for about 70 minutes, until the cheesecake is nearly set and when you jiggle it, the center shakes only a little bit.

Okay, now take it out, remove it from the water bath, and let it cool! Once it has cooled to room temperature, place it in the fridge to chill completely. For best results, let it set for at least 6 hours, or ideally overnight.

Step 3: Make Vanilla Frosty Whipped Cream.
When you're ready to serve the cheesecake, pour the cream into the CLEANED! (come on, guys) bowl of a stand mixer—but this time using the whisk attachment. Add the sugar and vanilla.

Start mixing on low speed to prevent splashing, then increase to medium/medium-high until the cream turns into a nice thick whipped cream. Once it's stiffening up, slowly stream in that room-temperature Frosty until it is all incorporated.

If you want to get fancy, you can get a piping bag and squirt some bougie decorations on top of your cheesecake. But you can also just serve beautiful slices with a big ol' dollop of whipped cream because it will, frankly, taste just as good, if not better.

Does My Cheesecake Need a Schvitz?

A water bath is a really cool technique in which, well . . . you bake something while it's also sitting in a water bath. What it does, though, is cook the filling super evenly and gently, allowing it to have that luscious, rich, custardy texture without getting rubbery and dry on the inside or cracked on top. #themoreyouknow

STOVETOP KIT KAT MAC 'N' CHEESE

For this recipe, we are using the Nicole style of classic Italian pasta cookery, in that we are finishing our cooked macaroni *in* the pan with the sauce, along with a splash of pasta water to help emulsify the sauce and create a cohesive dish. Oh, but we are doing one *slight* variation on the Italian pasta classics, because instead of making a sauce with ingredients like broccoli rabe, chicken stock, and pork sausage . . . we're going to use Kit Kats.

Place a pot of water over high heat and add a pinch of salt. Once the water comes to a boil, add the macaroni and cook according to the package instructions. Reserve 2 tablespoons of the pasta water and drain the noodles but DO NOT RINSE THEM—YOU ARE A FANCY ITALIAN NOW. Meanwhile, in a medium pot, combine the milk, mascarpone, chocolate chips, sugar, and the Kit Kats over medium heat. Bring to a simmer and cook, stirring constantly, until the chocolate has melted. Reduce the heat to a bare simmer and continue to cook, stirring regularly, until the sauce coats a spoon very well and drizzles slowly off it when lifted up, about 8 minutes.

Add the drained pasta and the reserved pasta water to the chocolate sauce and increase the heat to medium, stirring constantly until the sauce comes to a simmer. Continue stirring until the sauce has thickened and coats the noodles nicely, about 2 minutes.

Transfer to serving bowls (or one big boy) and then finish it with more crumbled Kit Kats. Eat it right away because classic Italian pasta is best eaten fresh, just like Nonna always says.

Serves 1 to 4 people, depending on how much Kit Kat Mac 'n' Cheese you usually eat

8 ounces dried elbow macaroni

1 cup whole milk

8 ounces mascarpone cheese

1¼ cups milk chocolate chips

½ cup sugar

Two 1.5-ounce packages Kit Kats (8 bars), finely chopped, plus more to crumble on top

MOVIE THEATER ICE CREAM SUNDAE

Home televisions are getting better and better. But while Martin Scorsese will tell you that home theaters will never re-create the cinematic experience of sharing a film with total strangers on a giant screen with huge speakers, we here at Mythical believe that the real issue is people's inability to re-create the concession stand at home. Sure, you could microwave some popcorn, buy a big Coca-Cola, and eat a giant box of candy . . . but it's just not the same.

So if you're watching a movie at home, why not improve the quality of your snacks and make an ice cream sundae that tastes like a night out at the movies? That's right, we are making no-churn buttered popcorn ice cream and butter-mounted Coca-Cola syrup, and then topping the whole thing with Raisinets. See you when *Avatar 9: Revenge of the Big-Ass Blue Flying Thing* comes out.

Step 1: Make the No-Churn Buttered Popcorn Ice Cream. First up, microwave the popcorn for *slightly less* time than it says on the package instructions (burned popcorn makes bad ice cream). Once it is popped, add it to a large pot and pour in the heavy cream. Cook, stirring occasionally, over medium heat. As soon as the mixture bubbles, about 6 minutes, reduce it to a simmer and keep on simmering, stirring frequently to prevent burning, for 5 minutes. Remove from the heat and let cool to room temperature. Once the popcorn mixture has cooled, cover the surface with plastic wrap and put it in the fridge to steep overnight (or transfer it to a container if needed for space purposes). (*Shhhhh . . . it's steeping . . .*) Meanwhile, place the bowl of a stand mixer in the fridge too. You want this thing nice and cold for its big day tomorrow.

And we're back! Strain the steeped cream, discarding the popcorn. Measure 2 cups of the popcorn-flavored cream, then pour it into the chilled bowl of the stand mixer. Fit your stand mixer with the whisk attachment and beat the cream on medium-high speed until you have stiff peaks, about 2½ minutes. Add the condensed milk and continue whipping until the mixture reaches a light, fluffy consistency, about 1 more minute. Fold in the vodka with a silicone spatula and transfer the ice cream to a container with a lid. Close it up and freeze the ice cream overnight.

Step 2: Make the Coca-Cola Syrup. Now that your ice cream is made, it's time to pair it up with some Coca-Cola syrup. Pour the Coca-Cola right into a medium pot over high heat and just start boiling the crap out of it until it has reduced by about 75 percent (½ cup), stirring it occasionally with a silicone spatula to prevent burning—but make dang sure you are keeping that butter in the fridge to stay cold while you do this.

As soon as the Coca-Cola is reduced, remove from the heat and add those cold butter chunks, a little at a time, stirring constantly until they are melted and incorporated.

Step 3: Top That Sundae! Scoop the ice cream into bowls and top with Raisinets, more popcorn, and a drizzle of Coca-Cola syrup. Then watch a superhero movie and tell Martin Scorsese that THIS IS CINEMA!

Makes 4 sundaes

No-Churn Buttered Popcorn Ice Cream
1 bag "extra butter" microwave popcorn
4 cups heavy cream
One 14-ounce can sweetened condensed milk
2 tablespoons vodka

Coca-Cola Syrup
Three 12-ounce cans Coca-Cola
½ cup (1 stick) cold unsalted butter, cut into small cubes

To Finish
Raisinets
More "extra butter" microwave popcorn, popped

Note: The Buttered Popcorn Ice Cream requires a little bit of planning. Expect to let the cream and popcorn steep overnight for maximum flavor. Then expect another night to let the ice cream freeze. So that's 2 days to make ice cream, but most of the time it's just sitting there not doing anything. It also requires a stand mixer.

COTTON CANDY MILKSHAKE

Hi, daddies! Cotton Candy Randy stopped by the ol' *GMM* one fine day, and after whispering sweet (and deeply unsettling) nothings into Rhett's and Link's ears, he also dropped off some cotton candy, so that they could find out "Is Anything Better Than Chocolate Milk?" Well, it turns out that cotton candy just completely dissolves into milk and then also makes it unreasonably delicious and colorful. So obviously we had to ramp things up a bit and create . . . *drumroll please* . . . oh . . . you already read the name of the recipe? Right, yeah, I guess it's just up there at the top. Anyway it's really great, and here it is!

Step 1: Decorate Your Glasses. If you, for some completely odd reason, don't have milkshake glasses, you can use any glass you like—wide-mouthed Mason jars would be pretty cool too.

Take that white frosting and get ready to frost the outside of the glass. We're not looking for a *rim*, like you would put on a margarita. We want to frost the whole top inch and a half or so of the *side* of the glass, from the rim on down. We want this to feel like you're at a millionaire toddler's birthday party.

Okay, now pour those sprinkles onto a plate and roll those frosted edges right through there, until you have frosted, sprinkled milkshake vessels.

Step 2: Make the Cotton Candy Milkshakes. Scoop the ice cream into a blender, then add the milk and cotton candy. Blend the whole thing on high speed until you've got a smooth milkshake.

Pour it into your decorated glasses and garnish it with cotton candy and tell that wealthy toddler that he has an IRRESPONSIBLE AMOUNT OF MONEY. Then drink your milkshake and take a deep breath because everything is totally fine and you're home and safe and there is no toddler. Take another sip. Everything is great.

Makes 2 big milkshakes

Elaborate Glass Decorating
¼ cup white frosting (we prefer Duncan Hines)
½ cup rainbow sprinkles

Cotton Candy Milkshake
1 pint vanilla ice cream
1 cup whole milk
2 ounces blue cotton candy, plus more for garnish

CINNAMON TOAST CRUNCH ROLLS

The great cereal makers of America have done an amazing job of tricking parents the world over into the idea that a bowl of dessert counts as "part of this complete breakfast," and for that, we salute you, four-star General Mills. While we're here, why hasn't Cap'n Crunch been promoted to Com'dore Crunch yet? Cookie Crisp, as it turns out, is just a bowl of cookies. Cocoa Krispies even brags about a cereal that has so much chocolate and sugar in it that it makes its own milk chocolate by-product. But Cinnamon Toast Crunch makes one of the best products out there, filling your bowl with dozens of tiny slices of extra-crunchy cinnamon toast. Well, we here at Mythical would like to applaud the fine people at CTC Incorporated (just kidding, it's made by General Mills) and help them with some brand integration by partnering them with Pillsbury (who they also own) to make quick, easy, delightful cinnamon rolls.

....

Step 1: Make Those Rolls. Preheat the oven to 375°F. Grease an 8 × 8-inch baking dish with some butter.

Add the Cinnamon Toast Crunch, butter, condensed milk, and brown sugar to the bowl of a food processor. Pulse it several times, scraping down the sides occasionally, until you have a well-mixed slurry with chunks of rustically misshapen bits of Cinnamon Toast Crunch in it—after all, if you destroy all the crunch, it's just . . . powdered cinnamon bread?

Meanwhile, crack open the can of pizza dough and unfurl it onto a clean work surface. Lift up the edges like you're putting a sheet on a bed and pull it out to stretch it a little bit thinner.

Spread the crunch filling evenly across the entire surface of the dough. Starting from one side, roll the whole thing up like a jelly roll. (Side note: if you are ever making a jelly roll, you're going to want to roll it up like a cinnamon roll. That's because when you're explaining

Makes 12 CTCRs (that's our shorthand for Cinnamon Toast Crunch Rolls, which in retrospect is already taking too long to explain—also, in case you're wondering, it's an initialism and not an acronym, which we just learned about a little while back on page 77)

Cinnamon Toast Crunch Rolls
½ cup (1 stick) unsalted butter, at room temperature, plus more to grease the pan
3 cups Cinnamon Toast Crunch
½ cup sweetened condensed milk
½ cup tightly packed light brown sugar
One 13.8-ounce can Pillsbury pizza crust

Cinnamon Glaze
1 cup powdered sugar
2 tablespoons whole milk
2 tablespoons unsalted butter, melted
½ tablespoon ground cinnamon

something in a cookbook, you can never just say the obvious thing; you have to compare it to a completely *different* obvious thing, even though it's not that helpful and, in this case, way more people make cinnamon rolls than jelly rolls.)

Okay, now that the dough is rolled up, use a serrated knife to cut it into 12 relatively even slices. Nestle them, cut side down, into the greased baking dish. Bake for 20 to 25 minutes, until cooked through and browned on the outside. Now you can move on to . . .

Step 2: Make the Cinnamon Glaze and Eat the Rolls. While the rolls are baking, whisk together the powdered sugar, milk, butter, and cinnamon in a large bowl until the mixture is all smooth and nice.

As soon as the rolls are out of the oven, pour and spread the glaze all over the top of the rolls, letting it drip and melt into the crevices while your mouth begins to water and even the person writing this cookbook right now sits up in their chair and gets a little excited. Okay, go on now. Take a bite. Is it too hot? Want me to blow on it for you? Uh . . . I mean . . . now you have completed the recipe, please enjoy.

OREO BISCUITS AND GRAVY

Lots of chefs out there, especially on the internet, have made a lot of things out of Oreos. They've stuffed Oreos into cookies, they've blended Oreos into a buttery spread, and they've even deep-fried them into funnel cakes. But has anyone other than us ever ground Oreos into flour, and used that flour to create a rich, buttery, flaky biscuit that gets sandwiched with a cream filling to then look like a giant Oreo-biscuit hybrid that is then covered in a sweet cookies-and-cream gravy? No, we're actually asking you, because we don't know. This was one of the first things we made on the *Mythical Kitchen* channel—and not only is it absolutely delicious but it also doubles as our audition to take over as the head of Cracker Barrel's culinary innovation kitchen. Cracker Barrel, as long as you have an open mind and a loose policy on background checks for your prospective employees, hit us up!

Note: A 3½-inch biscuit cutter is great here, but in a pinch you can also just use a cup, ideally with some pretty sharp edges on it.

Step 1: Make the Cream Filling. Set aside 1 tablespoon of the coconut oil. Then combine the rest of the coconut oil and the powdered sugar in a medium bowl and mix it all up until it's nice and smooth.

Next, set up a double boiler: fill a medium saucepan with about an inch of water and bring it to a gentle boil. Set a Pyrex or metal bowl snugly right on top of the pot—the goal is to have the steam hit the bowl but without the bowl touching the water. Put the white chocolate chips in the bowl, add the reserved tablespoon of coconut oil, and stir until the chocolate melts, while maintaining a nice simmer on the water.

Once the chocolate has melted, scrape it right into the bowl with the coconut oil and powdered sugar and then stir it all up with a lot of power and motion until you have something that kind of looks like fluffy Oreo cream! Okay, now line a baking sheet with a silicone baking mat or parchment paper. Spread the cream into an even layer about ½ inch thick, making sure it's wide enough to cut out 4 circles with a 3½-inch biscuit cutter. Then put the whole thing in the fridge, uncovered, to firm up and set, about 30 minutes.

Step 2: Make the Oreo Biscuits. Preheat the oven to 425°F. Line a baking sheet with parchment paper or ideally a silicone baking mat.

Drop the Oreos right into the bowl of a food processor and then whip those things through there for as long as it takes for them to have a sandy, flour-like texture. Measure out ¼ cup of the cookie crumbs and add them to a large bowl along with the flour, cocoa powder, sugar, baking powder, salt, and baking soda. Grab a whisk and whisk it all up until it's super-duper combined.

Add those cold, cold butter pieces and start using your hands to mix them all up, getting every piece of butter fully coated in the flour mixture, while still keeping them in individual chunks.

Stream in the buttermilk and then fold it all together, ideally with a silicone spatula, getting everything combined and incorporated but

Recipe continues

Cream Filling

1 cup coconut oil, melted

2 cups powdered sugar

¼ cup white chocolate chips

Biscuits

3 Double Stuf Oreo cookies

2¼ cups all-purpose flour, plus more for dusting

½ cup Dutch-process cocoa powder (or ideally black cocoa powder, if you can find it)

¼ cup granulated sugar

2 tablespoons baking powder

1 teaspoon salt

¼ teaspoon baking soda

1 cup (2 sticks) VERY cold unsalted butter, cut into pea-size pieces (keep it in the fridge until it's time to use it)

1 cup buttermilk

Gravy

2 tablespoons unsalted butter

2 tablespoons all-purpose flour

1 cup half-and-half

¼ cup powdered sugar

¼ cup white chocolate chips

1 Oreo cookie, cream removed (and hidden in your cheek for flavor), crumbled up by hand

⅛ teaspoon salt

not overworking the dough. Again, you want to still see those hunks of butter shining through—it's more about getting the flour to incorporate with the buttermilk.

Okay! Lightly flour a clean work surface, then plop the dough right onto it and knead it for about 10 seconds. Using a floured rolling pin, roll it out into a rectangle that's, like, ¼ inch thick. Cut it in quarters and stack them on top of each other to make a slab about 1 inch thick—this is a kind of "forced layering" that really, truly helps to make flaky, wonderful biscuits.

Roll it out again, to a thickness of about ¾ inch and a shape wide enough to cut out eight 3½-inch biscuits. Cut out the biscuits.

Space out those biscuits on the prepared baking sheet and bake until fluffy and risen to about ½ inch tall, about 15 minutes. Whew. Okay. Should we take a break? NO. THERE'S NO TIME LET'S GO.

Step 3: We're Making Gravy! But we're making sweet, sweet gravy. You may remember this "béchamel" technique from our earlier savory gravy recipes, like the Biscuit and Gravy Skillet Peetza (page 25). So this is that, but sugar.

Place a medium pot over medium heat and add the butter. Once it's melted, add the flour and cook, stirring, until it loses the raw flavor and smells toasty, about 2 minutes.

Slowly stream in your half-and-half, whisking constantly to prevent lumps. Let it come to a gentle simmer and then cook, stirring constantly, for about 1 minute.

Add the powdered sugar, white chocolate chips, cookie crumbs, and salt and stir it all together until it bubbles again, another 15 seconds or so. Remove it from the heat and set it aside while you assemble!

Step 4: Oreo Biscuits and Gravy, Assemble! Take your cream filling out of the fridge and cut out 4 cream circles with that biscuit cutter. Then sandwich them each between two Oreo biscuits, placing each sandwich on its own plate, then cover those suckers with all the beautiful gravy and enjoy that dessert-but-breakfast-but-dessert-but-breakfast-but-dessert with three of your closest friends. And by that we mean *literally* closest friends because you don't have time to pick anybody too far away—the food is ready right now.

Why Do We Steam?

Double boilers are essentially a method in which we use steam to gently and evenly cook things that might otherwise break, or separate (the water separates from the fat in an emulsified sauce) through normal cooking. Think: hollandaise, chocolate, and things like that. Steam power!

POP-TART LAVA CAKES

Way back in the year two thousand and twenty AD, we launched the world's most exclusive restaurant: The Gastro Pop. Why was it so exclusive? Well, first of all, it existed entirely inside an episode of *GMM*. Second, the only customers were Rhett and Link. But we did learn one truly important lesson that day: Pop-Tarts are absolutely supposed to be turned into lava cakes. It's sweet dough, it's frosting, and it's got a liquid center. Frankly, we are embarrassed for the rest of the people on the planet, who did not think of something so obviously delicious before we did. But we also worked incredibly hard to simplify this recipe down into a few easy steps. Okay, fine—we made it easy because we're using cake mix, strawberry jam, premade frosting, and Pop-Tarts—but something this easy has no right tasting this darn good.

....

Note: You WILL, however, need two 12-cup muffin tins in order to make the annoyingly slightly less than 24 individual cakes. You will also need a piping bag with a metal tip.

Preheat the oven to 350°F. Spray two 12-cup muffin tins with cooking spray.

Plop those Pop-Tarts into the bowl of a food processor and blend the heck out of them until they are as finely blended as you can get them.

Dump those crumbs into a large bowl with the cake mix, 1 cup water, the eggs, and oil. Use a whisk to whip it like crazy until it looks like cake batter.

Fill 22 of the prepared muffin cups about two-thirds of the way up with batter. Bake for 16 to 20 minutes, until a toothpick inserted into the center of a cake comes out nice and clean. For best results, rotate the pans after the 10-minute mark.

While the cakes are baking, pour the strawberry jam into a pastry bag fitted with a piping tip. Once the muffins are done, set them on the stove or a wire rack to cool, then tap your fingers impatiently while you wonder how long you *really* have to wait for things to cool before

Makes 22 individual lava cakes, serving 2 formerly lost backpackers who survived off foraged nettles for weeks or 22 people who have . . . not done that

Cooking spray or something similar, for greasing the muffin tins
6 frosted strawberry Pop-Tarts
One 15.25-ounce box yellow cake mix
3 large eggs
⅓ cup vegetable oil
2 cups strawberry jam
Two 16-ounce containers vanilla frosting (we prefer Duncan Hines)
½ cup rainbow sprinkles

you can start filling and frosting them, and then remember that time your friend Beth told you that she frosted her cupcakes too early and that's why they were all weird looking and runny at the party, but mostly how she *wouldn't stop talking about it*, and you were finally like, "Okay! Beth! Drop it! You're making things way worse, and after all, this seems like a weird thing to be bummed out about at your nephew's bris."

So yeah, wait about 20 minutes and then take them out of the tin. Poke the piping tip right through the top of each cake and pipe about a tablespoon or so of strawberry jam into the center. Wait another 5 minutes before using that handy (and cleaned) piping bag—now fitted with a star tip!—to pipe that frosting across the top of each cake (covering up that piping hole), and then finish them all off with rainbow sprinkles.

Now take these lava cakes to a bris and brag about how much better yours are than Beth's.

BEN & JERRY'S ICE CREAM BURRITO

We've all heard of ice cream sandwiches and Choco Tacos, but we believe that there should be way more options for ice cream delivery systems inspired by traditionally savory culinary vessels. Speaking of which, let us know in the comment section if you would buy a T-shirt that reads: "More Options for Ice Cream Delivery Systems Inspired by Traditionally Savory Culinary Vessels." What's that? There's still no comment section in a hard copy of a cookbook? Okay then . . . either way, let's make cherry crepes and use them to roll up Cherry Garcia ice cream and some homemade chipotle cherry compote.

....

Step 1: Make the Cherry Crepes. Crack those eggs into a large bowl and beat them until they are super whipped up with no big puddles of egg whites hiding in there. Add the milk and whisk that too. Pour in that cherry juice and whisk it in, watching the color swirl together in a surprisingly appealing fashion. Add the flour, whisking CONTINUOUSLY, to prevent lumps. Remember: lumps are bad. But on a more serious note: check for lumps on your body, too, and get them checked out. This actually isn't a joke; it's really important to do that regularly.

Okay, now that we're all safe and lump-free, keep on whisking until the batter is all smooth and the flour is incorporated, and then whisk in the melted butter too. Finally, whisk in the sugar and salt.

Okay, now take a 10-inch (or something close) nonstick skillet and place it over medium heat.

Spray it with cooking spray and then pour in ½ cup of the batter on the north side of the pan (aka the side that's farthest away from you). Quickly lift up the pan and tilt it around, trying to get the batter to fill in all the way around the surface of the pan. Let it cook until the wetness has solidified on top, about 30 seconds, then flip the crepe

Recipe continues

Makes enough crepes for, like, 5 burritos, which may seem like a lot until you try it, and then you start running down the street asking your neighbors who wants an ice cream burrito because it's so good

Cherry Crepes

3 large eggs
½ cup whole milk
¼ cup maraschino cherry juice, from a jar of maraschino cherries
1 cup all-purpose flour
2 tablespoons unsalted butter, melted
1 tablespoon sugar
¼ teaspoon salt
Cooking spray

Chipotle Cherry Compote

1 pound cherries, pitted and halved
½ cup sugar
¼ teaspoon ground chipotle pepper
½ teaspoon ground cinnamon
½ teaspoon salt
1 teaspoon cornstarch
1 tablespoon unsalted butter

To Finish

About ⅔ cup jarred hot fudge, at room temperature
2 pints Ben & Jerry's Cherry Garcia
Canned whipped cream, for serving

Can I Fill the Pit Inside My Soul by Removing the Pits from These Cherries?

If you want a super-fast, easy way to pit a cherry, all you need is a wide, sturdy boba straw. Simply slide the boba straw right through the center of the cherry and the pit will come right out. Then you can blow really hard through the straw to shoot a cherry pit at somebody, but only if they deserve it.

and hit the other side for about 30 more seconds. Transfer the crepe to a plate and repeat with the rest of the batter.

Once you're done, set those aside and move on to . . .

Step 2: Make the Chipotle Cherry Compote. Combine the cherries, ½ cup water, the sugar, chipotle, cinnamon, and salt in a medium saucepan and bring to a boil over medium-high heat. Once the mixture is bubbling, reduce the heat to a simmer and give it a nice stir. Let it keep on simmering, stirring occasionally, until half of the liquid has evaporated, about 15 minutes.

Meanwhile, in a small bowl, combine the cornstarch with 2 teaspoons water. Mix them up and then pour that slurry right into the pot and give it a stir to thicken—allowing it to simmer for about 1 more minute to activate the cornstarch. Remove from the heat. Finally, add the butter and stir until it has fully melted. You did it! Now set it aside and get ready to roll some burritos.

Step 3: Finish Him! Alright, it's time to party! Lay out your first crepe and smear on about 2 tablespoons of fudge. Then add 2 or 3 scoops of Cherry Garcia, depending on your scoop size. Roll it up like a burrito.

Finally, lay it seam side down on a plate. Drizzle the compote over the top and finish the whole thing with a few squirts of whipped cream. (Fun fact: Did you know that canned whipped cream in the UK is called squirty cream? Don't you just want to call it squirty cream now?)

Repeat this with the remaining burritos and then eat all the burritos, ideally before the ice cream melts.

ELVIS BREAD PUDDING

Makes 8 servings for young Elvis, or 1 serving for late-career Elvis

4 slices bacon
2 cups whole milk
4 large eggs
1 cup sugar
8 slices stale white bread
2 bananas, plus more
  for garnish
½ cup peanut butter
Caramel drizzle, for serving
Canned whipped
  cream, for serving
Scoop of vanilla ice cream,
  because why not?

Elvis Presley is known for many things, and the legacy he left in the music industry is nothing short of enormous. But the legacy he left in the culinary world may be just as formidable. Okay, it's not nearly as formidable, but he was a huge fan of putting bacon on foods that bacon isn't normally supposed to go on, which is why, of course, he's long been considered a patron saint of the Mythical Kitchen, up there with Tony Chachere and Iron Chef Hiroyuki Sakai. Many people know about his peanut butter, bacon, and banana sandwiches—the very same that we're taking inspiration from in this bread pudding—but the variation known as the Fool's Gold Loaf might be even more impressive. The ingredients are as follows: an entire loaf of French bread, an entire jar of blueberry jam, an entire jar of peanut butter, and an entire pound of bacon. Allegedly, Elvis and his friends took a private jet from Graceland to the Colorado Mining Company in Denver, where the sandwich originated, just to crush bottles of champagne and eat some Fool's Gold. Elvis, king of rock and roll, and king of surprise bacon, we salute you.

Normally we're not sticklers about the rules (hopefully we shouldn't have to explain that by now), but using stale bread for this recipe really does make a difference. Now, we're not saying you need to stare at your bread sitting in a half-opened bag for a week, watching it gradually lose moisture. Unless you're into that sort of thing? You can also throw the bread slices on a baking rack in the oven for an hour at 225°F. That's what WE'RE into. Not . . . not like in that kind of way. Anyway, make sure your bread is stale.

Preheat the oven to 350°F.

Cook some bacon. Make an extra slice or six for yourself. No one ever regretted a side of snacking bacon. Heat a sauté pan over medium heat, dice your bacon, toss it in the pan, and sauté until crispy and the fat is rendered, about 5 minutes. Do not throw the fat away! Good bacon fat is hard to come by these days. Let the bacon and grease cool in the pan, then make your custard.

Whisk together the milk, eggs, and sugar, then add your bacon bits and grease (please save at least 1 tablespoon of grease for later!) and

Recipe continues

continue whisking until combined. Cut the bread into 1-centimeter cubes (no idea why we switched to metric, but it's about 0.39 inches, and we WILL know if you go any smaller or bigger, and we WILL be disappointed) and toss the bread cubes into the custard. Slice your bananas and add them into the mixture as well. Give it a good toss with your hands, but try not to mash it around too much. You want to keep some of the bread's shape and structural integrity.

Grease up an 8 × 8-inch baking dish with that leftover bacon grease (told you it would come in handy) and add half of the bread-nana-custard mixture. You might be asking: Why only half? Great question, intrepid cooker-of-things—we're glad you asked. Use a teaspoon to dollop peanut butter gobs all around the top of the first custard layer. This creates molten peanut butter explosions in your mouth when you eat it, and it rules. If you want the peanut butter to stop sticking to the spoon and your hands, you can dip each periodically in a bit of warm water.

Top with the second half of the bread pudding mixture and gently press down on the top to make sure it's evenly spread out. Bake for 45 minutes, or until the top is golden brown, then let rest for at least 15 minutes before slicing into it. Heck, YOU should rest at least 15 minutes before slicing it. You had a big day, champ. Take a load off.

Okay, now serve it up with some caramel drizzle, whipped cream, more sliced bananas (because potassium!), and a scoop of vanilla ice cream (because . . . calcium?).

EAT SOMETHING THAT SCARES YOU

(CURIOUS)

Normal" is in the eye of the beholder. Why can you add the breast of a chicken to pretty much any salad in America—or order wings from every sports bar—but "Buffalo wild chicken feet" never took off? Meanwhile, cow tongue is totally normal at a Mexican taqueria, Japanese izakaya, or Jewish deli but seems conspicuously out of place at a Domino's. If anyone from Domino's corporate is reading this, we're begging for a cow tongue calzone!

We all have our comfort zones—the things we want that make us feel a certain way when life is getting us down. Maybe it's the food you ate as a kid, the TV show you watch over and over (and over) again, or the pair of jorts that I've never washed once, no matter how many cucumbers I've smuggled up there. But comfort can also be a devious trap. It's what keeps us in bad relationships, whether it be with a person or with a cereal bowl filled with boxed macaroni and cheese. Comfort is there for you when you *need* it but becomes less and less effective when it is ubiquitous.

That's why *adventure* is also part of living a Mythical life. If it can be reasonably considered a food, we've probably eaten it at Mythical. Sure, we've had a lot of laughs watching Rhett and Link retch while eating unseasoned pig anus—and they CERTAINLY learned something about themselves from those experiences—but it wasn't until we

launched a series called Food Fears that we really learned the power of bringing people out of their comfort zones. I'll personally never forget the initial fear in a guest's eyes as they stared down boiled turkey testicles and how that fear turned into pure elation when they ate them in the form of mac 'n' cheese. Rhett and Link said it best: being the person who ate something makes you inherently more interesting than the person who turned something down.

Trying new things and new experiences is also foundational to our growth as people. Does that mean you have to like everything? Heck no. In fact, we usually learn way more from the things we *dislike* than the things we like. Falling in love with someone you don't really know at all and then being rejected by them is deeply painful but not that educational because you never really found out if they were all that great for you. But going on an awful date and learning what you *really don't like* in a potential partner? That offers up *so much more* data to help you find the right person for you to spend your time with. Is it weird to compare dating to eating turkey testicles? We don't think so!

That's why we are big believers in not just *tasting* something you are scared of, but really *trying* it. If you've convinced yourself to try something new, and you gingerly place the tip of your tongue on the food, allowing a single taste bud to receive the information before pulling back, chances are your preconceptions will take over and make you think it's awful because you *want* to think it's awful. But that's just fear talking. So we say that if somebody offers you a slider filled with Nashville Hot Lamb Brains, you should put the whole darn thing in your mouth and really chew it, letting those flavors dance and swirl on your tongue, smacking you right in the face before that hunk of foodstuff glides down the back of your throat. Then and *only* then are you allowed to register an opinion on it. In fact, take a second bite, too, just to make sure.

But if you try two bites of a Squid Hot Pocket and absolutely hate it, that's okay too! That's all part of the experience, and part of learning more about yourself. Is there a chance you're going to absolutely LOVE Beef Testicle Ragù and it becomes a major problem for the people around you because you won't stop talking about it and cooking it and trying to serve it to everyone you know, and then when there's a nationwide shortage on beef testicles, you go into a deep depression spiral? Absolutely. But that's the journey of life, and you may as well make your journey an adventure—and a Mythical one at that.

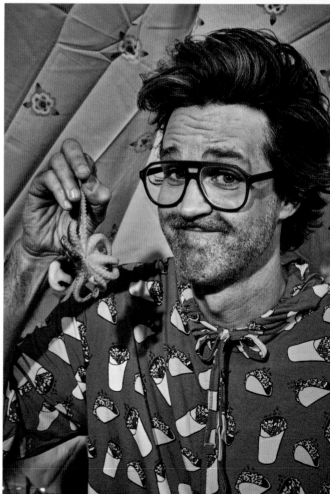

MUSTARD ICE CREAM

Makes about 1 quart; this is supposed to serve 6, but when it comes to mustard ice cream . . . mileage may vary

What is pleasure without something challenging to compare it against? What is vacation without the work that preceded it? What is dessert without dinner, or a shift beer without an eight-hour day standing on your feet?

On *GMM* we asked the question, "Will It Ice Cream?" and posited the premise around a scoop of Mustard Ice Cream. But perhaps what we were really asking is whether such stark contrasts could truly coexist. Is Mustard Ice Cream a punishable offense, like drinking on the job or working from your laptop on a family beach vacation? Can dinner find its way into dessert? Does Mustard Ice Cream expand your flavor horizons . . . or are you simply converting your kitchen into a Carnival of Curios and Oddities, while you bark at your friends to test their mettle? There's only one way to find out.

Oh and also, we find that covering it in salted pretzels makes it way better.

2 cups heavy cream

One 14-ounce can sweetened condensed milk

1½ tablespoons yellow mustard

1 tablespoon hot mustard powder, such as Colman's

1½ teaspoons ground turmeric

2 tablespoons vodka

Small to medium bag of salted mini pretzels, for serving

Place the bowl of a stand mixer in the freezer for at least an hour or so to get it nice and cold (this is optional, but really helps). Add the cream to your chilled bowl and fit your stand mixer with the whisk attachment. Beat the cream over medium-high speed until you have stiff peaks, about 8 minutes. Add the condensed milk, mustard, mustard powder, and turmeric and continue whipping over low speed until it begins to thicken, about 2 minutes. Then increase it to medium and whip it until it reaches a light, fluffy consistency, about 3 more minutes. Add the vodka and whisk it over low speed for another 30 seconds, then transfer it to a container with a lid. Close it up and freeze the ice cream overnight.

Open the bag of mini pretzels, and then use a moderately heavy object, like a rolling pin or a child's bowling ball, to very roughly break up the pretzels.

Serve the ice cream in scoops, topped generously with rustic pretzel shards.

PORK BLOOD TACOS

It all started with a pork blood taco, and it will all end with a pork blood taco. Well. Technically, it will all end with the entropic heat death of the universe whereby macroscale thermodynamic equilibrium is reached and the cosmos turns forever black, but that's not particularly noteworthy. Back to the pork blood taco.

Ever since I watched Rhett and Link gag trying to choke down a brick of coagulated pork blood in a stale hard taco shell, I knew I wanted redemption. You see, that was before my time, and I believe that if you strongly dislike a food, you just haven't had a good version of it. I also—unsurprisingly—enjoy coagulated pork blood, which goes by the English names blood curd, blood jelly, or blood tofu and is used in a lot of East Asian cookery. My favorite way to eat it is in large cubes, floating in the spicy Vietnamese soup bún bò Huế.

I put everything that I had into making a delicious taco infused with pork blood at every step. There was a blood tortilla, blood chile de arbol salsa, and the star—cubes of blood tofu—crisped up in oil and finished in the pan with some bright lime juice. Rhett loved it, and Link didn't gag, which made it one of the crowning moments of my career. And now you can replicate it at home in a much simpler, equally delicious way.

....

Cut the pork blood up into ½-inch cubes. Season them up with the salt, a few twists of pepper, and the chili powder.

Heat 2 tablespoons of the oil in a medium skillet over high heat. Once the oil is shimmering, place the cubes into the skillet and let them sear on the first side until crispy, about 2 minutes. Turn them and repeat until they are crisped on all sides, about 90 seconds per side.

Once they are all crisped, transfer them to a plate and squeeze the lime juice over them. Reduce the heat to medium and add the remaining 1½ teaspoons oil to the skillet. Cook the tortillas, one at a time, for about 6 seconds per side, just until warmed through and barely crispy at the edges.

Top the tortillas with the blood cubes, then hit them with onion, cilantro, and hot sauce and eat them right away.

Makes 6 tacos. Oh, did you think we were going to make some kind of joke here? Well, we're not. It just makes 6 tacos.

1 pound coagulated pork blood

2 teaspoons salt

Ground black pepper

1 teaspoon chili powder

2 tablespoons vegetable oil, plus 1½ teaspoons for the tortillas

Juice of half a lime, or 2 bad ones

6 corn tortillas

Finely chopped white onion, for garnish

Finely chopped cilantro leaves, for garnish

Hot sauce of your choice, for garnish

Where Do You Find Coagulated Pork Blood?

Sometimes it is called "pig blood curd" or "blood tofu." We buy ours at a popular chain grocery store here in California called 99 Ranch Market, but call around in your area to see where you can find it. East Asian grocery stores are usually a pretty good bet.

NASHVILLE HOT LAMB BRAINS

We get it. You might—*might*—be afraid of the idea of eating lamb brains. Maybe it's the jiggly texture. Maybe you, like us, watched the movie *Hannibal* when you were way too young and you're reminded of that one scene. You know the one. But there are many benefits to eating lamb brains. They are high in niacin, they are chock-full of vitamin B, and when you eat the brain of another creature, you absorb all its intelligence. You might think that you are already smarter than the average baby sheep, but when's the last time you were able to grow a self-sustaining and stylish jacket that covers every square inch of your body? That's what we thought. Fine, if that didn't convince you, hopefully you'll be persuaded by the fact that the lamb brain is crusted in Doritos, deep-fried, doused in spicy grease, then placed upon a pillowy and sweet King's Hawaiian roll. If you eat this, and *still* don't like it, then and ONLY then are you allowed to say, "I don't like lamb brains." Otherwise, we don't want to hear it.

Step 1: Brain Prep. First up, take a look at those lamb brains and then use a knife to cut off and remove anything that looks like a vein. Put the brains in a bowl with the buttermilk and salt and give it all a nice toss. Then put the bowl in the fridge and let it sit for 20 minutes to soak, mellow out, and extract any impurities. Also feel free to set up a camera to catch people's reactions when they open the fridge and see buttermilk lamb brains.

Meanwhile, pour your Doritos into the bowl of a food processor and blend them up until they have a nice crumbly texture. Scrape them into a wide bowl. Set up two more wide bowls, putting the flour in one and beating the eggs in the other one.

Once your brains are done soaking, lift them out, rinse them off, and pat them dry. Discard the buttermilk and then split them in half (they should peel easily) and peel off the connective tissue down the middle. Sprinkle them with a little more salt, then coat them in flour first, then egg, then Doritos crumbs and place them on a plate or baking sheet. Set them in the fridge to let the crumbs adhere and set while you . . .

Step 2: Make Josh's 4:1:1 Sauce. Oh boy here we go again you just put it all in a bowl and mix it up okay now you're done that was so easy.

Step 3: Make the Hot Lamb Brain Oil. Heat the oil in a small saucepan over medium-high heat. Keep on heating the oil until it is just shimmering—about 250°F. Meanwhile, mix together the cayenne, brown sugar, paprika, granulated garlic, and salt, then set aside about one-quarter of the mixture for future dusting. Once the oil hits the correct temperature, stir in the nonreserved seasonings and remove the pan from the heat.

Step 4: Nashville-Hot Those Lamb Brains. Heat your fry oil (using a deep fryer or a large, heavy-bottomed pot filled with at least 3 inches of oil, making sure that the pot is no more than two-thirds full) to 325°F. Line a baking sheet with a wire rack or a plate with some paper towels for draining.

Once the oil is heated, carefully lay the breaded brains into the oil, working in batches so you don't overcrowd the fryer or drop

Recipe continues

Lamb Brain Prep
4 lamb brains
1½ cups buttermilk
1 tablespoon salt, plus more to sprinkle
One 9.75-ounce bag Tapatío or Flamin' Hot Nacho Doritos
1 cup all-purpose flour
2 large eggs

Josh's 4:1:1 Sauce
½ cup mayo
2 tablespoons sriracha
2 tablespoons hot sauce

Hot Lamb Brain Oil
1 cup neutral oil
¼ cup cayenne
2 tablespoons light brown sugar
2 teaspoons paprika
1 teaspoon granulated garlic
1½ teaspoons salt

Nashville Hot Lamb Brains
Neutral oil, for frying

To Finish
8 King's Hawaiian rolls
16 slices bread-and-butter pickles

the temperature too much. Fry them until they are golden, crispy, and cooked through, about 5 minutes, then transfer them to your landing station.

Once they are all fried, pour your Hot Lamb Brain Oil right over those fried lamb brains to make them NASHVILLE HOT, just like Dolly Parton probably would have wanted you to eat lamb brains.

Step 5: Serve and Eat! Slather both sides of your rolls with that 4:1:1 sauce and then top each one with a lamb brain and 2 slices of pickles. Eat them while they're fresh. Serve them to your unsuspecting friends and neighbors and see what they think before you tell them it's not chicken.

Should I Lie to My Loved Ones?

We legally cannot tell you to lie to people about what they're eating so definitely don't do that unless you want to do it all on your own and it in no way has anything to do with what we think you should do okay that's it no take backs we're not liable for anything now goodbye enjoy your lamb brains.

FISH EGG QUESADILLAS

To be perfectly honest, we think that fish eggs (aka roe or caviar) are undeniably delicious and should not be in this section (see: Japanese ikuradon, caviar on potato chips, and more). But Rhett and Link disagree, and tiebreaker goes to the people with the most hair, so here we are. Every time someone had the idea to make a dish covered in fish eggs on *GMM*, it was like Christmas/Hanukkah come early for all of us in the Mythical Kitchen. While Rhett and Link were gagging over a fish egg quesadilla on set, all the Kitcheneers were in the kitchen throwing our own private caviar party. The caviar parties were beautiful, bacchanal affairs. We put caviar on leftover Domino's pizza, we put caviar on Dino nuggets, and when we got to the end of the jar, we'd just start scooping it out with our fingers and licking them clean. That's when we found out: dang, caviar really can go on anything if you're shameless enough. These tiny quesadilla rounds evoke the traditional pairing of caviar and blini but are way more fun because quesadillas are better than blini (COME AT ME, RICH BORING PEOPLE!).

....

Ready to make a giant quesadilla? (Note: you can also use smaller tortillas and make smaller quesadillas if you want to.) Heat a griddle or large skillet over medium-high heat. Toast each tortilla on both sides until it is softened and pliable, about 7 seconds per side.

Reduce the heat to medium, lay one of the tortillas right onto the skillet, and top it with the cheese in an even layer. Place the other tortilla on top and toast the quesadilla until the bottom is golden brown and the cheese has started to melt, about 2 minutes. Flip it over and toast the other side for another 2 minutes or so. Once both sides are golden and the cheese is melted, transfer it to a cutting board and let it sit for about 30 seconds to rest.

Take a 1-inch round cookie cutter and cut out 12 quesadilla circles. Just grab your remaining Frankenquesadilla frame and wear it on your face like a Hannibal Lecter skin mask before stabbing your tongue through the holes until you can suck it into your mouth and eat it.

Okay, now you dollop each quesadilla circle with 1 teaspoon crème fraîche and top it with 1 teaspoon caviar and a sprig of dill. Serve immediately, or just eat all of them yourself because Rhett and Link are wrong and fish eggs are awesome.

Makes 12 snack-size quesadilla bites, twice as many if you double the recipe (we actually think you could even triple it and end up with 36 of them, but that math is not 100 percent confirmed)

2 burrito-size flour tortillas
1 cup shredded Monterey Jack (about 4 ounces)
¼ cup crème fraîche or sour cream
¼ cup caviar
12 tiny sprigs dill

Note: Traditional beluga caviar can run you several hundred dollars, but you can generally find jars of trout or salmon roe for ten to fifteen dollars, and they taste just as fishy and delightful.

SPAGHETTI AND CRICKET MEATBALLS

Today on *Mythical Kitchen* we're showing you how to make Josh's favorite simple Italian meatballs to eat while watching a big International Cricket Council match with your friends! Wow, this is super normal—why would it be in this section of the cookbook?

Oh wait. It's the other kind of "cricket," isn't it?

Okay, let's make cricket meatballs with real crickets! Did you know that many people suggest that increasing our insect protein intake is a huge opportunity for more sustainable foodways? What if we told you that we were going to serve them with spaghetti and Marcella Hazan's iconic tomato-butter sauce . . . but also that you could substitute mealworms for spaghetti if you wanted extra protein? Okay great, we knew you'd be on board.

Step 1: Make Marcella's Tomato-Butter Sauce. Pour the tomatoes into a heavy-bottomed pot, then plop in the whole stick of butter, nestle in those onion halves, and season with salt. Bring to a simmer over medium-high heat, then reduce the heat to low and allow the sauce to simmer, covered, for about 45 minutes. Remove it from the heat, then take out the onions and either eat them whole over the sink or discard them.

Step 2: Make the Cricket Meatballs. Preheat the oven to 450°F. Line a baking sheet with parchment paper.

Put those crickets into the bowl of a food processor and pulse them up until they have a rustic texture, where maybe someone is thinking, "Wait, is that cricket in there . . . naaaah that's crazy—why would they do that?"

Transfer the rustic cricket bits to a large bowl along with the ground beef, garlic, milk, egg, bread crumbs, Pecorino Romano, olive oil, salt, crushed red pepper, oregano, and black pepper and mix them all up together, being careful not to overcompress the mixture. Lightly oil your hands and roll the cricket mixture in between your palms to shape it into 6 similarly sized balls. Place them on the prepared baking sheet and roast until they are just taking on some color and holding their shape, about 7 minutes. Transfer them to the pot of tomato sauce, bring it to a simmer over low heat, and cook them together until the meatballs are just cooked through, about 10 more minutes.

Step 3: Finish It All Up! Add the freshly cooked spaghetti or mealworms (straight from the package!) to three warmed pasta bowls. Place 2 meatballs in each bowl and ladle the sauce, dividing it evenly, over the pasta. Grate Pecorino over the top, then drizzle with olive oil and finish with a few leaves of basil. If you really want to make it funny, watch a game of cricket while you eat.

Serves 3 very environmentally conscious carnivores

Marcella's Tomato-Butter Sauce
One 28-ounce can whole peeled tomatoes, crushed by hand in a large bowl
½ cup (1 stick) unsalted butter
1 yellow or white onion, halved and peeled
Salt

Cricket Meatballs
1 cup roasted, salted whole crickets
1 pound 80/20 ground beef
2 garlic cloves, palm heel struck and finely chopped
¼ cup whole milk
1 large egg
⅓ cup Italian bread crumbs
¼ cup freshly grated Pecorino Romano (about 1 ounce)
1 tablespoon olive oil, plus more for your hands
1 teaspoon salt
½ teaspoon crushed red pepper
1 teaspoon dried oregano
½ teaspoon ground black pepper

To Finish
1 pound dried spaghetti, cooked in salted water and drained (you can also substitute 3 cups toasted mealworms)
Freshly grated Pecorino Romano, for serving
High quality extra-virgin olive oil, for serving
A few basil leaves, for garnish

PUMPKIN-SPICED PIGS' FEET

Makes 4 feet of flavor

4 pigs' feet—all four feet do not have to be from the same pig, but it is preferable

Three 20-ounce pumpkin-spiced lattes from your favorite coffee shop during the proper season

2 tablespoons salt, plus more to taste

Here's the thing: every time you eat bacon, that bacon comes from a pig. That pig has a belly (where the bacon comes from), but it also has blood (see Pork Blood Tacos, page 287), a tail, ears, kidneys, and yes—feet. You can also call them "trotters" if you want it to feel a little more playful.

But while there are *lots* of great recipes from around the world for pigs' feet, this is *Mythical Kitchen* after all, so we wanted to jazz it up a bit by braising our pigs' feet in a whole bunch of pumpkin-spiced latte. It may sound weird at first, but remember that milk-braising pork is a truly delicious technique, and that coffee-rubbed pork is also great.

In the end, this might well be the easiest recipe in the whole book, as long as you are willing to wait the full 3 hours for your pigs' feet to cook.

Take a deep breath and get ready for this one.

Put the pigs' feet in a large pot. Pour the pumpkin-spiced lattes over them. Add the salt. Bring to a boil over medium-high heat and reduce it to a gentle simmer. Simmer, covered, until the pigs' feet are cooked and fully tender, about 3 hours, stirring frequently to prevent burning, making sure that they stay completely submerged in liquid while they cook. Add water, if needed, to keep them submerged.

Transfer the pigs' feet to a plate to cool. Season to taste with salt and then eat them with a fork and knife, or if you really want to be a badass, with your bare gosh darn hands.

PEPPERONI SQUID POCKETS

This recipe follows a very simple premise: What if the delicious pastry shell of a Hot Pocket was replaced with the hollowed-out body of an entire animal? There were many different animals we could have chosen to conduct this experiment. Our first attempt at stuffing a whole, deboned cow resulted in an eight-foot crater filled with burning logs in our parking lot and an official warning from the Burbank fire marshal. No one knows who exactly is responsible for said hole and citation, but we are sure they are very sorry and will never try something like that again. They should definitely not be fired and should probably get a promotion, in fact. We eventually settled on squid—after passing on pig, chicken, duck, snake, alpaca, platypus, and kinkajou—because its body is naturally tube shaped, and it is a creature equally delicious and nightmarish. Also, this is loosely based on a very legitimate Sicilian squid-cooking technique, but we think it's funnier to call it a squid pocket, and then say it in Jim Gaffigan's voice over and over in your head while you're cooking it.

....

Preheat the oven to 400°F.

Stare at the squid and contemplate, "How in the fresh heck did I get myself here?" Heat 2 tablespoons of your olive oil in a sauté pan over medium heat, then add your shallots and garlic and cook, stirring occasionally, just until softened, about 4 minutes. If your garlic starts burning and turning brown, toss in about ¼ cup water to slow down the cooking process. When the aromatics are softened, remove the pan from the heat and let them cool. Oh my god, did the squid just look at you?

Let's clean some baby squid. If you can find whole, cleaned squid bodies, definitely just buy those, but we're assuming you went out and wrangled some baby squid fresh from the squid Jacuzzi yourself. Slice the tentacles off and reserve those for a lovely deep-fried snack later on. Reach your fingers up the squid body and remove the skeleton. You'll know when you find it—it feels almost like hard plastic. In one

Makes 12 baby squid, enough for 3 adult humans

12 whole baby squid (or you can buy them already cleaned)

4 tablespoons olive oil

2 tablespoons minced shallot

4 garlic cloves, palm heel struck and finely chopped

6 ounces pepperoni

8 ounces ground pork

¼ cup panko bread crumbs

2 tablespoons grated Parmesan

2 tablespoons chopped parsley

½ teaspoon salt, plus more for seasoning the squid

½ teaspoon crushed red pepper

½ teaspoon dried oregano

Your favorite tomato sauce, for serving

fluid motion, you should be able to remove the intestines and ink sac as well. Basically, remove everything from the inside of the squid tube that isn't white fleshy squid meat. Run some cold water through the squid bodies and let them dry on paper towels.

Mince up your pepperoni as finely as possible and add it to a large bowl with the ground pork, the cooled shallot and garlic mixture, bread crumbs, Parmesan, parsley, salt, crushed red pepper, and oregano. You want all that pepperoni grease to get trapped by the bread crumbs, the same way you trapped that baby squid with your bare hands when you went baby squid fishing.

To fill the squid bodies, you have a few options. A piping bag with a metal tip would work great—that way you can shove the tip inside the squid hole and squeeze (look, the term *squid hole* is a bit much, even for us, but what else are we supposed to call it?). You can also put some filling on the tip of a spoon and insert that into the squid hole (not even apologizing this time) and then use your fingers to

massage the filling toward the top. It doesn't matter how you do it, it just matters that you FILL. THAT. SQUID! (said in the cadence of *Extreme Makeover: Home Edition*'s catchphrase: "Move that bus!") Also, keep in mind that the filling expands a bit, so only fill the squid about 75 percent. Pinch the top to seal them shut.

Once the squid are filled up, season them with salt and then heat the remaining 2 tablespoons olive oil in an oven-safe sauté pan over medium-high heat. Add the squid, about 6 at a time, making sure not to overcrowd the pan, and sear for about 3 minutes on one side before flipping each squid. Put the pan in the oven and roast for about 10 minutes, until the internal temperature of the filling reaches 150°F. Serve topped with your favorite jarred tomato sauce.

For the full Hot Pocket experience, you would freeze the stuffed squid, then microwave them in a weird space-age cardboard sleeve until the internal temperature is both 4°F and 304°F, depending on where you bite it. (We do not recommend this.)

LIVER AND ONION DONUTS

Makes 6 donut sandwiches

6 jelly donuts (but also,
   using toast or crackers
   is just as good)
8 ounces chicken livers
1 cup whole milk
1 tablespoon vegetable oil
1 cup diced yellow
   or white onion
¾ cup peeled and diced apple
1½ tablespoons sugar
½ teaspoon ground
   black pepper
½ teaspoon dried thyme
2 tablespoons balsamic vinegar
Salt
4 tablespoons (½ stick)
   unsalted butter

Hey, it's me, Josh. I'm switching back to the first person here for personal reasons, and those personal reasons are that Rhett and Link have maligned liver for long enough, and I will no longer stand for it. Yeah, that's right, I've worked at Mythical Entertainment for years and have had plenty of opportunities to say this on camera, but I waited until the very last chapter of our long-awaited cookbook to grandstand about this. Liver is great. It is rich in vitamins and minerals, it is an inexpensive protein option, and I grew up eating it at every Jewish holiday gathering. Does it taste like bloody pennies that have been kicked through a hundred meters of dirt? Okay, yeah, sure, but that's why it's up to you as a chef to make it taste awesome! Chicken liver mousse on a nice piece of crusty bread with some sort of fruit preserve is one of my all-time favorite foods, and that combination of baked good, sweet fruit, and organ slop is made even better when you turn it into the most unholy filled donut you've ever had. Mazel tov! You've made a delicious monstrosity.

The first step is to get a couple of extra donuts from the donut shop and eat them alone in your car in the parking lot while glaring at the people around you peering into the car window. Everyone knows that's when donuts taste the best. The second step is to rinse the livers, dry them, and then remove the veins and tendons. This part is either more, equally, or less fun than eating donuts, depending on how much you like donuts and/or deveining livers. Use a paring knife to remove all the little bits from the liver that aren't pure, deep-reddish-brown liver flesh. Just get them out of there. Ain't nothin' to it but to do it. Get your chicken livers soaking in a bowl with the milk and place it in the fridge. There's a lot of myths surrounding WHY exactly a milk soak makes livers taste better. Some say it draws out "impurities"; some say the enzymes in milk change the chemical composition. But I do it because that's how my grandma did it, and sometimes, that's enough of a reason.

Recipe continues

While the livers are soaking (they should go for at least 30 minutes and up to 3 hours), heat your oil in a large sauté pan over medium heat. Add your onion and apple, and then the sugar, and cook, stirring occasionally with a wooden spoon, until you get some good caramelization on them, about 20 minutes. Both the apple and onion should be a deep, dark brown. If they start to get TOO dark, add some water to slow the cooking process. When you are satisfied with the color, add the pepper, thyme, and vinegar and cook for about 3 minutes, until the outside is seared but the inside is still juicy and medium.

Meanwhile, drain the chicken livers and dry them off well on paper towels. Add the chicken livers to the pan, season with a pinch of salt, and cook for about 5 minutes, stirring occasionally. The goal is to get the chicken livers cooked to a medium-rare consistency—if they're overcooked, the mousse is going to be an unappetizing gray color—but in our experience, people are going to be so disgusted by the fact that you've put liver inside a donut that the color is the least of their worries.

When the livers are done, transfer the pan's contents to a food processor and start processing on high. While the processor is running, throw in your butter, which will melt from the heat of the liver mush. Continue letting that bad boy run on high for 2 minutes, turning it off to scrape down the sides as needed and continuing until all the chunks and grains are blended smoothly. Press the mousse through a fine mesh sieve and into a bowl and let it rest in the fridge, covered, for at least 3 hours.

Listen, if you want to spread the liver mousse on toast, or some crackers, or, heck, maybe even some Doritos, we're all for it. But, to finish the donut, in an ideal world, you would put the mousse in a piping bag with a star tip, cut a jelly donut in half horizontally, and pipe the liver all around the rim of the bottom half of the donut before filling in the center and crowning it with the top half.

After consulting with our rabbi, we have been told that this is indeed not kosher for Passover. But it is delicious.

COCONUT DURIAN WAFFLES

Durian may not be allowed on public transportation in Singapore, but it is definitely allowed in the *Mythical* studio, because for those who don't know about the king of fruit's powerful aroma, it is absolutely hilarious to watch their reaction. Some describe the smell as rotting flesh that's been stuffed into the dumpster behind a Long John Silver's franchise, and some describe it as Josh after his second workout of the day after eating nothing but cabbage for the past six meals. But, if you can get past the smell—and you can; you truly can!—it has one of the most complex and delightful flavors of any fruit out there. In Southeast Asia, it's often turned into custards, ice creams, and candies, but why wait for dessert? Turn that big ol' spiky death fruit into some waffles for breakfast, and start your day off with a powerful odor that tells people around you, "I am a strong and confident individual, and I don't care what anyone thinks of me."

....

Step 1: Make the Durian Butter. Add the butter, sugar, and durian to a food processor and process on high speed until the mixture is fluffy and pale yellow, about 1 minute, then scoop it into a bowl. DO NOT CLEAN THE FOOD PROCESSOR YET! TRUST US!

Assuming you didn't eat all the sweet, sweet, stanky durian butter straight out of the food processor, you should get to . . .

Step 2: Make the Waffles. Mix together your flour, coconut flakes, sugar, baking powder, baking soda, and salt in a large bowl. In your dirty food processor (SEE?!?!), put your eggs, milk, and durian and blend until smooth. Pour the liquid mixture into the dry ingredients, then whisk together until fully combined. Finally, add the melted butter and whisk to incorporate.

Heat a waffle maker and lube it up with some cooking spray. Add enough waffle batter so that at least ½ cup of it spills over the sides of the machine and you frantically try to wipe it up with a paper towel

Makes 4 waffles

Durian Butter
- ½ cup (1 stick) salted butter, at room temperature, plus more for greasing the waffle iron
- 3 tablespoons sugar
- 4 ounces thawed frozen seedless durian

Durian Waffles
- 2 cups all-purpose flour
- ½ cup toasted coconut flakes, plus more for serving
- ½ cup sugar
- 2½ teaspoons baking powder
- 1½ teaspoons baking soda
- ½ teaspoon salt
- 2 large eggs
- 1½ cups whole milk
- 8 ounces thawed frozen seedless durian
- ½ cup (1 stick) unsalted butter, melted
- Cooking spray
- Sweetened condensed milk, for serving

going, "Ah, crap, ooh, ow, why?" as you inevitably get burned by the appliance that you had to dig out of the storage closet. Okay, no, don't do that— probably add about ½ cup of waffle batter, but also I don't know how big your waffle maker is.

Remove the waffle from the iron once it's crispy and golden brown on the outside, then repeat the process until you have 4 waffles. And then stop immediately. Even if you have more waffle batter left over, DO NOT MAKE MORE THAN 4! (He's not looking anymore, quick, make more than 4!)

Top each waffle with a hefty drizzle of condensed milk, followed by a spoonful of whipped durian butter, followed by toasted coconut flakes. Eat on a public bus while celebrating the fact that the United States, at the time of this writing, has no antidurian transportation laws.

What About Fresh Durian?

If you can get your hands on fresh durian—some large Asian markets will carry it during the summer—absolutely do it! You crack it open and scoop the custardy flesh from around the hard seeds, and it is truly one of the most memorable food experiences you could ever have. Even if you don't like it, you definitely won't forget it! But, for this recipe, frozen durian thawed to room temperature will do just fine.

BEEF TESTICLE RAGÙ

"Ox testicles actually have an incredibly clean and pure beefy flavor." Those words almost escape your mouth at the party. You look around and assess your surroundings. You imagine how every person within earshot will react to that statement. Will it be positive? Almost assuredly not. Will they run away in horror? Also, likely no—that's dramatic. But will there be a slightly disgusted glint in their eye, causing them to look at you differently every single time they see you again? Bingo. But, testicles are commonly eaten, both in America and around the world, so it's flat-out ignorant to be disgusted by them. And if your sentiment is both true and virtuous, don't you have a moral imperative to say it aloud? You take another sip of your beer to stall. "My favorite food is chicken Parmesan," you say a little too loudly. You have taken the coward's way out.

Needless to say, this is based on a true story. Even though we've used testicles as a gag on *GMM* for a long time—c'mon, it's funny, they're balls!—when cooked and prepped properly, they offer a really unique texture and incredible flavor. As far as sourcing fresh testoculars goes—we've always gotten them from our local outpost of 99 Ranch Market, a fantastic Taiwanese grocery store. But if you're friends with any cowboys, getting those bovine beanbags fresh after castration is the way to go!

Oh boy. We hope this is the first and last time you're ever going to have to read this sentence: first, you need to peel your testes (crosses legs and shudders in fear). You'll notice several coiled veins underneath a thin, semitranslucent membrane. You want all that to be gone so you can get to that sweet, sweet nut meat. Bring about a quart of water to a boil in a large saucepan over high heat, then make a small incision, about 1 inch long, anywhere through the testicular membrane (vomits uncontrollably). Blanch the testicles for about 30 seconds and add to an ice bath and let sit for about a minute. Use your fingers to peel the membrane off the testicles (blacks out and enters the netherrealm) and let the meat dry on a paper towel. Add the naked testicles to a food processor and process on high until they become a nice, wet nut slurry (Mom, I'm scared, can you pick me up?). Reserve this for later.

Heat your oil in a large pot over medium-high heat, then add your bacon. Give it a stir and allow it to cook until some of the

Makes enough testy rags for 8 people!

1 pound beef testicles

2 tablespoons vegetable oil

8 ounces bacon or pancetta, diced

1 medium yellow or white onion, diced

2 medium carrots, diced

3 stalks celery, diced

6 garlic cloves, palm heel struck and finely chopped

1 pound 80/20 ground beef

1½ teaspoons salt

½ cup white wine

One 28-ounce can crushed tomatoes

2 tablespoons tomato paste

1 bay leaf

½ teaspoon dried oregano

½ teaspoon crushed red pepper

1 pound dried penne

1 cup grated Parmesan (about 4 ounces)

fat has rendered, 3 to 4 minutes. Add your onion, carrots, celery, and garlic and cook until softened and fragrant, about 5 minutes. Add your ground beef and liquefied testicle slurry (AAAAAAAAAAAAAAAHHH!!!), along with your salt, and sauté, stirring frequently with a wooden spoon, until the meat is browned and cooked through, 8 to 9 minutes.

Crank the heat to high, and when you hear the meat start to sizzle, deglaze the pan with your white wine, scraping up the browned bits at the bottom of the pan (you must extract all the testicle flavor!) with the spoon. Cook until some of the alcohol evaporates, about 3 minutes, then add your crushed tomatoes, tomato paste, bay leaf, oregano, crushed red pepper, and 3 cups water. Simmer on low until it has reduced

substantially and has the texture of a nice, thick sauce, about 2 hours. Or, if you want to contain the testicle smell to a smaller area, you can alternately throw the uncovered pot in a 325°F oven for 2 hours.

When the ragù is ready, boil the penne in heavily salted water. You can use whatever noodle you like, but the penne and testicles is funny, and if there's anything we've learned in the Mythical Kitchen, it's that you should always make the sex pun while cooking. Toss the penne in the ragù, let it hang out for about 5 minutes, so some of the sauce can absorb into the pasta, then serve and top with the Parmesan. We initially thought there was a pun to be made with Pecorino Romano (like, PECKER-ino?) but ultimately decided that was a bridge too far.

ACKNOWLEDGMENTS

They say writing a book is like starting a family. First, you need love. Then, you need a bunch of trees to make the paper, and you're probably going to need four hundred to five hundred squids so you have enough ink, and that's going to require a very large net. As it turns out, writing a book is nothing like starting a family, but it does take a heck of a lot of people to make it happen. Here is an incomplete list of all the people who I am terribly indebted to, both metaphorically and literally.

First, my bookie, Karl. Dude, I'm good for the money, I just need more time. Nine times out of ten, Boston College wins that women's lacrosse championship.

Second, the fearless Mythical Kitcheneers: Nicole Enayati, Trevor Evarts, Vianai Austin, and Lily Cousins. Y'all are the best ragtag team of incredibly smart professional food doofuses in the entire game. You inspire me constantly, and I can't thank you all enough for trusting in the process, both for this book and all the shenanigans we have accomplished on *Mythical Kitchen*. Special shout-out to Lily for testing the baked bean recipe, like, six times.

My coauthor, Noah Galuten, who showed up to every writing session with random citrus fruits that he bought at the farmers' market. The Meyer lemons were good, dude, thank you!

Stevie Wynne Levine, Brian Flanagan, Gabriel Blanco, Kevin Kostelnik, and all the other folks at Mythical, whose fearless leadership always puts us in position to be as creative as we possibly can be.

Mike Pasley, for creative directing the pants off this book (and for literally putting me IN pants during the photo shoot).

Matthew Dwyer, Julien Hill, Chappie, and Zack Rezowalli, for taking the absolute stupidest illustration and design requests and turning them into magic on the page.

Jessie Lamworth and Caitlin Johnson, for, among many things, making "a weirdly aggressive sentient toaster" come to life.

Annaliese Kassebaum and Mindy Castillo, because, without them keeping the whole team on track, you wouldn't have been able to buy this book until 2036.

Our whole dang photo team: Andrea D'Agosto, Ashli Buts, Lauren Anderson, Michaun "Snax" Barner, and Alicia Buszczak. It's amazing what you can pull off with a talented group of creative people and a bag of thirty live crickets.

Stephanie Fletcher and the entire team at Harvest Books, for your tireless commitment to excellence and meaningful involvement throughout.

Brandi Bowles and the entire team at UTA, for believing in this project from day one.

Adam Kaller, Ryan Pastorek, and the entire legal team at HJTH.

Guy Fieri. Technically, he didn't do anything for this book, but his spiky hair and shining personality has always been my North Star, pointing me toward the promised land.

And, of course, every dang Mythical Beast—past, future, and present—who has supported us at every turn.

UNIVERSAL CONVERSION CHART

OVEN TEMPERATURE EQUIVALENTS

250°F = 120°C

275°F = 135°C

300°F = 150°C

325°F = 160°C

350°F = 180°C

375°F = 190°C

400°F = 200°C

425°F = 220°C

450°F = 230°C

475°F = 240°C

500°F = 260°C

MEASUREMENT EQUIVALENTS

Measurements should always be level unless directed otherwise.

⅛ teaspoon = 0.5 mL

¼ teaspoon = 1 mL

½ teaspoon = 2 mL

1 teaspoon = 5 mL

1 tablespoon = 3 teaspoons = ½ fluid ounce = 15 mL

2 tablespoons = ⅛ cup = 1 fluid ounce = 30 mL

4 tablespoons = ¼ cup = 2 fluid ounces = 60 mL

5⅓ tablespoons = ⅓ cup = 3 fluid ounces = 80 mL

8 tablespoons = ½ cup = 4 fluid ounces = 120 mL

10⅔ tablespoons = ⅔ cup = 5 fluid ounces = 160 mL

12 tablespoons = ¾ cup = 6 fluid ounces = 180 mL

16 tablespoons = 1 cup = 8 fluid ounces = 240 mL

INDEX

ABOUT THE AUTHOR

JOSH SCHERER is the chef behind *Good Mythical Morning* and *Mythical Kitchen*, the author of *The Culinary Bro-Down Cookbook*, and a cohost of the award-winning podcast *A Hot Dog Is a Sandwich*. He was a zero-time All-American hammer thrower at UCLA, where he learned more about the merits of deep-fried burritos than political science. His writing has appeared in *Los Angeles* magazine, *GQ, Maxim, LA Weekly,* and Vice Munchies, and he loves grocery store sushi. Seriously, it's gotten a lot better over the years. You'd be surprised.

ABOUT MYTHICAL

Founded by comedy duo Rhett & Link, Mythical is home to the internet's most-watched daily talk show, *Good Mythical Morning*, as well as the culinary-focused spin-off channel, Mythical Kitchen. Mythical's owned and operated YouTube channels have amassed more than 31 million subscribers and 12 billion lifetime views. Born in North Carolina and best friends since the first grade, Rhett & Link also cowrote the *New York Times* bestsellers *Book of Mythicality* and *The Lost Causes of Bleak Creek*. Rhett loves beans. Link hates tomatoes. They are both staunch advocates for the healing properties of bacon.

RHETT & LINK PRESENT: THE MYTHICAL COOKBOOK. Copyright © 2024 by Mythical Entertainment LLC. All rights reserved. Printed in Canada. No part of this book may be used or reproduced in any manner whatsoever without written permission except in the case of brief quotations embodied in critical articles and reviews. For information, address HarperCollins Publishers, 195 Broadway, New York, NY 10007.

HarperCollins books may be purchased for educational, business, or sales promotional use. For information, please email the Special Markets Department at SPsales@harpercollins.com.

FIRST EDITION

Designed by Leah Carlson-Stanisic

Photography copyright © 2024 by Andrea D'Agosto

Illustrations copyright © 2024 by Charlotte Holden: Will It Taco? (page xi), Food Experiments (pages 158–59); Julien Hill: The Tale Of Horrible, No-Good, Grumpy Old Smoothie Man (pages 28–29); Matthew Dwyer, Caleb Hartsfield: Bacons of Tomorrow (pages 100–101); Katrina "Chappie" Chaput: Our Official Guide to Kitchen Safety (pages 191–95); Zack Rezowalli: Crispee Towne Business Plan (pages 222–23)

Photographer: Andrea D'Agosto

Photo Assistant and Cricket Wrangler: Ashli Buts

Food Stylist: Lauren Anderson, StoneColdStyleLA

Food Stylist Assistant: Michaun "Snax" Barner-Page

Prop Stylist: Alicia Buszczak, Caitlin Johnson

Set Decoration: Caitlin Johnson, Jessie Lamworth

Props provided by The Surface Library

Photo Studio: Historic Hudson Studios

Custom hot dog sculpture created by Sienna DeGovia

Library of Congress Cataloging-in-Publication Data has been applied for.

ISBN 978-0-06-332396-4

24 25 26 27 28 TC 10 9 8 7 6 5 4 3 2